Economy and Social Inclusion

Creating a Society for All

This series provides a forum for theoretical, empirical, historical, and experimental analysis of issues related to economy and social inclusion and exclusion. Included are the interconnected problems of alienation, deprivation, discrimination, economic inequality, polarization, and prejudices caused by or related to abusive behavior, aging, depopulation, disability, the educational gap, the gender gap, natural disaster, poverty, rare diseases, war, and various other economic and social factors. The common theme of the series is to examine how we can create an inclusive society that accommodates as many people as possible and promotes their welfare. We believe this should be the main goal of economics as a discipline. Society need not passively observe its inequality, social exclusion, and decline. Policy, institutions, and our actions matter. The series aims to enrich academic discourse, influence economic and social policy, and enlighten a global readership. Methodologies adopted in this series are mainly economic theory, game theory, econometrics, statistical analysis, economic experiments, and disability studies. Psychology, sociology, legal studies, and medical sciences, among other disciplines, are also considered important related fields of study. The interdisciplinary research taken up in the series utilizes these existing methodologies for the common goal of creating a society for all. Furthermore, progress in such interdisciplinary studies will contribute new insights to the development of economic studies. The major geographical targets of the series are Japan and other Asian countries but are not restricted to those areas. At the same time, however, the goal is to amplify the findings therein to universally applicable insights and knowledge.

More information about this series at http://www.springer.com/series/13899

Yasuyuki Sawada · Michiko Ueda
Tetsuya Matsubayashi

Economic Analysis of Suicide Prevention

Towards Evidence-Based Policy-Making

Springer

Yasuyuki Sawada
Faculty of Economics
The University of Tokyo
Bunkyō, Tokyo
Japan

Tetsuya Matsubayashi
Osaka School of International Public Policy
Osaka University
Toyonaka, Osaka
Japan

Michiko Ueda
Faculty of Political Science and Economics
Waseda University
Shinjuku, Tokyo
Japan

ISSN 2509-4270 ISSN 2509-4289 (electronic)
Economy and Social Inclusion
Creating a Society for All
ISBN 978-981-10-1499-4 ISBN 978-981-10-1500-7 (eBook)
DOI 10.1007/978-981-10-1500-7

Library of Congress Control Number: 2017953802

Printed on acid-free paper

This Springer imprint is published by Springer Nature
The registered company is Springer Nature Singapore Pte Ltd.
The registered company address is: 152 Beach Road, #21-01/04 Gateway East, Singapore 189721, Singapore

Preface

As social scientists who are familiar with Japan and as members of society, we have been seriously concerned with the problem of suicide in Japan. Suicide is part of everyday life in Japan: there is not a single day when news media do not report stories on suicide deaths; commuters in the Tokyo Metropolitan area experience train schedule disruptions almost every day because railway and metro suicides are so frequent. In fact, from 1998 to 2011, more than 30,000 people lost their lives by suicide every year. This means that more than 80 individuals died by suicide per day on average during this period. Japan's suicide rate, defined as the number of suicide deaths per 100,000 people, reached 27.0 in 2003, which was the highest among the OECD nations with a similar level of economic development. Although the suicide rate in Japan had declined to 18.9 by 2015, it remains relatively high compared with that of other OECD countries.

These striking numbers led us to ask ourselves several questions. Why did such a large number of people have to end their lives by themselves? What is an implication of high suicide counts to society? Should the government intervene to stop people from taking their own lives? What are the effective policies to prevent suicide? Has the suicide rate in Japan recently declined because the Japanese government initiated a national suicide prevention program in 2007 or simply because society recovered from an economic recession? And what can we, as researchers, do to stop this tragedy?

This book is a part of our effort to address these questions as social scientists. Over the last 10 years, we as a team have been studying the causes and consequences of suicide as well as the effectiveness of suicide prevention programs. Because our academic background is in economics and political science, our focus mainly lies in examining the socioeconomic factors of suicide and suicide prevention policies that target societal factors, rather than addressing individual mental and physical disorders as risk factors of suicide. However, this is not to play down the role of these individual risk factors. Suicide is a complex phenomenon that involves a multitude of causes and factors, and we believe that understanding both micro (individual)- and macro (societal)-level determinants is essential for effective suicide prevention.

The findings of our studies have been published as articles in international and Japanese academic journals and as a book. The book was titled "Jisatsu no nai shakaihe" and published by Yuhikaku Publishing. It received the Nikkei Prize for Excellent Books in Economic Science in 2013. This volume combines the findings of our published works into a single volume in the hope of contributing to an understanding of suicide from a social science perspective. It also contains some of the unpublished recent findings and updated results of our previous studies. Although the evidence presented in this book comes primarily from Japan, we believe that our conclusion offers important implications for other countries as well.

Our ultimate goal is to achieve society in which nobody is forced to die by suicide. We sincerely hope that the collection of studies included in this volume helps readers in Japan and other countries achieve this goal.

Bunkyō, Japan Yasuyuki Sawada
Shinjuku, Japan Michiko Ueda
Toyonaka, Japan Tetsuya Matsubayashi

Acknowledgements

We thank for financial assistance from the following sources:
Yasuyuki Sawada

- Center of Excellence (COE) Grant for Faculty of Economics, University of Tokyo, "the Research Center for the Relationship between Market Economy and Non-market Institutions," JSPS and Ministry of Education and Science, Government of Japan, 2003-2008
- JSPS Funding Program for Next Generation World-Leading Researchers "Evidence-Based Policy Study on Poverty Dynamics in Japan and the World" # LZ003, JSPS, Feb 2011-March 2014. (PI Yasuyuki Sawada)
- Ministry of Health, Labour and Welfare (MHLW) Project entitled "Interdisciplinary and International Approaches to the Study of New Policy Developments for Comprehensive Suicide Countermeasures"

Michiko Ueda

- JSPS Grants-in-Aid for Scientific Research Grant Number 17H02541
- Waseda University Grant for Special Research Projects (2016S-180)
- Sumitomo Life Insurance Research Grant

Tetsuya Matsubayashi

- JSPS Grants-in-Aid for Scientific Research Grant Number 26870326
- The Itochube Foundation Grant.

Contents

About the Authors

Yasuyuki Sawada is chief economist of the Asian Development Bank and a professor of economics at the University of Tokyo. He has previously been a visiting fellow at the Bangladesh Institute of Development Studies (BIDS) and a visiting professor at Stanford University. In his research, Prof. Sawada uses microlevel data from developed and developing countries to analyze risk-coping strategies of individuals, households, and firms, particularly in response to natural and man-made disasters. He received his M.A. in international development policy and Ph.D. in economics, both from Stanford University. He is also a co-recipient of the Jiro Enjoji Memorial Prize and the 56th Nikkei Prize for Excellent Books in Economic Science of the Japan Center for Economic Research and the Ishikawa Prize of the Japanese Economic Association.

Michiko Ueda is associate professor in the Faculty of Political Science and Economics at Waseda University. Prior to joining Waseda University, she was an assistant professor at the California Institute of Technology, a research assistant professor at Syracuse University, and a visiting researcher at the University of Tokyo, Waseda University, and the Economic and Social Research Institute in the Cabinet Office. Her research interests include suicidology and suicide prevention, public health, and political science, and she has published articles in the areas of public health, medicine, and political science. She has received the 56th Nikkei Prize for Excellent Books in Economic Science as well as the Best Paper Award by the Japanese Association of Electoral Studies and the Jewell-Loewenberg Award by the Legislative Studies section of the American Political Science Association. She received her Ph.D. in political science from the Massachusetts Institute of Technology in 2006.

Tetsuya Matsubayashi is associate professor of Osaka School of International Public Policy (OSIPP) at Osaka University, Japan. After receiving a Ph.D. in political science in 2007 from Texas A&M University, he worked as an assistant professor at the University of North Texas until 2013. His areas of research include mass political behavior, political representation, racial and ethnic politics, and public health. His work has appeared in the *American Journal of Political Science*, *American Political Science Review*, *British Journal of Political Science*, *Political Research Quarterly*, *International Journal of Epidemiology*, *Social Science and Medicine*, and others. He is a co-recipient of the 56th Nikkei Prize for Excellent Books in Economic Science.

Chapter 1
Introduction

1 Introduction

Suicide is a significant social issue. The World Health Organization (WHO) reports that over 800,000 people die by suicide each year. Although suicide rates have consistently been highest in the elderly, suicide is among the leading causes of death of youths in many countries.

There may be a cultural aspect to attitudes towards suicide. For example, in Japan there is a long history of ritual suicide. Thus, Japanese society may seem more accepting of suicide when compared to other societies. However, views towards suicide often transcend such cultural or geographical boundaries and can be very diverse simply because different people view suicide differently. Furthermore, attitudes towards suicide may generate controversy because they are often based upon each individual's own sense of morality. For example, some may claim suicide is a personal choice made by individuals, and the government and others should not intervene in their decisions.

In this book, rather than debating whether suicide is a choice, we seek to understand the causes and consequences of suicide from the perspective of economics. We argue that the risk of suicide can be shaped by economic and institutional settings. Thus, our approach here differs from those in the medical, psychiatric, epidemiological, and sociological studies of suicide that tend to focus on the personal causes of suicide.

In the following chapters, we examine those economic and institutional causes of suicide, and what strategy the society and government should choose to prevent suicide in the constraint of scarce resources. What is more, we argue that suicide imposes a tremendous economic cost on society and therefore that suicide prevention could alleviate a massive substantial economic burden. We also argue that the risk of suicide changes dramatically in the event of economic and natural disasters, and also when the government implements policies with certain economic implications. The relevance of school-related issues for the risk of suicide in school

Y. Sawada et al., *Economic Analysis of Suicide Prevention*, Creating a Society for All, DOI 10.1007/978-981-10-1500-7_1

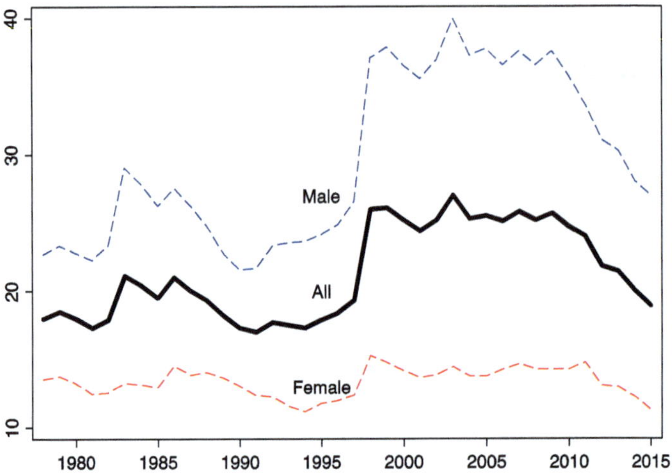

Fig. 1 Suicide rate in Japan, 1978–2015

children and adolescents is also discussed. In addition, we consider effective prevention strategies to prevent railway and subway suicides as well as effective public awareness campaigns. Ultimately, this book contributes to the understanding of the socioeconomic aspect of suicide and to the development of evidence-based policy proposals.

When testing hypotheses on the link between economic and institutional settings and suicide, we use data from Japan and other high-income nations. Suicide is a particularly serious problem in Japan, as more than 30,000 people died by suicide each year from 1998 to 2011. Figure 1 shows the suicide rate in Japan (per 100,000 people) between 1978 and 2015, based on data by the National Police Agency.[1] In the figure, the solid line indicates the total suicide rate, and the dashed lines indicate the suicide rates by gender. Figure 1 shows that the suicide rate increased sharply from 1997 to 1998, and thereafter, more than 30,000 people died by suicide each year for 14 years in succession. In other words, approximately 80 people died from suicide each day on average during this period. Furthermore, Fig. 1 shows that men have a much higher suicide count than women. Finally, the graph indicates that the suicide rate started to decline in 2010 and that the number of suicide victims continued to decrease to 24,025 in 2015.

Figure 2 displays the 20 highest age-adjusted suicide rates in 2012 around the world. The top panel indicates that the suicide rate in Japan for men and women combined is the 18th highest in the world and 3rd highest among the OECD countries. The middle panel shows that the male suicide rate in Japan is the 20th highest in the world and 4th highest among the OECD countries. The female

[1] The suicide rate is the total number of suicide victims in a year divided by the population of the same year and then multiplied by 100,000.

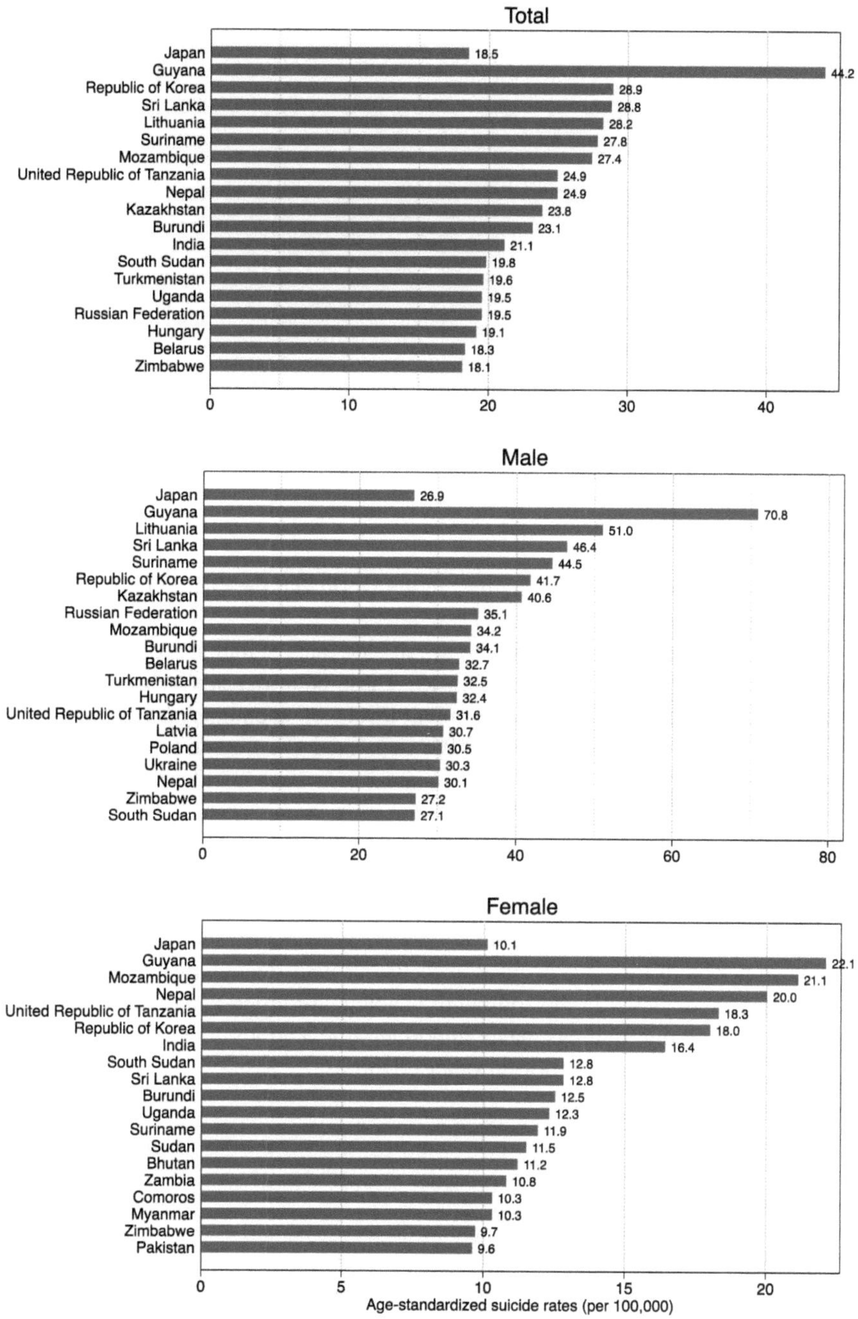

Fig. 2 Cross-national comparison of suicide rates

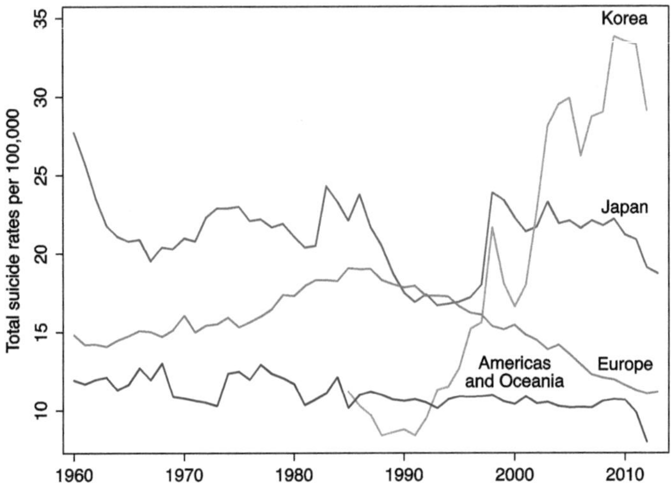

Fig. 3 Temporal comparison of suicide rates

suicide rate in Japan is the 18th highest in the world and the 2nd highest among the OECD countries.

Figure 3 displays temporal shifts in the suicide rates of four sets of countries that belong to OECD between 1960 and 2013. These countries were chosen for comparison because they experienced similar levels of economic development and political stability in those 50 years. We separated the countries into 4 groups: European, Americas and Oceania, Japan, and Korea. The suicide rate in Japan was the highest of the groups from 1960 up to the early 2000s, when it was exceeded by Korea's suicide rate. The suicide rates in the European nations and Americas and Oceania have declined in the last two decades.

Japan has had a long struggle with suicide. Coupled with the fact that individual death records and aggregated suicide counts are available for sub-regions and for an extensive period of time, we decided to focus our investigation on suicide in Japan. While most hypotheses in the following chapters are tested against data in Japan, we believe that our findings have important implications to suicide prevention literature and suicide prevention in other countries.

2 Book Outline

The remaining chapters of this book are divided into two parts. Part I includes Chaps. 2–6 and Part II consists of Chapters 7–9. Part I considers why policy interventions by the government are necessary and examines the factors that shape suicide risk in different subpopulations. Chapter 2 discusses the need to reduce suicide by focusing on the negative externalities that suicide generates. Negative externalities here include the effect on the bereaved, the so-called Werther effect, and the economic costs that suicide imposes.

In Chaps. 3 and 4, we show that suicide is linked to socioeconomic factors. Suicide has long been known to be caused by personal factors such as depression or other mental illnesses. However, we think that behind depression can lie a socioeconomic environment that can generate depression. For example, people may lose their job as a result of recession, fall into economic distress, and then become depressed, which increases suicide risk. In such cases, if the economic shock caused by recession can be mitigated through policy intervention, the risk of suicide can be reduced. Chapter 3 spotlights economic crises as a form of human-generated disaster, and Chap. 4 focuses on the effect of natural disasters on suicide.

Chapter 5 looks at suicides by adolescents and young adults. Because the majority of adolescent suicide victims are students, we examined the effects of school-related risk factors on the timing and rates of suicide in young individuals. Chapter 6 focuses on railway suicides that are prevalent in Japan. We start by presenting descriptive data of railway suicides in Japan which includes the annual frequencies, demographic characteristics of the deceased, and the timing of occurrence. We then discuss the economic costs imposed by railway suicides and overview our studies that examined the effectiveness of prevention strategies, such as blue light-emitting-diode (LED) lamps on platforms and platform screen doors (PSD).

The second part of this book explores prevention policies that may contribute to reducing the number of suicides, using cross-national data as well as data from Japan. In Chap. 7, we examine the influence that government policies have on people's levels of life satisfaction and on suicide rates by looking at the ideology of the ruling party as comprehensive indicators of government policies. Furthermore, Chap. 8 uses panel data from the 47 prefectures in Japan to examine whether the expansion of economic and welfare policies by prefectural governments can reduce suicide rates.

Chapter 9 highlights the importance of government suicide prevention efforts. We evaluate the effectiveness of comprehensive suicide prevention programs developed by national government in 21 OECD nations. Moreover, we discuss the effectiveness of suicide prevention programs led by subnational governments in Japan since 2009. In addition, we look at the effectiveness of public awareness campaigns by using data from Nagoya City, Japan.

Chapter 2
Rationale Behind Suicide Prevention Policies

1 Introduction

Article 25(1) of the Constitution of Japan stipulates: "All people shall have the right to maintain the minimum standards of wholesome and cultured living." However, data on suicide in Japan suggest that not all people enjoy this right. According to "About deaths by suicide among recipients of livelihood assistance," a report released by the Ministry of Health, Labour and Welfare in July 2011, the suicide rate among recipients of livelihood assistance was 54.8 per 100,000 people in 2008, 62.4 in 2009, and 55.7 in 2010, more than twice the national average of 25.3, 25.8, and 24.9 respectively (Public Assistance Division, Social Welfare and War Victims' Relief Bureau, Ministry of Health, Labour and Welfare 2012). Furthermore, according to data from the National Police Agency, suicides caused or triggered by "economic and livelihood issues" in 2010 totaled 7,438. Of these, 1,649 were caused or triggered by "hardships in life" (Community Safety Planning Division, Community Safety Bureau, National Police Agency 2011). Moreover, of these 1,649, 1,049 were unemployed. As we shall explain in Chap. 3, the suicide rate among unemployed people, including jobless and pensioners, is much higher than in those who have a job. These facts indicate that destitution is an obstacle to attaining the "minimum standards of wholesome and cultured living." Thus, policy interventions to prevent suicide may be justified from the point of view of the Constitution.

However, in addition to constitutional views, this chapter argues that suicide prevention is necessary for economic reasons. The first is the negative externalities and social costs of suicide, the second is the lifetime work-loss costs of suicide, and the third is market imperfections and incentive distortions that contribute to suicide.

The rest of this chapter is organized as follows: Sects. 2, 3, and 4 discuss the negative externalities that suicide generates, and we argue that these externalities

---

The original version of this chapter was revised: Final corrections have been incorporated. The erratum to this chapter is available at https://doi.org/10.1007/978-981-10-1500-7_10

Y. Sawada et al., *Economic Analysis of Suicide Prevention*,
Creating a Society for All, DOI 10.1007/978-981-10-1500-7_2

can be a basic rationale for preventing suicide. Section 2 will show our estimates of the number of bereaved family members of those who died by suicide, Sect. 3 discusses the so-called Werther effect, i.e., suicides induced by media reports on celebrity suicides, and Sect. 4 examines the social costs of suicides arising from railway suicides, loss of individuals, and lifetime work-loss costs, which may justify active policy interventions to prevent suicide. Section 5 shows that socioeconomic factors such as insurance and credit market imperfections, and distortions in incentives can be behind suicide, necessitating carefully designed policy interventions. Finally, potential caveats are discussed in the concluding section.

2 Bereaved Family Members of Suicide Victims[1]

Key to preventing suicides is identifying high suicide-risk groups. In the US National Strategy for Suicide Prevention, risk factors for suicide are divided into three categories. Among these, family history of suicide is one of the biopsychosocial risk factors. Relational or social loss is one of the environmental risk factors, and exposure to and influence of others who have died by suicide is one of the socio-cultural risk factors (U.S. Department of Health and Human Services 2001). Hence, family members of suicide victims belong to all three categories. In a resource for general physicians (World Health Organization 2000), the World Health Organization itemizes eight clinically useful individual and socio-demographic risk factors associated with suicide, as documented by Gunnell and Frankel (1999), and among them is family history of suicide and bereavement in childhood. Yet, little is known about those "left behind" family members. In particular, there is little information on the number of family members of suicide victims.[2] Although some studies attempted to estimate the costs of suicide, estimates of the number of family members of suicide victims in such studies were made only on the basis of ad hoc assumptions or small-scale case studies (Coggan et al. 1997; Clayton and Barcelo 1999; O'Dea and Tucker 2005). Although often neglected, information on the number of family members of suicide victims is valuable in evaluating the cost-effectiveness of suicide prevention programs and in designing appropriate policies.

The next section presents a study by Chen et al. (2009), which was designed to fill in the existing literature. The study developed a method to estimate the number of family members of suicide victims on the basis of aggregate level data and then applied it to the Japanese data.

---

[1]Discussions in this section are based on Chen et al. (2009).

[2]In this chapter, family members are defined as first-degree relatives: spouses, parents, siblings, and children.

2.1 Estimating the Number of People Who Became Bereaved in 1993–2006

The number of suicide victims by gender and 5-year age group from 1993 to 2006 was taken from Vital Statistics data, compiled by the Japanese Ministry of Health, Labour and Welfare.[3] The number of bereaved family members for each relationship, gender and age group, and year was estimated using the estimation procedures described below.

Spouses

Data for the marital status of suicide victims in 1995 and 2000 were published by the Ministry of Health, Labour and Welfare in the "2004 Special Report of Vital Statistics."[4] The number of spouses of suicide victims, *SP*, was estimated using Eq. (1)[5]:

$$SP_{t,a,s} = \alpha_{t,a,s} \cdot SCD_{t,a,s} \tag{1}$$

where t, a, and s represent year, age group, and gender, respectively. α is the marriage rate of suicide victims, and *SCD* is the number of suicide victims. Note that because marriage rates are available only for 1995 and 2000, the marriage rates for other years were interpolated linearly using Eq. (2):

$$\alpha_{t,a,s} = \frac{\alpha_{t_2,a,s} - \alpha_{t_1,a,s}}{t_2 - t_1}(t - t_1) + \alpha_{t_1,a,s} \tag{2}$$

where $t_1 = 1995$ and $t_2 = 2000$.

Siblings

The number of bereaved siblings was estimated using the total fertility rate in the year in which the suicide victims were born, taking into account the survival rate for

[3]Suicide victims of unknown age are excluded. This should not affect the estimates because they account for less than 1% of all suicide victims.

[4]Marital status is classified into 5 categories: married, single, widowed, divorced, and unknown.

[5]Data on suicide victims are divided into 19 age groups up to age 90 years and above, while data on marital status are divided into only 17 age groups up to age 80 years and above. To adjust for this difference, the same marital status was used for all suicide victims age 80 years and above.

the siblings.[6] The probability γ_{t_1,t_2} that a person who was born in t_1 was alive in t_2 was calculated using Eq. (3)[7]:

$$\gamma_{t_1,t_2} = \frac{POP_{t_2,t_2-t_1}}{B_{t_1}} \tag{3}$$

where $POP_{t,a}$ is the number of people of a years old in year t, and B_t is the number of births in year t.[8] The number of bereaved siblings was then computed using Eq. (4):

$$BS_{t,a} = \gamma_{t-a,t}(\beta_{t-a} - 1)SCD_{t,a} \tag{4}$$

where β is the total fertility rate, and SCD is the number of suicide victims of both genders.

Parents

The average age of women who give birth to median birth-order children is about 30 years.[9] The probability δ_{t_1,t_2} that a person who was 30 years old in t_1 was still alive in t_2 was calculated using Eq. (5):

$$\delta_{t_1,t_2} = \frac{POP_{t_2,t_2-t_1+30}}{POP_{t_1,30}} \tag{5}$$

The number of bereaved parents was then computed using Eq. (6):

$$PR_{t,a} = 2\delta_{t-a,t}SCD_{t,a} \tag{6}$$

Children

The fertility rate of women by 5-year age group was used to estimate the number of bereaved children. Let $FR_{t,i}$ be the fertility rate in year t of women in age group

---

[6]The birth year for suicide victims was calculated by subtracting the mid-point of their age group from the year of suicide. Note that suicide victims of age 90 years and above were treated as people of age 92 years.

[7]Whenever γ became larger than 1, it was set to 1. γ can be larger than 1 due to immigration and missing observations.

[8]Data on population and birth rates are taken from "Population Statistics of Japan 2008," published by the National Institute of Population and Social Security Research.

[9]The average age of women at childbirth was calculated based on "Average Age of Women at Birth by Birth Order" in Population Statistics of Japan 2008 by the National Institute of Population and Social Security Research.

i. The average number of children of mothers in age group i who died by suicide in year t was calculated using Eq. (7)[10]:

$$\xi_{t,a_I} = \sum_{i=0}^{I-1} \Delta a FR_{t-a_I+i\Delta a,i} + \frac{\Delta a}{2} FR_{t-a_I+I\Delta a,I} \tag{7}$$

where $\Delta a = 5$ is the width of the age group interval and a_i is the midpoint of age group i. To take into account the discrepancy between the actual age at suicide and the upper cutoff for age group i, the width of the age group was divided in half. The average number of children of fathers in age group i who died by suicide in year t can be safely assumed to be the same as that of a mother because the average age difference between husband and wife was about 3 years during the sample periods (Chen et al. 2009).

Note that for some age groups, the average marital status is different between the suicide victims and the general population. To take that into account, the estimated number of bereaved children was adjusted by the ratio of the unmarried percentage of suicide victims, *NMS*, to that of the general population, *NM*[11]:

$$\eta_{t,a} = \frac{NMS_{t,a}}{NM_{t,a}} \tag{8}$$

Substituting in the results from Eqs. (3), (7), and (8) above, the number of living bereaved children, *CH*, was computed using Eq. (9)[12]:

$$CH_{t,a} = \eta_{t,a}\xi_{t,a}\gamma_{t-a+a_c,t}SCD_{t,a} \tag{9}$$

The number of minor children was also calculated. The index function for minor children whose parents died by suicide in year t is defined by Eq. (10):

$$\theta_{t,a} = 1[a - a_c < 20] \tag{10}$$

where t and a index the year and age at which a person dies by suicide. Therefore, the number of minor children who lost their parents to suicides was computed using Eq. (11):

$$CHJ_{t,a} = \theta_{t,a}CH_{t,a} \tag{11}$$

[10]Data on fertility rates are divided into 7 age groups from 15 to 49 years.

[11]The average unmarried rates in 1995 and 2002 in Japan were taken from the "Census" of the Ministry of Internal Affairs and Communications. The unmarried rate for suicide victims was taken from the "2004 Vital Statistics' Special Report of Japan" of the Ministry of Health, Labour and Welfare. The data for other years were calculated through linear interpolation in a similar manner as Eq. (2).

[12]By using this approach, children who lost a parent who was less than 30 years old are assigned an age of less than 0 years old. In these cases, the survival rate was set to 1.

2.2 *Estimating the Total Number of Living Bereaved Family Members in 2006*

To estimate the total number of bereaved family members who were still alive in 2006, the family members who became bereaved from 1993 to 2006 were aggregated with an adjustment for survival rates. Next, the number of all family members who became bereaved before 1992 was estimated. Finally, the number of all the above family members who were still alive in 2006 was estimated.

Estimating the Total Number of Living Family Members Who Became Bereaved from 1993 to 2006

The "2000 Prefectural Life Table" was used to calculate the survival rate in 2006, that is, the probability of a bereaved person being alive in 2006.[13] The probability that a person who was a_1 years old at the time of the suicide becoming a_2 years old was calculated using Eq. (12):

$$p_{a_1,a_2} = \prod_{k=a_1+1}^{a_2} q_k \tag{12}$$

where q_a is the probability of survival from $a_{1\text{-}1}$ year to a_1 years. The ages of spouses and siblings were assumed to be the same as those of the suicide victims. The parents of suicide victims were assumed to be 30 years older than the suicide victims, and the children of suicide victims were assumed to be 30 years younger than the suicide victims.

Estimating the Total Number of Living Family Members Who Became Bereaved Before 1992

Due to data limitation only the total number of bereaved family members was estimated, as opposed to the relationship-by-relationship estimates described above. By using the age assumptions in the previous section, together with the relationship-specific estimates of bereaved family members for 1993 to 2006 as calculated above (Table 1), the average age of bereaved family members was calculated to be 47. Since the average life expectancy of a Japanese individual is about 80 years, going back about 35–45 years provides a good estimate of the total number of family members alive in 2006.[14]

[13]These data were published by the Ministry of Health, Labour and Welfare.

[14]The survival rate is thought to have increased over time. On the other hand, the birth rate is thought to have decreased over time. This chapter assumes that the latter has a greater effect than the former. Although it is not certain that the birth rate increases continuously back through the time period evaluated, even if this factor is changed, the results remain intact.

Table 1 Estimated numbers of bereaved family members 1993–2006

Year	Suicide victims	Spouses	Wives	Husbands	Siblings	Parents	Children	Minor children	Total
1993	20,516	10,070	6,896	3,174	35,970	16,990	35,583	9,284	98,612
1994	20,923	10,050	6,993	3,057	39,020	17,745	36,350	9,005	103,165
1995	21,420	10,350	7,127	3,223	39,429	18,189	37,441	9,304	105,409
1996	22,138	10,747	7,488	3,259	41,495	18,672	38,815	9,717	109,728
1997	23,494	11,434	8,045	3,389	41,547	19,860	41,075	10,199	113,916
1998	31,755	15,490	11,319	4,171	53,152	27,130	51,423	12,659	147,196
1999	31,413	15,255	11,258	3,997	57,017	27,150	51,557	12,684	150,979
2000	30,251	14,722	10,919	3,803	54,254	26,222	49,653	11,762	144,850
2001	29,375	14,290	10,643	3,647	52,888	25,598	48,598	11,374	141,375
2002	29,949	14,600	10,923	3,678	50,333	26,436	49,736	11,912	141,105
2003	32,109	15,397	11,576	3,821	48,746	29,466	49,354	12,344	142,963
2004	30,247	14,345	10,758	3,587	49,951	27,623	46,839	11,757	138,759
2005	30,553	14,338	10,780	3,558	48,813	28,730	46,745	12,345	138,626
2006	29,921	13,973	10,349	3,624	47,769	27,796	45,899	11,954	135,436
Total	384,064	185,062	135,074	49,988	660,386	337,604	629,067	156,300	1,812,119

Table 2 Estimated numbers of bereaved family members per suicide 1993–2006

Year	Spouses	Wives	Husbands	Siblings	Parents	Children	Minor children	Total
1993	0.49	0.34	0.16	1.77	0.83	1.75	0.46	4.85
1994	0.48	0.34	0.15	1.88	0.86	1.75	0.43	4.97
1995	0.49	0.34	0.15	1.86	0.86	1.76	0.44	4.96
1996	0.49	0.34	0.15	1.89	0.85	1.77	0.44	5.00
1997	0.49	0.35	0.15	1.79	0.85	1.77	0.44	4.89
1998	0.49	0.36	0.13	1.69	0.86	1.63	0.40	4.68
1999	0.49	0.36	0.13	1.83	0.87	1.66	0.41	4.85
2000	0.49	0.36	0.13	1.81	0.87	1.66	0.39	4.83
2001	0.49	0.37	0.13	1.82	0.88	1.67	0.39	4.85
2002	0.49	0.37	0.12	1.69	0.89	1.67	0.40	4.75
2003	0.48	0.36	0.12	1.53	0.92	1.55	0.39	4.49
2004	0.48	0.36	0.12	1.66	0.92	1.56	0.39	4.62
2005	0.47	0.36	0.12	1.61	0.95	1.54	0.41	4.57
2006	0.47	0.35	0.12	1.60	0.93	1.54	0.40	4.55
Average	0.49	0.35	0.13	1.74	0.88	1.66	0.41	4.78

The average numbers of bereaved family members per suicide are referred to as "bereavement coefficients" in the remainder of the chapter. The bereavement coefficients of all family members decline gradually over time (Table 2). On the basis of the results for 1993 to 2006, the bereavement coefficients of all family members were assumed to be 5 in 1992 and to increase by 0.5 for each 15 years into the past. Multiplying the bereavement coefficients with the numbers of suicide victims, the number of all family members who became bereaved in and before 1992 was estimated. The last step was to account for the survival rates of those family members. First, the survival rate of bereaved family members in 1993 was set equal to the actual survival rate in 1993, which is approximately 0.847.[15] Second, three different geometric series for the survival rates were computed, which become zero at 81, 86, and 91 years, respectively.[16]

2.3 *Results*

Estimate of the Number of People Who Became Bereaved in 1993–2006

Estimates of the total and average numbers of family members of suicide victims are presented in Tables 1 and 2. The bereavement coefficients for total family

[15]This number can be calculated using information from Tables 1 and 3.

[16]The "Life Table" shows that the probability of death for the elderly increases approximately in a geometric progression.

members are between 4 and 5 during the period of 1993–2006 and decline gradually. The bereavement coefficients for siblings and children both decline gradually; this may reflect the declining birth rate in Japan. The coefficients for parents increase gradually; this may reflect the prolonged life span in Japan. The coefficients of spouses are almost constant.

Estimate of the Total Number of Bereaved Family Members Who Were Living in 2006

As shown in Table 3, as of 2006 there were 1.7 million family members who became bereaved in 1993–2006. Among them, the number of minors who lost their parents to suicide is 86,000. Soeda (2001, 2002) estimated the number of bereaved minors to be about 77,000 in the 14 years from 1986 to 1999, about 10% less than the present study's estimate. However, the number of suicides for the present study period (1993–2006) is approximately 17% more than that for the period of 1986–1999, suggesting that Soeda's number may overestimate the number of total bereaved children. Furthermore, Soeda postulates that the age of bereaved children follows a uniform distribution. Yet, in reality, the age distribution of suicide victims is skewed to an older age, and thus the age distribution of the bereaved children is also skewed to an older age. Because the present study considers the age distribution explicitly, there is a discrepancy between Soeda's estimate and the present study due to the difference in treatment of the age distribution.

An estimate of the number of family members who became bereaved before 1992 is shown in Table 4. By looking at both Tables 3 and 4, it is estimated that the number of all bereaved family members alive in 2006 ranges from 2.92 to 3.46 million. Therefore, considering that the population of Japan was 127.77 million in 2006, 2.31% to 2.71% of Japanese are estimated to be bereaved family members.

Costs of Suicides in Japan

Table 3 indicates that 123,482 (135,436 minus 11,954) Japanese working-age family members were affected by suicide in 2006. Chen et al. (2009) also estimated direct loss of productivity because of absence of family members. They assumed that a family member would be away from work for a week (O'Dea and Tucker 2005). Japanese GNP per working-age population in 2006 was 7,644,962 JPY, which results in an average weekly income of 159,270 JPY or approximately 1,600 USD. The total direct cost was then computed as the product of 1,600 USD and the estimated number of adult bereaved family members, which is 197 million USD.

Three main findings emerge from Chen et al. (2009). First, there are approximately five bereaved family members per suicide. Second, in 2006, there were about 90,000 children who had lost a parent to suicide. Third, in 2006, there were about 3 million family members bereaved by suicide. On the basis of these results and the assumption that each adult family member would be absent from work for a

Table 3 Estimate of the total number of living family members who became bereaved 1993–2006

Year	Suicide victims	Spouses	Wives	Husbands	Siblings	Parents	Children	Minor children	Total
1993	20,516	8,420	5,923	2,497	30,234	10,366	34,566	892	83,586
1994	20,923	8,522	6,065	2,457	33,625	11,532	35,396	2,559	89,074
1995	21,420	8,908	6,263	2,645	34,504	12,136	36,588	2,622	92,136
1996	22,138	9,396	6,678	2,717	36,869	12,889	38,077	2,746	97,230
1997	23,494	10,137	7,246	2,891	37,192	14,065	40,403	3,072	101,797
1998	31,755	14,076	10,449	3,627	48,297	20,332	50,765	3,445	133,470
1999	31,413	14,043	10,496	3,547	52,850	21,195	50,978	6,831	139,066
2000	30,251	13,732	10,301	3,431	50,935	21,181	49,205	6,619	135,053
2001	29,375	13,474	10,121	3,352	50,233	21,527	48,249	6,732	133,482
2002	29,949	13,928	10,491	3,437	48,253	22,940	49,470	7,190	134,591
2003	32,109	14,923	11,280	3,643	47,246	26,711	49,177	7,466	138,058
2004	30,247	14,042	10,565	3,477	48,952	25,988	46,722	11,757	135,704
2005	30,553	14,188	10,684	3,504	48,342	27,912	46,689	12,345	137,131
2006	29,921	13,973	10,349	3,624	47,769	27,796	45,899	11,954	135,436
Total	384,064	171,761	126,911	44,850	615,301	276,570	622,182	86,230	1,685,815

Table 4 Estimate of the total number of living family members who became bereaved before 1992

Year	Number of suicides	Factor	Bereaved family members	Survival rate1[a]	Survival rate2[a]	Survival rate3[a]	Bereaved family members1	Bereaved family members2	Bereaved family members3
1962	16,724	6	100,344			0.00			
1963	15,490	5.5	85,195			0.02			2,001
1964	14,707	5.5	80,889			0.08			6,642
1965	14,444	5.5	79,442			0.14			10,902
1966	15,050	5.5	82,775			0.19			15,647
1967	14,121	5.5	77,666		0.00	0.24			18,463
1968	14,601	5.5	80,306		0.04	0.28		2,928	22,766
1969	14,844	5.5	81,642		0.11	0.33		8,575	26,657
1970	15,728	5.5	86,504		0.17	0.37		14,595	31,743
1971	16,239	5.5	89,315		0.23	0.40		20,354	36,169
1972	18,015	5.5	99,083	0.00	0.28	0.44		28,024	43,664
1973	18,859	5.5	103,725	0.05	0.33	0.47	5,557	34,631	49,193
1974	19,105	5.5	105,078	0.14	0.38	0.51	14,317	40,064	53,152
1975	19,975	5.5	109,863	0.21	0.43	0.54	23,258	46,726	58,832
1976	19,786	5.5	108,823	0.28	0.47	0.56	30,532	50,735	61,310
1977	20,269	5.5	111,480	0.34	0.50	0.59	38,283	56,208	65,729
1978	20,199	5	100,995	0.40	0.54	0.61	40,475	54,486	62,036
1979	20,823	5	104,115	0.45	0.57	0.64	47,175	59,581	66,364
1980	20,542	5	102,710	0.50	0.60	0.66	51,445	61,904	67,705
1981	20,096	5	100,480	0.54	0.63	0.68	54,709	63,401	68,291
1982	20,668	5	103,340	0.58	0.66	0.70	60,379	67,919	72,222
1983	24,985	5	124,925	0.62	0.68	0.72	77,527	85,153	89,566
1984	24,344	5	121,720	0.65	0.70	0.73	79,572	85,727	89,337

(continued)

Table 4 (continued)

Year	Number of suicides	Factor	Bereaved family members	Survival rate1[a]	Survival rate2[a]	Survival rate3[a]	Bereaved family members1	Bereaved family members2	Bereaved family members3
1985	23,383	5	116,915	0.68	0.73	0.75	79,967	84,803	87,678
1986	25,667	5	128,335	0.71	0.74	0.76	91,321	95,595	98,169
1987	23,831	5	119,155	0.74	0.76	0.78	87,791	90,920	92,828
1988	22,795	5	113,975	0.76	0.78	0.79	86,595	88,890	90,305
1989	21,125	5	105,625	0.78	0.80	0.80	82,467	84,032	85,006
1990	20,088	5	100,440	0.80	0.81	0.82	80,343	81,368	82,011
1991	19,875	5	99,375	0.82	0.82	0.83	81,228	81,848	82,236
1992	20,893	5	104,465	0.83	0.84	0.84	87,055	87,352	87,530
Total	520,856		2,700,051				1,199,994	1,475,820	1,724,154

[a] Three different geometric series of survival rates were computed: Survivalrate1, Survivalrate2, and Survivalrate3, which become zero at 81, 86, and 91 years, respectively

week (O'Dea and Tucker 2005), in 2006 the estimated direct loss of production because of absence of family members alone is around 197 million USD. This number can be interpreted as a lower bound estimate because it does not include indirect costs such as psychological counseling or other expenditures.

3 The Werther Effect

In some cases, the "negative externalities" of suicide not only affects bereaved family members and acquaintances, but can also impact a broad range of people outside of the deceased's immediate circle of influence. In particular, suicides by celebrities, family suicides, or suicides resulting from bullying, which receive considerable media coverage, may induce a series of related suicides once they are publicized.

Since the 1970s, many studies have been carried out on the influence that media reporting on suicides by celebrities has on the general public. For example, Phillips (1974) compared the number of suicides in a month when suicide stories were published on the front pages of American newspapers with the number of suicides in a month in which no suicide stories appeared on the front pages, and found that the number of suicides tends to increase when suicide stories are featured prominently in the newspapers. This "Werther effect" (named after a novel by Goethe) has been confirmed by many of the subsequent studies (e.g., Wasserman 1984; Stack 1987). These studies generally indicate that the suicide rate tends to increase following the media reports on celebrity suicides, suggesting that suicides that receive considerable media coverage have an extremely large social impact.

However, because most of the previous studies employed monthly data on the number of suicides, the timing and duration of the Werther effect continues to be understudied. Moreover, because many of the existing studies used only a few celebrity suicide cases for analysis, they show only the impact of suicides by those specific celebrities, which makes it difficult to generalize their findings. As for studies on celebrities in Japan, only a limited number of studies have examined the impact of media reports on their suicides (Ishii 1991; Stack 1996). Bearing this in mind, Ueda et al. (2014) estimated the effect that media reports on suicides by 109 nationally "well-known figures" in Japan had on the total number of suicides. The 109 well-known figures included not just entertainment celebrities, as in typical past studies, but also politicians, business owners, and athletes. In addition, as opposed to monthly data, they used daily death records for a period of 22 years from 1989 to 2010. Then they compared the number of suicides occurring in the three-week period before and after the suicide stories were publicized, with that of a period without any suicide stories. In their estimations, they controlled for the effects that other factors, including seasons and economic conditions, have on suicide.

Figure 1 shows the estimation results. The vertical axis of the graph shows the percent changes in the number of suicides compared with the baseline period in which there was no media reports on celebrity suicides. The horizontal axis shows

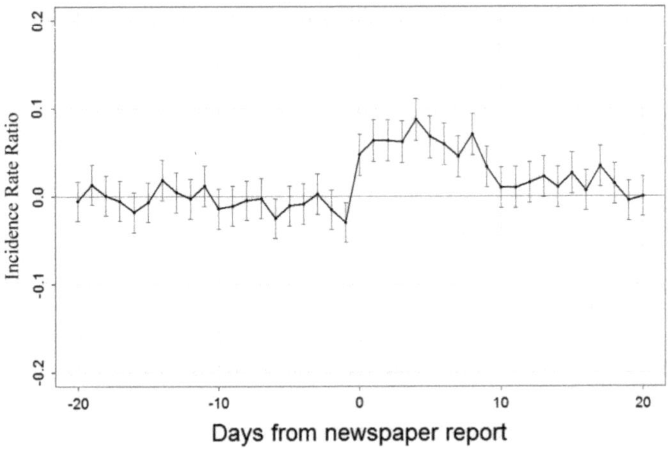

Fig. 1 Percentage increase in total suicides before and after the media reports on celebrity suicide *Source* Ueda et al. (2014)

the number of days from media reports on celebrity suicides, with positive and negative values indicating a post- and pre-reporting period, respectively. The vertical lines around the estimated figures indicate a 95% confidence interval. Thus, if the vertical lines do not cross the horizontal line at 0 in the post-reporting period, it indicates that media reports on celebrity suicides had a statistically significant effect on actual suicides in the general population.

According to the results, the number of suicides increases by around 7% immediately after the publication of celebrity suicide stories and the effect lasts for around 7 days. About a week after the stories are publicized, the effect is halved (approximately 4%) but the number of suicides remains elevated for around 20 days after the publication of such suicide stories. As expected, there was no increase in the number of suicides before celebrity suicide stories were publicized (left half of the graph). These results suggest that some individuals' decisions to take their lives are clearly affected by the media reports on celebrity suicides, indicating large negative externalities of prominent suicides.

In summary, the negative externalities of suicide affect not only the deceased's bereaved family members but also a wider segment of the population. Thus, suicide prevention measures can lead to saving lives of not only those at risk of suicide but also many others in a much broader scale.

4 Social Costs of Suicide

4.1 Social Losses Caused by the Loss of Individuals

Thus far, we have examined the negative externalities generated by suicide in the surrounding environment. In this section, we would like to consider the implication of losing individuals due to suicide from a different perspective. Losing members of society due to suicide is itself a loss to society as a whole. Furthermore, because those members are no longer able to participate in economic activities, their suicides can affect the country's overall economy. We start this section by considering how many years of individual lives have been lost in Japan due to premature deaths by suicide. Then, we will discuss lifetime work-loss cost caused by the loss of individuals due to suicide.

Potential Years of Life Lost (PYLL)

An indicator called Potential Years of Life Lost (PYLL) is often used to measure the consequences caused by the death of an individual sooner than his or her life expectancy. PYLL is used not only for suicides but also to measure the degree of losses caused by premature deaths due to diseases. In the case of suicides, PYLL is used to calculate the "years lost" by suicide based on an estimate of the average years a person would have lived if he or she had not died by suicide. More specifically, it is calculated by summing the life expectancies of all suicide victims. Because life expectancies vary by age and sex, PYLL is usually calculated by taking into consideration the age and sex of the suicide victims.

To calculate PYLL in this book, we first obtained age-specific PYLL by multiplying the number of suicide victims by their life expectancies for each age. Then, we aggregated the age-specific PYLL of all ages to obtain the total PYLL in Japan for each year. In terms of data, we used the numbers of suicides from the Vital Statistics that are available every 5 years from 1950 to 2010 and data on the life expectancies from the Life Tables (Ministry of Health, Labour, and Welfare, annually). Age groups under 9 or over 99 were excluded from the calculation because the number of suicides in those age groups is extremely low.

According to our estimations of PYLL due to suicide in 2010, the total PYLL of men of all ages was 590,000 years, while that of women was 260,000 years. In other words, 850,000 years' worth of life was lost from the future of Japan by the suicides that occurred in merely 1 year.

Next, we look at age-specific PYLL of year 2010 by 5-year age group. Figures 2 and 3 show PYLL of suicides in 2010 by sex. According to Fig. 2, men in the age group 35–39 have the longest PYLL. The number of potential years of life lost by this age group alone amount to 70,000 years. Figure 2 also shows suicide rates by age group in 2010 (right axis). As expected, the elderly had the highest suicide rate. However, those in their 30 s and early 40 s had much greater PYLL than the elderly, indicating that suicides among the younger generations have a large impact on society.

In addition, according to Fig. 3, which shows PYLL of female suicides in the same period, the PYLL values of women were generally lower than those of men. This is due to the fact that the number of suicides is lower among women (8,626 women versus 21,028 men, according to the 2010 Vital Statistics). Figure 3 also indicates that as is the case for men, women in their 30 s have the highest PYLL.

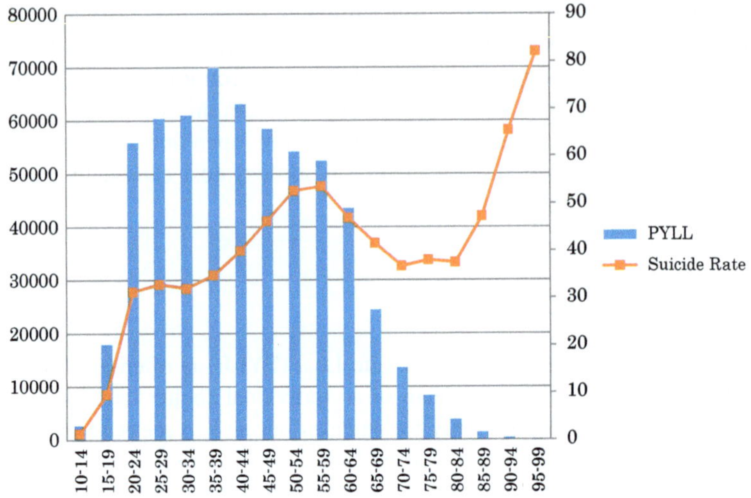

Fig. 2 Potential years of life lost (PYLL) due to suicide and suicide rates by age groups in Japan (Male, 2010)

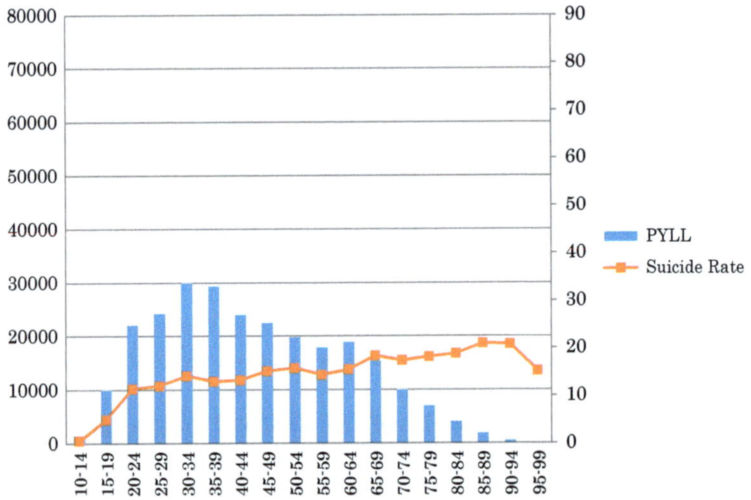

Fig. 3 Potential years of life lost (PYLL) due to suicide and suicide rates by age groups in Japan (Female, 2010)

The PYLL of women aged 30 to 34 is approximately 30,000 years, nearly 60,000 years for women in their 30 s, and 50,000 for women in their 20 s.

When women in their 20 s and 30 s die, those who may have given birth in the future have been removed from the life cycle. Although this factor is not included in this estimation, we expect that PYLL of the next generations resulting from this will not be trivial. This indicates that even though suicide rates among young women are

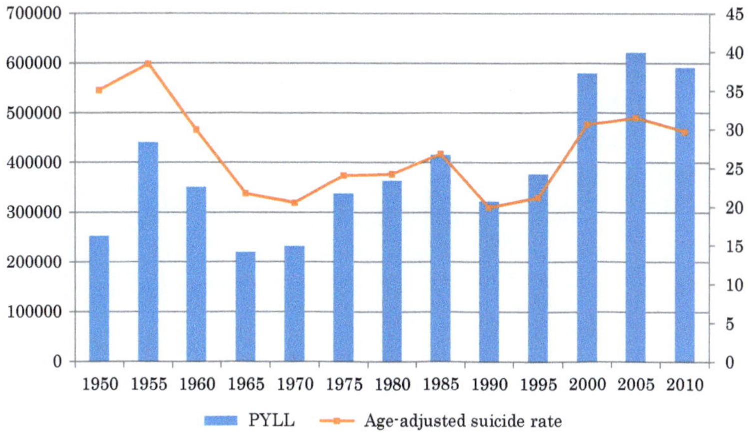

Fig. 4 PYLL due to suicide in Japan (Male, 1950–2010)

lower than women in older age groups, suicide prevention measures targeted at young women are important when considering their profound cross-generational impact.

Next, in order to understand trends in PYLL over the last 60 years, we also calculated PYLL for men from 1950 to 2010. The results are shown in Fig. 4. For reference, Fig. 4 also contains the "age-adjusted suicide rates," in which the differences in age distribution are controlled for to make better comparisons over time. According to Fig. 4, PYLL peaked in 1955, because there were many suicides among young people in their 20 s in that year.

Next, to see the shifts in the age distribution of the suicide victims, PYLL and the ratios of the suicide victims by 10-year age group are shown in Figs. 5 and 6,

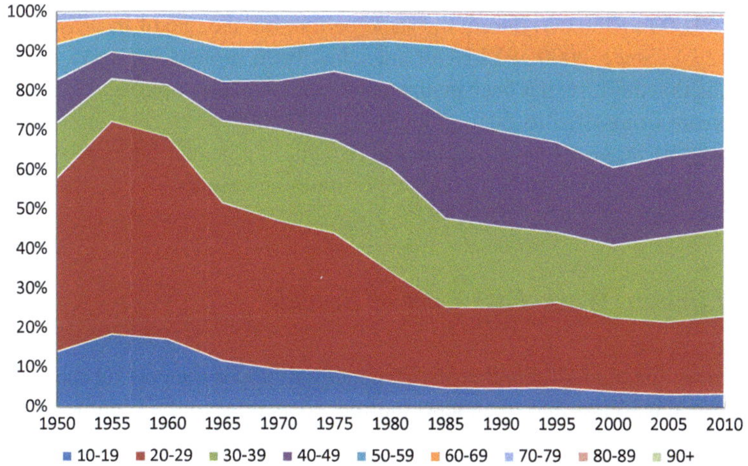

Fig. 5 PYLL in Japan by age group (%, Male, 1950–2010)

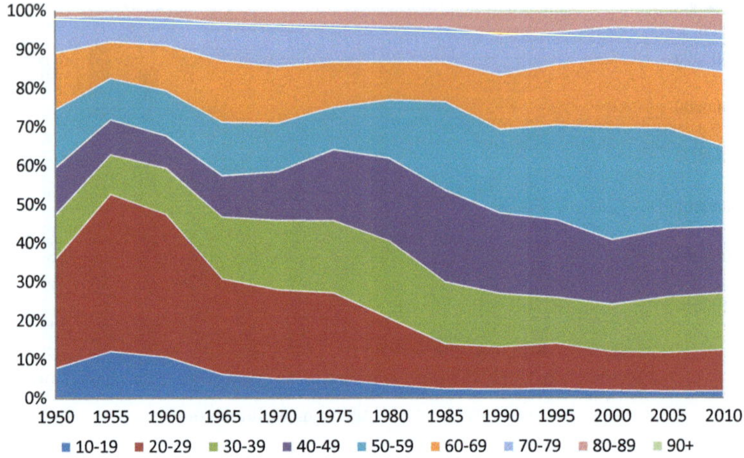

Fig. 6 Suicide deaths in Japan by age group (%, Male, 1950–2010)

respectively. According to Fig. 5, the number of suicides of those in their teens and 20 s was highest in 1955, and as shown in Fig. 6, teens and those in their 20 s accounted for nearly 50% of all suicide victims in that year. Because these age groups have long life expectancies, PYLL of those in their teens and 20 s accounted for 70% of PYLL for all ages (Fig. 5). Suicides among these age groups are decreasing today after peaking in 1955. However, suicides by those in their 30 s and 40 s are increasing. Because the life expectancies of these groups are also relatively long, PYLL for these age groups account for 40 to 50% of PYLL for all ages since 1980. In recent years, along with the sharp increase in the number of suicides from 1997 to 1998, PYLL increased drastically between 1995 and 2000. PYLL for men was approximately 380,000 years in 1995 and rose to about 580,000 years in 2000, a 53% increase. PYLL for women increased from about 190,000 to 250,000 during the same period, but the rate of increase was not as high (32%). Since 2000, PYLL for men has been around the level of 600,000. Assuming that this level has been maintained since 1998, the cumulative PYLL for men for 13 years from 1998 to 2010 amounts to 8,000,000 years. The fact that such an overwhelming number of years of life and amount of potential future productivity are lost should justify implementing suicide prevention measures.

4.2 *Lifetime Work-Loss Cost of Suicide*

Suicide has direct and indirect costs. Direct costs include the cost for the dispatch of ambulances, autopsy, and treatment. Indirect costs refer to the lifetime income that one is no longer able to receive in the future because of suicide.

Table 5 Suicide-related medical and work-loss costs in the United States in 2010

		Suicide	Self-harm	
			Hospitalized	Treated and released in emergency department
Number of cases		38,364	316,572	134,202
Medical cost	Average	$4,015	$11,116	$3,459
	Total	$154,032,000	$3,519,174,000	$464,155,000
Work loss cost	Average	$1,160,484	$19,903	$1,088
	Total	$44,520,795,000	$6,300,746,000	$145,992,000
Combined cost	Average	$1,164,499	$31,019	$4,546
	Total	$44,674,827,000	$9,819,920,000	$610,147,000

Source Centers for Disease Control and Prevention, National Center for Injury Prevention and Control

To gauge the scale of the cost of suicide, we consider the estimated lifetime work-loss and medical costs of suicide in 2010, estimated by the Centers for Disease Control and Prevention (CDC), a governmental organization in the United States. The CDC's website gives detailed information on the costs associated with deaths as a result of injuries, including homicides and suicides. By entering the manner of injury (for example, suicide, homicide, unintentional injury), age group of the injured person, sex, cause (for example, firearm, fall), and so on, the CDC's Web-based Injury Statistics Query and Reporting System (WISQARS) determines the estimated costs of the incident. Only medical costs are included as direct costs in the CDC's calculation. Table 5 shows the average medical and lifetime work-loss costs per case and the total of all the cases in the country. The total cost is the combined medical and work-loss cost. To calculate work-loss for each suicide death, the age-specific probability of surviving to a given age was multiplied by the mean earnings of the persons of that age, assuming that no one would live beyond 102 years of age. In the case of self-harm, costs from reduced working hours due to injury and so on are included in the calculation. The value of domestic tasks is also included in the calculation as earnings. Because there are differences in wage and probability of surviving between men and women, sex is also taken into account in the CDC estimation.

According to Table 5, the average medical cost per suicide is about $4,000 (around 450,000 yen at the exchange rate of February 2017), and the average lifetime work-loss cost is about $1,100,000 (around 124,000,000 yen at the same exchange rate). A total of 38,364 suicides occurred in 2010 in the United States, which means the total cost to the country is around $44.67 billion (approximately 5 trillion yen). In addition, in the same period in the United States there were more than 450,000 cases of self-harm (more than 11 times the number of suicides) (Table 5). Although the total cost of self-harm is lower than that of completed suicides, the cost of self-harm to the entire nation was still $10.4 billion (around 1.2 trillion yen). The medical cost of self-harm alone amounts to more than $3.9 billion (approximately 440 billion yen).

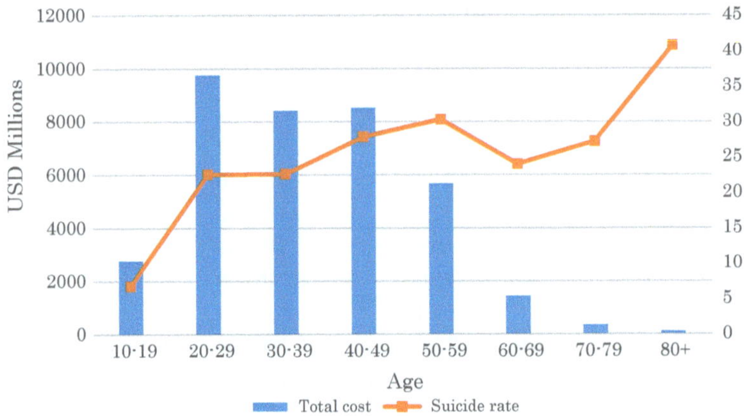

Fig. 7 Estimated total costs of male suicide in the United States in 2010 by age-group *Source* Centers for Disease Control and Prevention, National Center for Injury Prevention and Control

As in the case of PYLL, suicide-associated costs vary by age and gender. Figure 7 shows the estimated total cost (combined total of medical cost and lifetime work-loss cost) of male suicide in the Unites States. It seems that the total cost owes much to suicides by men in their 20 s to 40 s, demonstrating the profound impact these age groups have on society.

The estimates by the CDC include only the earnings of those who died from suicide or those who attempted suicide; they do not pay attention to the impact of the individuals' inability to participate in economic activities in the macro economy. Thus, the actual social costs are likely to be much higher than the above estimates. Taking this into account, Yoshihiro Kaneko and Itaru Sato, at the National Institute of Population and Social Security Research in Japan, made improved estimates of the social costs of suicides in Japan. In their estimation, they took into consideration the impact of the suicide victims' consumer activities and participation in the labor market, in addition to lost potential future earnings. Therefore, their estimates seem more comprehensive than other approximations. According to their estimates, in 2009 the lifetime income of the entire country would have increased by 1.9028 trillion yen if no suicides had occurred. Furthermore, if there were no suicides or depression in 2010, the GDP could have increased by 1.7 trillion.

However, it must be noted that these estimates were intended to capture only the lifetime incomes lost by suicide. They do not quantify a wide range of losses, including mental distress suffered by bereaved family members. This fact makes these the lowest possible estimates of the costs of suicide.

Naturally, suicide prevention carries a cost of its own. Some people may be doubtful about the usefulness of allocating financial resources to suicide prevention. Under severe financial conditions, it may be difficult for some localities to secure budgets for suicide prevention. However, the problem of suicide cannot be dealt with as a personal matter, as we have discussed; it is a problem of society as a whole and has a profound impact on a wide range of life aspects. If suicide prevention measures are effective, it can reduce the burden of massive social and economic costs and losses. The findings discussed in this chapter indicate that the benefits yielded by a decrease in the number of suicides are likely to exceed the costs necessary for suicide prevention. (We will discuss the actual costs necessary for suicide prevention in Chap. 9)

5 Market Imperfections and Distortions in Incentives

In basic economic theory, it is known that if the market is functioning well, market prices will be adjusted in a direction preferable to society. However, if the market is not functioning well, various problems can occur. In economics, this is called "market failure." In this section we discuss the possibility that such market failures are related to decisions to take one's own life. Furthermore, we consider why the correction of market failures is justified by means of suicide prevention.

To begin, there is a possibility that friction in the labor market causes involuntary unemployment. As will be discussed in depth in Chap. 3, there is a strong correlation between unemployment rates and suicide rates. According to Chen et al. (2015), this likely represents a causal relationship between unemployment and suicide. Thus, it seems in order to prevent suicides, the issue of unemployment must be addressed. Furthermore, policies that facilitate public job-placement offices in providing mental health and legal consultations in addition to employment consultations may also help prevent suicides triggered by unemployment.

5.1 Credit Market Imperfections

Credit market imperfections and liquidity constraints, in which loans are demanded but cannot be given, may be related to suicide. Chen et al. (2010) have shown theoretically a relationship between cosigner agreements and suicide from the perspective of ex-post welfare loss. When small and medium-sized businesses and micro-enterprises obtain loans in Japan, it is common for a third party, such as the business owner or a relative of the business owner, to become a co-signer for the borrower. It has been pointed out that there is a problem when a third party, such as relatives who are not experts in management or finance, become co-signers.

In theory, this co-signer system in Japan operates through the same mechanism as the microcredit concept initiated by Dr. Muhammad Yunus, founder of Grameen Bank. In a situation where there is an information asymmetry between borrowers and lenders (making the market imperfect) and borrowers who do not have collaterals face liquidity constraints, the co-signer system can ease such liquidity constraints and mitigate the problems of adverse selection in uncollateralized loans, moral hazards, and strategic debt defaults. However, according to Chen et al. (2010), the co-signer system can also attach a significant social stigma to the primary debtor if a "bad state" occurs afterwards, and may impose an excessive burden on primary debtors who feel a strong sense of altruism toward the co-signer. This entails virtually unlimited liability and therefore may induce suicides by the primary debtors. In fact, according to the "1,000-Person Suicide Survey" carried out by the Japanese nonprofit organization (NPO) Lifelink, co-signer problems led to 17 of the 52 suicides of self-employed workers. On the other hand, co-signer problems led to suicide in only 9 out of 253 non-self-employed workers. Furthermore, Rotating Savings and Credit Associations (ROSCAs) use a similar mechanism that forces contracts to be fulfilled and it has been reported that some cases led to suicide (Besley 1995). One could argue that the co-signer problem is generated by the perverse form of contracts adopted to mitigate credit market imperfections. However, if this "perverse" form of contract can induce suicide to a significant extent, then removing this form of contract should be a suicide prevention strategy.

Another example of market-related issues contributing to suicide is consumer loan group life insurance. Consumer loan group life insurance can be interpreted as an interlinkage contract (combined contract) consisting of both a loan contract granting a consumer loan to a borrower who faces liquidity constraints, and a life insurance contract. This type of interlinkage contract is generally considered as a mechanism that corrects the distortions in incentives caused by market imperfections. Consumer credit group life insurance is a contract that mitigates liquidity constraints faced by the debtor. However, it strengthens incentives towards suicide to make repayments for the debt incurred. Thus, in this sense, it is not a desirable form of contract. The "Results of the survey on consumer credit group life insurance" published by the Financial Services Agency in October 2006 summarizes the data on five major consumer loan companies in Japan. According to the survey, the number of cases of this type of insurance, in which the benefits were actually paid as a result of suicide, was 6,110, 5,074, and 3,476 respectively in 2004, 2005, and 2006. They account for 23.15%, 22.25%, and 19.39% respectively of the 26,388, 22,804, and 17,928 cases in which the causes of death are known and the benefits were paid. If these suicides were caused by imperfections inherent in the credit market and triggered by life insurance contracts designed to overcome such imperfections, then in efforts to further suicide prevention, other forms of contract must be adopted.

5.2 *Life Insurance Market Imperfections*

If the problem of information asymmetry exists between the insurers and the insured in the life insurance market, there is a theoretical possibility that adverse selection and moral hazard can occur. Thus, suicide can be induced by the presence of life insurance. In Japan, benefits from private life insurance companies are paid for deaths by suicide only after the suicide exemption period expires. The period set by major life insurance companies in Japan was 1 year until 1999 and 2 years from 2000 onward, and the period has been extended to 3 years since 2005. The benefits paid by a major life insurance company as a result of suicide increased by 50% from

1995 to 2004 and that 10% of all the insurance benefits paid are paid as a result of suicide-related deaths (Mainichi 2005). Shiromizu (2011) indicates that periods with low suicide rates during the exemption period shifted toward the right along with the extension of the exemption period, indicating that there is a close relationship between suicide and life insurance.

The only studies that discuss the relationship between suicide and insurance contracts, to our knowledge, are Tseng (2006) and Choi et al. (2015). Tseng (2006), using data provided by the Society of Actuaries (SOA) in the United States, found that suicide rates were three times higher after the life insurance exemption period had expired.

Choi et al. (2015) investigated the life insurance exemption periods from 1980 to 2002 using data on 26 OECD countries and analyzed the relationship between suicide rates and average life insurance policy premiums per capita using cross-national data. The results of this study show that there is a positive correlation between the two variables (Fig. 8). They also demonstrate that the shorter the life insurance exemption period, the higher the per capita life insurance premium. These results are consistent with the hypothesis that insurance contracts increase the number of insurance policy holders with a high risk of suicide (adverse selection problem) and lead to an increased risk of suicide after the purchase of insurance policies (moral hazard problem). These results correspond with the fact that many life insurance companies have extended the suicide exemption periods since 1999. Therefore, extension of the suicide exemption periods should be regarded by considering how the extension of exemption periods can prevent people from purchasing insurance policies to receive benefits as a result of suicide.

The above discussions emphasize the need to carefully reconsider, from the perspective of suicide prevention, the current system of co-signer contracts, and the design of insurance contracts that have complemented the functions of the markets.

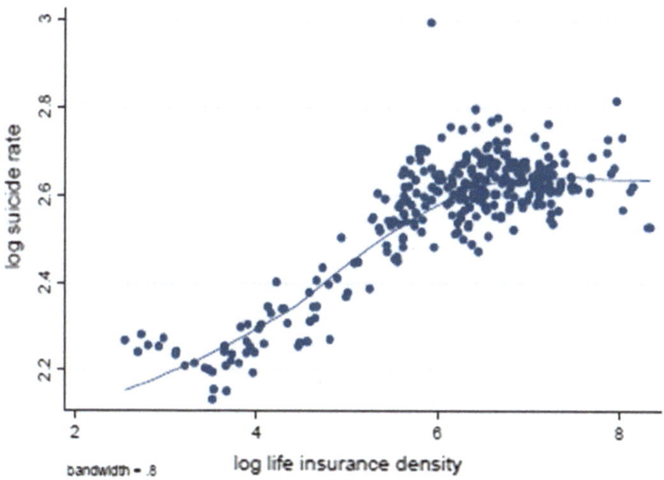

Fig. 8 Suicide rates and average life insurance policy premiums per capita *Source* Choi et al. (2015)

6 Conclusion

In this chapter, we have discussed why suicide prevention is necessary from various perspectives. The first rational basis for implementing suicide prevention measures is ensuring "the minimum standards of wholesome and cultured living" as stipulated in the Constitution of Japan. Furthermore, we also argued that suicide prevention can be justified by serious negative externalities and social costs generated by suicide as well as market imperfections.

In this chapter, we made arguments for suicide prevention by casting a spotlight on the fact that suicide is thought to significantly increase the risk of suicide among bereaved family members who are estimated to be 2.92 to 3.46 million people in 2006. Furthermore, we discussed the "Werther effect", the extremely high number of Potential Years of Life Lost (PYLL), and the seriousness of the lifetime work-loss costs of suicide. In addition, we have seen that involuntary unemployment caused by imperfections in the labor market could contribute to suicide. Other potential causes of suicide include credit market imperfections as well as life insurance market imperfections such as the loan co-signer system, consumer loan group life insurance, and life insurance exemption periods. We believe that these justify proactive suicide prevention. In summary, although people may be forced into suicide with personal problems unique to each individual, suicide is also induced by imperfections in various markets within society and generates serious negative externalities.

However, there are a few points that require careful interpretation. The first is the supposed causal relationship between unemployment and suicide. Even under the extreme assumption that all suicides are caused by unemployment, the number of suicides would account for 0.9% of the total number of the jobless. In other words, the number of suicide deaths is low even among the jobless.[17] Thus, even if there is a causal relationship between unemployment and suicide, various individual factors are believed to exist before unemployment leads to suicide. In the future, we must develop and implement more in-depth measures by understanding the reality of suicide among the jobless and identifying various factors that exist between the state of unemployment and suicide.

The second regards co-signer agreements in loans and consumer loan group life insurance policies. If these collateral supplementation systems were not offered, there is a possibility that borrowers could not get a loan in the first place, which could put them in a worse situation. The primary goal of life insurance policies is to provide a form of security to protect the livelihoods of bereaved family members from the risk of financial difficulties, irrespective of the cause of death. Therefore,

[17]This is based on the following facts and assumptions. The total population of Japan is 127 million; the population of the labor force is 65 million; 5% of the labor force is jobless; and the number of suicides is 30,000. The suicide rate calculated using the total population as the denominator would be 0.024% and the number of suicides would account for 0.9% of the total number of the jobless.

the appropriateness of these systems must be weighed against the fact that they may lead to an unfortunate consequence, namely suicide.

Despite its seriousness as a worldwide social problem, the costs of suicide are severely under-investigated and there is a serious lack of data. Further data are necessary to fully understand the true cost of suicide to society.

References

Besley, T. (1995). Savings, Credit and Insurance. In Chenery, H. & Srinivasan, T. N. (eds.), *Handbook of Development Economics*, *3*, 36, 2123–2207. Elsevier.

Centers for Disease Control and Prevention. (2010). *Web-based Injury Statistics Query and Reporting System (WISQARS)*.

Chen, J., Choi, Y. J., Mori, K., Sawada, Y., & Sugano, S. (2009). Those who are left behind: An estimate of the number of family members of suicide victims in Japan. *Social Indicators Research*, *94*(3), 535–544.

Chen, J., Choi, Y., & Sawada, Y. (2010). Joint liability borrowing and suicide: The case of Japan. *Economics Letters*, *109*(2), 69–71.

Chen, J., Choi, Y. J., Mori, K., Sawada, Y., & Sugano, S. (2015). An Analysis of Suicides in Japan, 1997–2007: Changes in Incidence, Persistence, and Age Profiles. *Social Indicators Research*, *121*(1), 253–272.

Choi, Y. J., Chen, J., & Sawada, Y. (2015). Life insurance and suicide: Asymmetric information revisited. *B. E. Journal of Economic Analysis & Policy, 15*(3), 1127–1149.

Clayton, D., & Barcelo, A. (1999). The cost of suicide mortality in New Brunswick, 1996. *Chronic Diseases in Canada, 20*(2), 89–95.

Coggan, C., Fanslow, J., Miller, B., & Norton, R. (1997). *Economic costs associated with suicide and attempted suicide in New Zealand*. Auckland: Injury Prevention Research Centre, Department of Community Health, University of Auckland.

Financial Services Agency. (2006). Shōhisha shin'yō dantai seimei hoken no chōsa kekka ni tsuite [Results of the survey on consumer credit group life insurance]. Available at http://www.fsa.go.jp/news/18/20061006-1.html.

Gunnell, D., & Frankel, S. (1999). Prevention of suicide: aspirations and evidences. *British Medical Journal, 308*, 1227–1233.

Ishii, K. I. (1991). Measuring mutual causation: Effects of suicide news on suicides in Japan. *Social Science Research*, *20*(2), 188–195.

Lifelink. 1000-Person Suicide Survey. Available at http://www.lifelink.or.jp/hp/research.html.

Mainichi. (2005). Jisatsu-sha kyūzō de seiho ga menseki enchō [Rapid increase in suicide rates leads to extended exemption period in life insurance], 2005, Oct 4, Mainichi shimbun.

Ministry of Health, Labour and Welfare, (all years). Life Tables. The Vital Statistics Report.

Ministry of Health, Labour and Welfare (2012). The number of suicide of welfare recipients.

National Police Agency. (2011). Heisei 22 nenjū ni okeru jisatsu no gaiyō shiryō. [Outline of Suicide in 2011].

National Institute of Population and Social Security Research. (2010). Jisatsu utsu taisaku no keizai-teki ben'eki (jisatsu ya utsu ni yoru shakai-teki sonshitsu) [The economic benefits of suicide and depression prevention policies (The social costs of suicide and depression)].

O'Dea, D., & Tucker, S. (2005). *The cost of suicide to society*. Wellington: Ministry of Health.

Shiromizu, Tomohito. (2011). Sakkon no jisatsu dōkō to seimei hoken [Current suicide trends and life insurance]. *Nihon hoken-i gakkaishi*, *109*(2), 102–119.

Stack, S. (1987). Celebrities and suicide: A taxonomy and analysis, 1948–1983. *American sociological review*, 401–412.

Stack, S. (1996). The effect of the media on suicide: evidence from Japan, 1955–1985. *Suicide and Life-Threatening Behavior*, *26*(2), 132–142.

Soeda, Y. (2001). On the children of suicide victims. In Y. Soeda & I. Shoten (Eds.), *Sociology of death* (pp. 195–210). Location: Publisher (in Japanese).
Soeda, Y. (2002). On the children of suicide victims reconsidered. *Mother and Child Research, 22,* 21–37. (in Japanese).
Tseng, S. H. Y. (2006). The effect of life insurance policy provisions on suicide rates, Chapter 2, Ph.D. dissertation, Three Essays on Empirical Applications of Contract Theory, Department of Economics, University of Chicago.
Ueda, M., Mori, K., & Matsubayashi, T. (2014). The Effects of media reports of suicides by well-known figures between 1989 and 2010 in Japan. *International Journal of Epidemiology, 43,* 623–629.
U.S. Department of Health and Human Services. (2001). *National strategy for suicide prevention: goals and objectives for action.*
Wasserman, I. M. (1984). Imitation and suicide: A reexamination of the Werther effect. *American sociological review*, 427–436.
World Health Organization. (2000). *Preventing suicide, a resource for general physicians, mental and behavioural disorders.*

Chapter 3
Socioeconomic Causes of Suicide

1 Introduction

Many studies on suicide in Japan and other countries have looked into the issues mainly from the health and medical point of view. Many of these studies also attempted to identify effective measures against suicide. We can set three broad categories to divide these existing studies: sociological and psychological studies; epidemiological studies; and medical studies. These studies basically highlight the seriousness of mental health conditions such as depression in causing suicidal behaviors. Because risks of depression and suicide are likely to be induced by one's economic position within a society, it would be plausible to consider that suicide and mental illnesses and suicide result not only from the individuals' characteristics but also from socioeconomic conditions. Yet, the social and economic factors behind depression have attracted little attention in the existing literature.

A notable case of suicides induced by economic factors is the year 1998 in Japan, when a reported 34.73% increase in the number of suicides—from 24,391 to 32,863—shocked the nation (Fig. 1).[1] Since then, in Japan—which has a total population of 127.5 million—more than 30,000 people have died by suicide in each of 12 consecutive years (i.e., 1998–2010). Despite the facts that some economic recovery occurred in 2003 and 2004 and that numerous preventive measures had been implemented by the government and suicide experts, the persistence of suicide remains a vexing problem for Japanese society.

A great deal of medical research has been conducted on the problem of suicide, and how severe depression or mental disorders are the major causes of suicide.[2] The Japan National Police Agency (NPA) reports that the most frequent reason for suicide in 2008 was health problems, and the main cause of breakdowns vis-à-vis various health problems was depression. In contrast, relatively little attention has been given to the underlying causes of depression itself—e.g., financial difficulties,

[1]Japan National Police Agency (NPA), Annual Report on Suicide (2009).
[2]See Mann et al. (2005) as an example.

Y. Sawada et al., *Economic Analysis of Suicide Prevention*, Creating a Society for All, DOI 10.1007/978-981-10-1500-7_3

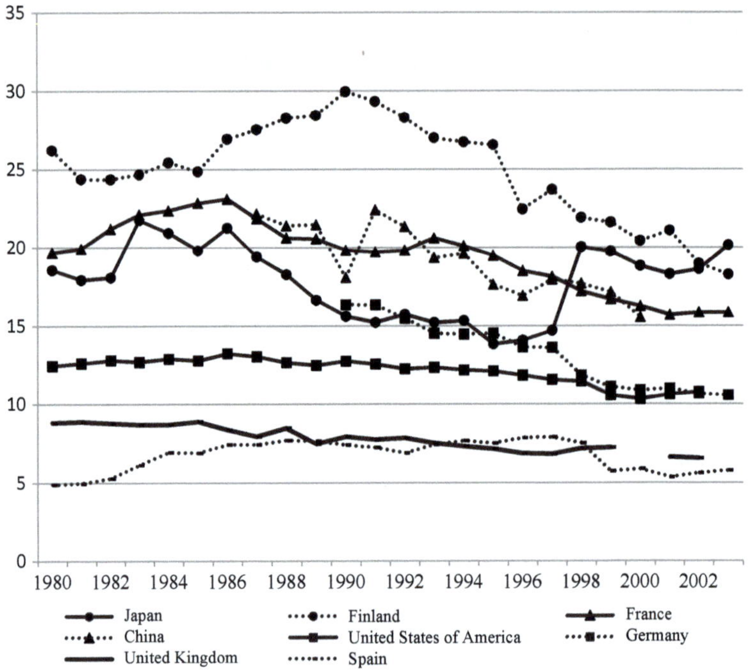

Fig. 1 Age-adjusted suicide rates, 1982–2004 (per 100,000 population) *Note* The age-adjusted suicide rate is a weighted average of the age-specific suicide rates per 100,000 persons, where the weights are the proportions of people in the corresponding age groups of the European Standard population*Source* WHO Mortality Database (2006); World Health

problems in the workplace, and family problems—and their relationships to suicide. As a matter of fact, by examining individual-level data, the Suicide Investigation Team (2008) finds that people who killed themselves had typically suffered from multiple—four, on average—risk factors for suicide. Therefore, an effective suicide prevention measure requires a more general understanding of suicide that transcends oversimplified medical perspectives.

On the other hand, it has been suggested that Japan has a "suicide tradition." Some argue that certain Japanese cultural elements—such as *samurai*, *kamikaze*, groupism, shame culture, and authoritarian familism—have contributed to Japan's remarkably high suicide rate compared to that of other industrialized countries. Such a claim is not necessarily supported by empirical analysis. For example, in conducting cross-country panel regression analysis, Chen et al. (2009) empirically identify how suicide in Japan is different from suicide in other OECD countries. They show that the suicide rate in Japan is more markedly affected by economic variables such as female labor participation, per capita gross domestic product, and unemployment rate than is the case in other OECD countries. Further, it has been found that life insurance contracts in Japan may have provided financial incentives for suicide, as life insurance policies there pay death benefits even in cases of suicide (Chen et al. 2008).

Despite there being a long list of studies linking socioeconomic variables to suicide, the disturbing upsurge of suicide in Japan in 1997 or on the persistently high number of suicides afterwards are understudied.[3] As a matter of fact, little is known of how Japanese suicides since 1998 can be characterized and to what extent Japanese suicides can be attributed to certain demographic and socioeconomic changes. Studying the suicide problem in Japan is particularly important from an economic perspective, because the Japanese economy has been suffering from a series of economic recessions. Especially in 1997, in the aftermath of the 1990 burst of the financial bubble, a number of financial institutions could not afford the massive bad loans, and they subsequently collapsed. As the banks were calling back loans and becoming unwilling or unable to lend money, consequently, many of the companies facing credit constraints faced bankruptcy, which in turn led to high unemployment across Japan.

In this chapter, we explore socioeconomic determinants of suicides. First, we sort out the results of the existing studies and discuss the socioeconomic factors that are among the risk factors for suicide. Then, using cross-national data, we clarify that the suicide rate in Japan is high and also that socioeconomic factors have a much greater impact on suicide in Japan than in other countries. By analyzing the chronological data in Japan, we will demonstrate that suicide in Japan has four characteristics: (1) a "sharp increase" from 1997 to 1998, (2) a "consistently high level" in the annual number of suicides in excess of 30,000 per year for 14 years since 1998, a continuous increase in suicide of "young people" aged 20–39, and (4) a recent decline in overall suicide since the year 2010. Lastly, we will clarify that these four characteristics are closely related to economic conditions.

We use the decomposition method and explore what contributed to the 1998 upsurge in the number of suicides in Japan, as well as the persistence in the high suicide rate thereafter. Decomposition was applied to the 1997–1998 change and to the cumulative changes from 1998 to 2007; the results thereof revealed how each group (i.e., by gender and age profile) contributed to changes in the number of suicides in the 1997–2007 period. This set of results showed that while the abrupt increase in the number of suicides in 1998 can be mainly attributed to middle-aged men aged 40–59, it was the suicides of young people aged 20–39 that contributed to the persistently high number of suicides after 1998. This finding suggests that the age profile of suicide in Japan has been changing recently, in a transition from middle-aged to young suicides.

To shed more light on changes in the age profile of suicides in Japan during this period, we further decomposed suicide growth according to the reasons for committing suicide. While a large proportion of the 1997–1998 suicide upsurge can be attributed to the economic and financial problems of middle-aged men, it is not as important a factor in explaining persistently high suicide rates after 1998. In

[3]For a survey of the literature on suicide and socioeconomic variables, see Chen et al. (2012a).

addition, decomposition by employment status showed that while self-employed persons contributed significantly to the 1997–1998 suicide upsurge, their contribution has been declining in recent years. Finally, supporting the assertion that there had been a change in the suicide age profile in Japan, the data also revealed a clear transition in the means of suicide. While hanging accounted for most of the 1997–1998 suicide upsurge, gas poisoning—a means of suicide that has been widely discussed on the internet—has become prominent in more recent years.

To strengthen the link between economic hardship and suicide in Japan, aggregate data analyses as well as prefecture-level panel regressions were used to examine the presumption that bankruptcies and unemployment following the 1997 credit crunch had played an influential role on both the abrupt increase in suicide in 1998 and the persistence of suicide afterwards. The regression results indicate that, first, the unemployment rate is positively correlated with the suicide rate. Second, the personal bankruptcy rate was also a significant predictor of the total male suicide rate. Third, among middle-aged men, a higher personal bankruptcy rate was found more likely to increase the suicide rate. Furthermore, the impact of personal bankruptcy on suicide rate was found to be stronger for men aged 40–59 than for males of all ages.

2 Factors of Suicide Viewed from an Economic Standpoint

In this section, we will first review the results of various empirical studies on suicide carried out in the discipline of economics. Because it is difficult for researchers to use individual data on suicide, empirical studies are typically carried out using macro data aggregated by area or by country. Many of the existing studies have used socioeconomic variables as explanatory variables and the suicide rates by country or area as dependent variables, attempting to explain the relationship between the socioeconomic variables and suicide rates through regression analysis. Although there are a variety of socioeconomic variables, researchers have mainly used variables that represent income or wealth, such as per capita income level; variables that represent the conditions of the labor market, such as unemployment rate and jobs-to-applicants ratio; and variables that represent demographic structures, domestic situations, or health conditions. These data are not individual data, but rather, they are country- or area-level macro data. Therefore, they do not necessarily allow us to precisely understand the relationship between economic conditions of individuals and suicide rates. Despite these limitations, many studies have elucidated the correlation between the macroeconomic variables and suicide rates tabulated by region or country. Hereinafter, we will examine some of the key economic variables discussed in the existing studies—income and its inequality, economic growth and economic crisis, and employment situation.

2.1 Income and Its Inequality

Hamermesh and Soss (1974) published a pioneering research article in the field of economics on the theme of suicide. They consider suicide to be an action resulting from a rational choice, and conclude that a person chooses to die by suicide when his or her expected lifetime utility falls below a certain threshold. In economics, it is generally believed that the higher the income, the higher is the level of utility attained. Based on this theory, the probability of suicide becomes lower when one's income is higher. In other words, if people have a high income, they have a higher standard of living, which makes them more satisfied with their lives and less suicidal. In the existing empirical studies, per capita GDP or per capita real income are used as data that represent income. Many studies have demonstrated that countries and regions with low incomes have higher suicide rates (Chen et al. 2012a). On the other hand, it is also known that the relationship between income and suicide rates vary by gender and age. Chen et al. (2009) have demonstrated that income has a negative relationship with suicide rates across all age/gender groups, but it has a more negative relationship with the suicide rates among men aged 45–64 and women aged 65 and over.

In addition to income itself, income inequality and income gaps have been considered to have effects on suicide. The Gini coefficient is often used as a variable that represents income inequality. Existing studies have found that countries and regions with high income inequality have higher suicide rates (Chen et al. 2012a).

2.2 Economic Growth and Economic Crisis

In addition to inequality of gross income and income, economic growth or economic trends can also affect suicide rates. This is because the outlooks for future employment and household economy are bright when the economy is showing growth, and such positive economic conditions are believed to contribute to lowering suicide rates. Indeed, many empirical studies have found a significantly negative correlation between economic growth and suicide rates, demonstrating that countries and regions that show economic growth have lower suicide rates. On the other hand, some studies claim that financial difficulties and economic crises are associated with suicide (Chen et al. 2012a). However, it must be noted that not all the existing studies have necessarily produced consistent and robust findings.

2.3 Employment Situation

Unemployment has a profound effect on the decision to die by suicide. This is because unemployment not only causes difficulties in one's short-term living environment, but also precludes a clear future forecast of income and creates a decline in lifetime income. It is therefore expected that higher unemployment rates will be a factor leading to an increase in the number of suicides and attempted suicides, based on the theory presented by Hamermesh and Soss (1974). Furthermore, unemployment is often associated with mental or physical disorders, which increases the risk of suicide in a complex and serious manner. In reality, many empirical studies have demonstrated a correlation between high unemployment rates and high suicide rates.

Chen et al. (2012a) used a method called meta-regression analysis,[4] and verified the robustness of the empirical research findings reported by the existing studies. This study revealed three points as tendencies commonly seen in the existing studies. First, the impact of income on suicide rates tends to be overestimated. Second, when the level of income inequality becomes higher, suicide rates tend to be higher in general. Third, there is a positive correlation between unemployment and suicide rates. "Biased publication of findings from academic research (publication bias)" is observed particularly in the existing studies (Chen et al. 2012a). Specifically, we see a tendency to find that income has a negative relationship with suicide rates, that the level of income inequality and divorce rates have a positive relationship with suicide rates, and that these relationships are statistically significant (Chen et al. 2012a). Therefore, we must pay attention to the robustness of the analysis results reported when interpreting the research findings.

3 Suicide Trends in Japan Through Cross-National Comparison

With a basis established for the need to examine trends in suicide causation, let us analyze the suicide trends in Japan based on the leading causes of death by age group provided in the *2011 White Paper on Suicide Prevention* of Cabinet Office of Japan. According to this report, suicide is the number one cause of death in men aged 20–44 and women aged 15–34 and is the second leading cause of death in men aged 15–19 and 45–49 and women aged 35–49. In other words, according to the death statistics in Japan, suicides among young and middle-aged generations are the most prevalent cause of death irrespective of gender.

With this in mind, we shall examine the characteristics of suicides in Japan from an international point of view. The suicide rate in Japan for the total population is approximately 24 per 100,000 people, which is extremely high by international standards. According to data from the year 2009, the suicide rate in Japan for men and women combined ranks eighth in the world and third among the OECD countries, after South Korea and Hungary. In terms of the number of male suicides,

[4]Meta-regression analysis is a method that performs another regression analysis using the results of an earlier regression analysis, as the basic data.

Japan ranks 10th in the world (third among the OECD countries), whereas in terms of the female suicide rate, Japan ranks third in the world and second among the OECD countries, after Korea, which is quite serious.

The chronological trends are also revealing. Figure 3 of Chap. 1 shows the shifts in the suicide rates per 100,000 population members in Japan and Korea, as well as in OECD countries combined. The suicide rate in Japan rose through the end of the 1990s, particularly between 1997 and 1998, a sharp increase to nearly twice the average of OECD countries excluding Japan. What also draws attention here is the sharp increase in the suicide rate in Korea after the financial crisis in 1997 and 1998. Korea has the highest suicide rate among the OECD countries today. On the other hand, the suicide rate in Europe has continued to drop since 1980's, in contrast to Japan and Korea. It is vital to explore the determinants of suicide that can explain these differences when thinking about effective suicide prevention measures.

Chen et al. (2009) examined the socioeconomic factors of suicide in Japan through cross-national comparison using the data provided by the World Health Organization (WHO). In this study, multiple linear regression analysis was conducted based on data for 21 OECD countries from 1980 and 2000 that allow for an international comparison using the suicide rate as a dependent variable and various socioeconomic indices as explanatory variables.[5] The explanatory variables include per capita GDP levels, per capita GDP growth rates, unemployment rates, female labor participation rates, birthrates, divorce rates, and the Gini coefficient, which measures income inequality.[6] Furthermore, this paper made its estimates based on regression analysis, taking into the possiblity that these factors could affect Japan differently than other countries, and the international comparison based on such analysis has revealed three trends seen in suicides in Japan and in the world.

First, correlation between socioeconomic variables and the suicide rate varies by gender and age group worldwide. In particular, suicide rates for men show a stronger correlation with socioeconomic variables, whereas suicide rates for women and older people show a relatively weak relationship with socioeconomic variables.

Second, the suicide rates are generally lower in countries with better economic conditions, which have achieved high economic growth or whose people enjoy high income, as well as in countries where income equality has been achieved. The negative correlation between income levels and suicide rates is especially notable in the cases of middle-aged and older men (45–64 and 65 and over). Furthermore, a low economic growth rate shows a correlation with high suicide rates, and this is especially notable in the cases of middle-aged and older men (those aged 45–64 and those aged 65 and over) and women aged 25–44. These groups are highly likely to be vulnerable to the risks associated with income reduction.

[5]See Choi et al. (2009) for data sources and details of the analysis.

[6]Furthermore, in order to eliminate false correlations due to time trends and features unique to individual countries, fixed effects for countries and yearly linear trends are also added. See Chen et al. (2009) for details of the analysis and data sources.

Third, the suicide rate in Japan has a stronger correlation with economic conditions compared with other OECD countries. In other words, economic variables such as low per capita GDP levels, large income gaps, recessions, high unemployment rates, etc., have significantly stronger correlations with the suicide rates in Japan than in other countries.[7] What is notable here is that the correlation between income gaps and suicide rates is particularly high in Japan, in comparison with other OECD countries. This indicates the possibility that a stigma resulting from income gaps has a stronger connection to suicides in Japan. Furthermore, these analysis results suggest the possibility that the Japanese government must play a significant role in terms of suicide prevention; there is much to be done, particularly from the perspective of targeting observable economic indices.

According to the analysis results obtained by Chen et al. (2009), given the positive correlation observed between high unemployment rates and high suicide rates in Japan, e.g., that for men, a 1% point rise in the overall unemployment rate could lead to an approximately 25-per-100,000-person increase in the number of suicide victims. The study shows that particularly for men aged 65 and over, a 1% point rise in the overall unemployment rate could lead to an approximately 39-per-100,000-person increase in the number of suicide victims. On the other hand, this correlation is not statistically significant for women. Additionally, around 19% of the differences in suicide rates between Japan and other OECD countries from 1980 to 2000 can be explained by a stronger influence by the unemployment rate on the suicide rate in Japan.

In addition, the suicide rate and the female employment rate show a positive correlation in Japan. This tendency is especially notable for the suicide rate among older men (aged 65 and over) and the suicide rate among younger women (aged 25–44). Kohara (2010) indicates that when the head of household (typically a husband) loses a job against their will, their spouses' (typically wives') labor supply is apt to increase; this is particularly true among poor households with low levels of financial assets. Therefore, the female employment rate may strongly reflect households' poverty levels, and the positive correlation between the female employment rate and the suicide rate observed here may indirectly point to a correlation between economic difficulties caused by spousal unemployment and the suicide rate.

4 Suicide Trends in Japan Viewed Chronologically: Jump, Inertia, Age Change, and Decline

By looking further into the chronological changes in suicide trends in Japan, the three characteristics described at the beginning of the chapter are evident. First, the "sharp increase" from 1997 to 1998; second, the "consistently high level" in the annual number of suicides in excess of 30,000 per year for 14 years since 1998,

[7]On the other hand, divorce rates in Japan had a statistically significant relationship only with the suicide rate for men aged 22–44.

with the number remaining high; third, the "increase in younger suicide victims," which is advancing over the years (Chen et al. 2015), and the recent decline. Due to such characteristic features, suicide is recognized as one of the most serious social problems in Japan, and various measures to prevent it are now being implemented. Here, let us examine these four characteristics in depth.

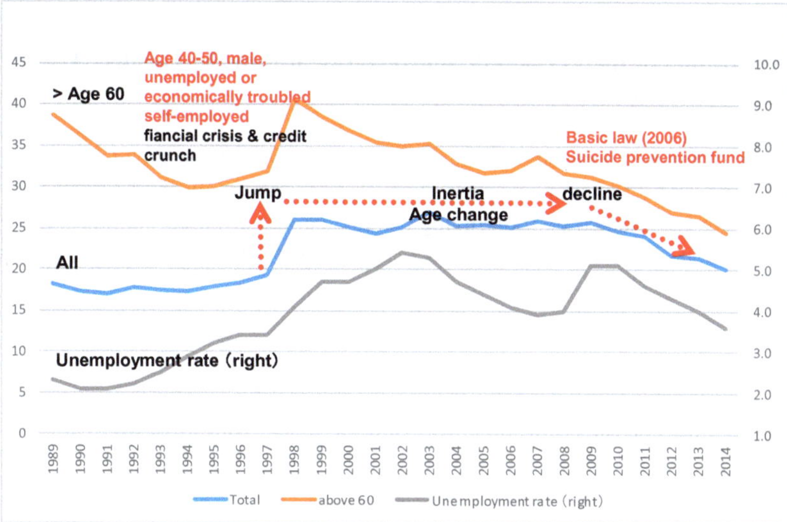

4.1 Decomposition of Japanese Suicides

Using a decomposition method, we explored Japanese suicide data from 1997 to 2007 (Chen et al. 2015). In Japan, the Ministry of Health, Labour, and Welfare (MHLW) and the NPA publish suicide data independently.[8] Whereas MHLW data are based on death certificates submitted to local offices, NPA data are constructed from jurisdictional police records. Although there are minor discrepancies between these two dataset series, the correlation coefficient between them is almost 1.[9] Neither of the two datasets provides individual suicide records; rather, released information includes suicide counts in terms of categories such as age, gender, and reasons for committing suicide.

From MHLW data, we obtained annual data on suicide numbers, classified by age, gender, and the means of suicide. From the NPA data, we extracted data on annual suicides by employment status and reasons for suicide—two categories not available

[8]MHLW data are published in the Vital Statistics, while NPA data are published in the Annual Report on Suicide.

[9]In general, NPA data report slightly higher suicide numbers than MHLW data.

from the MHLW data.[10] Finally, population data made available in the Population Estimates by Japan's Ministry of Internal Affairs have been combined with MHLW suicide data in order to control for effects arising from demographic changes.

4.2 Increase in the Number of Suicides from 1997 to 1998

Decomposition of the 1997–1998 Suicide Growth Rate, by Gender, Age, and Population Structure

First, we conducted a decomposition of the 1997–1998 suicide growth rate data, by gender, age, and population structure. Note that the total number of suicides at time t (SCD_t) can be obtained by multiplying the suicide rate of group j at time t ($SR_{j,t}$) by the population of group j at time t ($POP_{j,t}$), and then summing them over J groups:[11]

$$SCD_t = \sum_{j=1}^{J} SR_{j,t} \cdot POP_{j,t}. \tag{1}$$

Taking the derivative of the logarithm of SCD_t with respect to t, one can decompose the total suicide growth rate in terms of changes in the population and changes in age group-specific suicides:

$$\begin{aligned} \frac{\Delta SCD_t}{SCD_t} &\cong \sum_{j=1}^{J} \left(\frac{SR_{j,t}}{SCD_t} \cdot \Delta POP_{j,t} + \frac{POP_{j,t}}{SCD_t} \cdot \Delta SR_{j,t} \right) \\ &= \sum_{j=1}^{J} \left(cd\_POP_{j,t} + cd\_SR_{j,t} \right), \end{aligned} \tag{2}$$

where $cd\_POP_{j,t}$ and $cd\_SR_{j,t}$ are, respectively, the effect (degree of contribution) of changes in the number of population of group j at time t and the effect of changes in the number of suicides of group j at time t, on the total suicide growth rate. Equation (2) was applied separately to male and female suicides, and the results thereof are presented in Table 1.[12]

[10] There are limitations in examining NPA suicide data in terms of the reasons for dying by suicide. First, since 2007, the NPA has been recording multiple reasons for each suicide, which makes it impossible to decompose into individual categories of suicide data in terms of those reasons. Second, from 1999 to 2006, the reasons for suicide were not identified for those individuals who did not leave suicide notes or other writings. As a result, the sample from each year is reduced to only one-third of the total suicides in this period, perhaps incurring sample-selection problems. Until and including 1998, the NPA suicide data covered almost all suicides in terms of reasons for suicide.

[11] For details on the decomposition formula, see Mori et al. (2012).

[12] Note that there were some discrepancies between the actual suicide growth rate, 35.16%, and the sum of the degrees of contribution, 34.834%, due to the approximation of derivatives by first differences. We report this discrepancy as a residual, at the bottom of each table.

Table 1 Decomposition of the 1997–1998 suicide growth rate by gender, age, and population structure (Unit: %)

Age group (years)	Sum of the degrees of contribution (A). (A) = (B) + (C) + (D) + (E)	Male		Female	
		cd_SR (B)	cd_POP (C)	cd_SR (D)	cd_POP (E)
00–19	1.156	0.828	–0.034	0.375	–0.014
20–39	7.135	5.297	0.124	1.671	0.043
40–59	15.148	13.097	0.106	1.89	0.056
60–79	9.856	6.391	0.467	2.737	0.262
80 and above	1.538	0.756	0.136	0.417	0.229
Total	34.834	26.37	0.799	7.09	0.575

Suicide growth rate: 35.163; Residual: 0.329
Notes cd_SR and cd_POP denote, respectively, the degree of contribution of the change in the age group-specific suicide rate and the degree of contribution of the change in the population to the suicide growth rate from 1997 to 1998
The sample does not include suicide victims of unknown age
Source Vital Statistics, Japan Ministry of Health, Labour, and Welfare; Population Estimates, Japan Ministry of Internal Affairs

The decomposition results in Table 1 suggest that, first, the 40–59 age group experienced the most dramatic increase in the number of suicides, followed by the 60–79 and 20–39 age groups. Second, 78% of the suicide growth (i.e., 27.17% of 34.83%) can be attributed to men; the men aged 40–59, in themselves, contributed 37.9% of the suicide growth rate (i.e., 13.2% of 34.83%). Third, from the demographic perspective, the effect of the change in population on the number of suicides was of a substantially smaller magnitude, compared to the effect of age group-specific suicide changes. This is not surprising, because we were examining change within 1 year, during which there was little change in the population structure. However, for the age groups of 60–79 and 80 and above, the effects of population change on suicide growth were relatively higher than those of younger groups. Other things being equal, this implies that the aging population structure in Japan is expected to continuously fuel the suicide growth rate in the future. Finally, despite the decline in the population of young people aged up to 19 years—a decline that contributed negatively to suicide growth from 1997 to 1998—the combined effect (i.e., changes in population and suicide together) to the suicide growth rate was small, but positive.

Decomposition of the 1997–1998 Suicide Growth Rate, by Gender, Age, and Reasons for Suicide

To gain more insight into the upsurge in the number of suicides, using the NPA dataset, we decomposed the suicide growth rate from 1997 to 1998 by gender, age, and reasons for suicide. Note that the total number of suicides at time t (SCD_t) can be obtained by:

$$SCD_t = \sum_{j=1}^{J} SCD_{j,t}, \tag{3}$$

where $SCD_{j,t}$ is the number of suicides in the jth cell of gender–age–reasons, $j = 1, \ldots, 56$, at time t.[13] Hence, the decomposition is performed via the following formula:

$$\begin{aligned} \frac{\Delta SCD_t}{SCD_t} &= \sum_{j=1}^{J} \left(\frac{\Delta SCD_t}{SCD_t} \right) \\ &= \sum_{j=1}^{J} cd\_SCD_{j,t}, \end{aligned} \tag{4}$$

where $cd\_SCD_{j,t}$ is the effect (degree of contribution) of changes in the number of suicides of the jth group on the total suicide growth rate.

The decomposition results are shown in Table 2.[14] First, notice that suicides associated with economic and financial problems contributed the most (i.e., 39.2%) to male suicide growth (10.39% of 26.5%), but it contributed little (i.e., 7.28%) to female suicide growth (0.58% of 7.97%). Second, especially, the percentage of men in the 40–59 age group who died by suicide for economic and financial reasons increased dramatically; they alone accounted for 18.83% of the 1997–1998 suicide growth rate (6.49% of 34.47%). This finding is consistent with the presumption that bankruptcies and unemployment, followed by the unprecedented 1997 credit crunch, had played an influential role in this upsurge in suicide. Third, the male group aged 60 and above with health problems was the second-largest contributor to suicide growth (4.05% of 34.47%), followed by the male group aged 40–59 with health problems (3.37% of 34.47%).

Decomposition of the 1997–1998 Suicide Growth Rate, by Employment Status and Reasons for Suicide[15]

Using the NPA data, we also decomposed the suicide growth rate from 1997 to 1998, by employment status and reasons for suicide. Equation (3) is used to carry

[13] $J = 2$ (genders) $\times$ 4 (age groups) $\times$ 7 (reasons for suicide) = 56.

[14] Tables 1 and 2 use different age-group categorizations, due to categorization differences between the MHLW and NPA datasets. The data in Table 2 exclude those of unknown age or for unidentified reasons.

[15] The term "employment status" used throughout the chapter is somewhat of a misnomer; we followed the categorizations offered by each of the data sources.

Table 2 Decomposition of the 1997–1998 suicide growth rate, by gender, age, and reasons for suicide (Unit: %)

Gender	Age group	Sum of the degrees of contribution (A). (A) = (B) + (C) + (D) + (E) + (F) + (G) + (H)	Economic and financial problems (B)	Family (C)	Health (D)	Relationships (E)	School (F)	Work (G)	Others (H)
Male	00–19	0.58	0.031	0.048	0.215	0.044	0.092	0	0.149
	20–39	5.436	1.721	0.452	1.221	0.29	0.114	0.926	0.711
	40–59	12.879	6.49	0.918	3.368	0.11	0	1.44	0.553
	60 and above	7.61	2.147	0.676	4.048	0.018	0	0.202	0.518
	Subtotal	26.504	10.389	2.094	8.852	0.461	0.206	2.569	1.932
Female	00–19	0.364	–0.004	0.066	0.026	0.048	0.101	0.009	0.119
	20–39	1.822	0.004	0.338	0.953	0.228	0.026	0.162	0.11
	40–59	1.914	0.369	0.479	0.869	–0.031	0	0.088	0.141
	60 and above	3.868	0.211	0.571	2.951	0.018	0	0.009	0.11
	Subtotal	7.97	0.58	1.453	4.799	0.263	0.127	0.268	0.479
Total		34.474	10.969	3.548	13.652	0.725	0.334	2.837	2.411

Note The sample does not include suicide victims of unknown age or with unspecified reasons
Source Annual Report on suicide, Japan National Police Agency

out this decomposition, except that $SCD_{j,t}$ denotes the number of suicides in the jth cell of employment status and reasons for suicide, for $j = 1, \ldots, 42$.[16]

Table 3 presents the decomposition results. First, we found that suicides prompted by economic and financial problems contributed second-most to the 1997–1998 suicide growth rate (10.97% of 34.4%), following suicides for health reasons (13.63% of 34.4%). Second, those who were unemployed, employed, and self-employed accounted for 89.11% of the suicide increase in 1998 (30.66% of 34.40%). Third, except for the housewife or househusband, student, and unemployed categories, suicides for financial problems contributed most to the 1997–1998 suicide upsurge; furthermore, it was most significant for those who were self-employed. Since there are relatively fewer self-employed workers in Japan compared to those who are employed, this high degree of contribution by self-employed suicides for financial problems underscores the significance of the impact of the credit crunch event during this period on this subset of the data sample. This finding indicates that bankruptcies triggered by the 1997 financial crisis would be a significant factor to growth in the suicide rate.

Decomposition of the 1997–1998 Suicide Growth Rate, by Gender and Means of Suicide

The number of suicides, $SCD_{j,t}$, can be obtained by summing the various numbers of suicides categorized by the means of suicide; therefore, Eq. (3) also applies here, with j indicating each means of suicide. In the original MHLW data, there are 25 categories of suicide means, by gender.[17] For simplicity, we reduced these to seven categories.[18] The decomposition results are presented in Table 4.

Table 4 indicates that most of the increased number of suicides from 1997 to 1998 had been by individuals who hanged themselves. Note that these events took place before knowledge of relatively new suicide means—e.g., carbon monoxide poisoning and the use of homemade hydrogen sulfide gas—became widespread and readily available through internet chat rooms and bulletin boards.

4.3 *The Persistence of Suicide Since 1998*

Following the same set-up and using the same decomposition method as that used in the previous subsection, we looked into the long-term effects of gender, age,

---

[16] $J = 6$ (employment status) $\times$ 7 (reasons for suicide) = 42.

[17] According to the 10th Revision of the International Statistical Classification of Diseases and Related Health Problems (ICD-10) from Japan's Vital Statistics, these 25 categories correspond to Categories X60–X84.

[18] We follow the same categorization as that in Table 22 of the Vital Statistics Special Report (2004): Hanging, X70; gas poisoning, X67; drugs, X60–X66, X68, and X69; drowning, X71; jumping (others), X80; jumping (towards a moving object such as a train), X81; and others, X72–X79 and X82–X84.

Table 3 Decomposition of the 1997–1998 suicide growth rate, by employment status and reasons for suicide (Unit: %)

Employment status	Sum of the degrees of contribution (A). (A) = (B) + (C) + (D) + (E) + (F) + (G) + (H)	Economic and financial problems (B)	Family (C)	Health (D)	Relationships (E)	School (F)	Work (G)	Others (H)
Employed	9.392	2.976	1.116	2.262	0.423	0.004	2.099	0.512
Housewife or househusband	2.174	0.181	0.586	1.31	0.022	0	0.022	0.053
Management	0.825	0.428	–0.026	0.159	0.013	0	0.256	–0.004
Self-employed	5.697	3.625	0.472	1.199	0.018	0	0.154	0.229
Student	0.75	0.018	0.031	0.229	0.031	0.273	0.013	0.154
Unemployed	15.566	3.739	1.429	8.471	0.212	0.053	0.3	1.363
Total	34.403	10.967	3.607	13.63	0.719	0.331	2.844	2.306

Note The sample does not include suicide victims of unknown employment status, age or with unspecified reasons
Source Annual Report on Suicide, Japan National Police Agency

Table 4 Decomposition of the 1997–1998 suicide growth rate, by gender and means of suicide (Unit: %)

Means	Sum of the degree of contribution (A). (A) = (B) + (C)	Male (B)	Female (C)
Drowning	0.396	0.26	0.136
Drug overdose	–0.272	–0.136	–0.136
Gas poisoning	1.434	1.349	0.085
Hanging	30.702	24.083	6.619
Jumping (towards a moving object such as a train)	0.145	0.094	0.051
Jumping (others)	2.145	1.328	0.817
Others	0.613	0.468	0.145
Total	35.163	27.446	7.717

Source Vital Statistics, Japan Ministry of Health, Labour, and Welfare

Table 5 Decomposition of the 1998–2007 cumulative suicide growth rate, by gender, age, and population structure (Unit: %)

Age group	Sum of the degrees of contribution (A). (A) = (B) + (C) + (D) + (E)	Male		Female	
		cd_SR (B)	cd_POP (C)	cd_SR (D)	cd_POP (E)
00–19	–0.659	–0.336	–0.255	0.064	–0.132
20–39	2.606	2.117	–0.301	1.048	–0.257
40–59	–4.393	–2.530	–0.897	–0.745	–0.220
60–79	0.796	–2.261	3.914	–2.474	1.616
80 and above	0.167	–1.064	1.658	–2.159	1.731
Total	–1.483	–4.074	4.119	–4.266	2.738

Cumulative growth Rate: –1.918; residual: –0.435

Notes

(1) cd_SR and cd_POP denote, respectively, the degree of contribution of the change in the age group-specific suicide rate and the degree of contribution of the change in the population to the suicide growth rate, from 1998 to 2007

(2) The sample does not include suicide victims of unknown age

Source Vital Statistics, Japan Ministry of Health, Labour, and Welfare; Population Estimates, Japan Ministry of Internal Affairs

population structure, the reasons for suicide, employment status, and the means of suicide on cumulative suicide growth since 1998. By comparing the decomposition results here with those from the 1997–1998 decomposition, we can shed some light on the changing factors that affect the suicide rate in Japan and the persistence of the suicide problem in Japan.

Decomposition of the Cumulative Suicide Growth Rate from 1998 to 2007, by Gender, Age, and Population Structure

To examine the long-term effects of gender, age, and population structure on the cumulative suicide growth rate in Japan, we first applied the same decomposition technique to each year's data. After obtaining the annual degrees of contribution of changes in population and age group-specific suicide on the annual suicide growth rate, we aggregated them over the years to compute the cumulative degree of contribution of a particular component $x_{j,t}$ from t_1 to t_2, i.e., $\sum_{t=t_2}^{t_2-1} cd\_x_{j,t}$.

Table 5 indicates that the cumulative suicide growth rate was negative, i.e., –1.92%, which suggests that despite a marginal decrease, the overall number of suicides from 1998 to 2007 resided at the new plateau established by the suicide upsurge in 1998. This showed that the large number of suicides persisted during that period.

The decomposition results indicated that the persistently large number of suicides was promoted by suicide increases among those of the younger generation (age 20–39) and the older generation (age 60 and above); nonetheless, there were qualitative differences in their contributions. First, unlike the 1997–1998 suicide upsurge—which was mainly attributed to the increase of suicide among middle and older generations (those aged 40–59 and 60–79)—it was the increase in suicide among the relatively younger generation (20–39 years) that led to persistence in the high number of suicides. Since the population of this age group has been decreasing, the contribution of the demographic component of this age group, POP_{20-39}, to the cumulative overall suicide growth rate has been negative (–0.301 and –0.257 for males and females, respectively). Therefore, holding the population of this age group constant, the increase in the suicide rate within this group would have been 3.17% instead of 2.61%, or 21.45% higher. This finding is consistent with the suicide-age migration claim that, after the 1997–1998 suicide upsurge, the incidence of suicide shifted from the middle-aged group to the young group, i.e., to people in their 20 and 30s. This is very different from the public perception that middle-aged males contribute most to Japan's high suicide rate. Our results here revealed that, in terms of the age profile, suicides by younger people explain the persistence of the high suicide rate after 1998. Second, population aging has also been a serious problem that has led to persistence in the number of suicides. Holding the age-group-specific suicide rates constant, the population-aging effect in the groups of men and women aged 60–79 and 80 years and above would result in a cumulative suicide growth rate of 8.92%.

Decomposition of the Cumulative Suicide Growth Rate from 1999 to 2006, by Gender, Age, and Reasons for Suicide[19]

To gain greater insight into the persistence of suicide in Japan, we conducted a decomposition of the cumulative suicide growth rate, by gender, age, and reasons

[19] In the last section, we used MHLW data from 1998 to 2007, as well as NPA data from 1999 to 2006. As mentioned, only the NPA data contain information on the number of suicides

for suicide. The same decomposition method as that used in the last section was applied to the NPA data for the period from 1999 to 2006; cumulative degrees of contribution were calculated and are reported in Table 6.

First, in the comparison of the decomposition results in Tables 2 and 6, we found that health problems and economic and financial problems were still the main reasons for suicide. Together, these two reasons account for 69.1% of the suicide growth (8.97% of 12.98%). Second, in comparison to the decomposition results in Tables 5 and 6, we confirmed that the persistence of high suicide rates was due to a change in the age profile of suicides from the middle-aged (40–59 years) to the young generation (20–39 years), and to suicide among the non-weary members of the older generation (age 60 and above). These two facts hold, regardless of the use of different datasets. Moreover, while men aged 60 and over killed themselves mainly because of financial and health problems and men aged 40–59 did so because of family problems, young people aged 20–39 committed suicide for a variety of reasons, including family and work-related problems.

On the other hand, the decomposition results in Table 6 (and in Table 7, below) should be carefully interpreted, because the samples are limited to suicide victims whose motives and reasons are known. Within that group, the number of suicides had grown by 12.98% from 1999 to 2006. Since the suicide numbers had been almost constant or slightly declining within this period, the results may be subject to sample-selection bias.

Decomposition of the Cumulative Suicide Growth Rate from 1999 to 2006, by Employment Status and Reasons for Suicide

We also decomposed the cumulative suicide growth rate from 1999 to 2006, by employment status and reasons for suicide; we did so using the NPA data. The results thereof are shown in Table 7. First, we found that suicides due to financial problems contributed second-most to suicide growth (3.25% of the 12.72% increase), trailing suicides for health reasons (5.58% of the 12.72% increase). Second, the unemployed accounted for most of the suicide growth, followed by the employed, and housewives or househusbands. Interestingly, while financial problems constituted the number one reason for suicide among the employed, health-related problems were the main cause of suicide among the unemployed.[20] Third, suicide among the self-employed showed negative growth between 1999 and 2006—a completely different picture from its significantly positive contribution to suicide growth from 1997 to 1998 (Table 3). However, there may be

by reason and by employment status; due to changes in the NPA's categorization system in 2007, we were limited to the use of data from 1999 to 2006.

[20]One possible interpretation is that the unemployed include not only individuals who lost their jobs, but also individuals who were retired due to old age or for other reasons. Also, unemployed people may have already suffered from depressive illness at the same time they lost their jobs; hence, in this group, health becomes a dominant reason for suicide.

Table 6 Decomposition of the 1999–2006 cumulative suicide growth rate, by gender, age, and reasons for suicide (Unit: %)

Unit: % Gender	Age group	Sum of the degrees of contribution (A). (A) = (B) + (C) + (D) + (E) + (F) + (G) + (H)	Economic and financial problems (B)	Family (C)	Health (D)	Relationships (E)	School (F)	Work (G)	Others (H)
Male	00–19	−0.065	−0.012	0.078	−0.014	−0.083	−0.072	0.01	0.028
	20–39	4.324	0.955	0.602	1.529	0.121	0.189	0.594	0.333
	40–59	0.543	0.01	0.861	−0.29	0.122	0.001	0.228	−0.389
	60 and above	3.898	1.365	0.638	1.611	0.059	0.001	0.063	0.162
	Subtotal	8.701	2.318	2.179	2.837	0.218	0.119	0.896	0.134
Female	00–19	−0.035	−0.014	−0.068	0.105	−0.082	0.035	0	−0.011
	20–39	2.055	0.05	0.281	1.582	−0.035	0.031	0.176	−0.031
	40–59	0.81	0.472	−0.174	0.525	−0.032	0	0.096	−0.077
	60 and above	1.446	0.506	0.206	0.592	0.02	−0.001	0.034	0.089
	Subtotal	4.275	1.014	0.245	2.804	−0.13	0.065	0.307	−0.029
Total		12.976	3.331	2.425	5.64	0.089	0.184	1.202	0.105

Note The sample does not include suicides of unknown age or for unspecified reasons
Source Annual Report on Suicide, Japan National Police Agency

Table 7 Decomposition of the 1999–2006 cumulative suicide growth rate, by employment status and reasons for suicide (Unit: %)

Employment status	Sum of the degrees of contribution (A). (A) = (B) + (C) + (D) + (E) + (F) + (G) + (H)	Economic and Financial Problems (B)	Family (C)	Health (D)	Relationships (E)	School (F)	Work (G)	Others (H)
Employed	4.993	2.145	1.175	0.889	0.172	–0.01	0.787	–0.165
Housewife or househusband	1.341	0.367	0.048	0.962	–0.051	0	–0.02	0.037
Management	–0.422	–0.379	0.048	–0.292	0.038	0	0.214	–0.051
Self-employed	–1.544	–1.822	0.148	0.19	–0.015	0	–0.023	–0.022
Student	0.578	0.074	0.047	0.294	–0.094	0.204	0.008	0.045
Unemployed	7.769	2.869	0.882	3.535	0.032	–0.009	0.251	0.21
Total	12.716	3.253	2.348	5.578	0.081	0.185	1.216	0.054

Note The sample is limited to suicide victims whose reasons/motives are known and does not include those of unknown employment status, age or with unspecified reasons

Source Annual Report on Suicide, Japan National Police Agency

sample-selection bias arising from the omission of individuals who had died by suicide without leaving written evidence indicating their motivation. Therefore, using the same NPA data, we decomposed all suicides solely by employment status, regardless of will availability. Table 8 confirms the negative suicide growth among the self-employed, which contributed to decreases in the overall suicide numbers. This result indicated that while the self-employed had been seriously affected by the 1997 credit crunch, it was suicide among the employed that accounted for the persistently high level of suicide after 1998. Finally, a comparison of the results in Tables 3 and 7 also suggests that while financial problems were the main contributor to an increase in suicide among the self-employed from 1997 and 1998, they actually led to a *decrease* in suicide among the self-employed from 1999 to 2006. On the other hand, for those employed and unemployed, suicide due to financial problems always plays a significant role in the increases in suicide from 1999 to 2006.

Decomposition of Cumulative Suicide Growth Rate from 1998 to 2007, by Gender and Means of Suicide

Accessibility to the means of suicide is a cost component when making decisions vis-à-vis suicide. Easy access to a particular means of suicide lowers the cost of suicide. Table 9 shows the decomposition of the MHLW suicide growth rate from 1998 to 2007, by gender and means of suicide.[21] The results suggest that there was a change in the main means of suicide, from hanging (as shown in Table 4) to gas poisoning (for example, carbon monoxide poisoning by burning charcoal or via car exhaust). Furthermore, gas poisoning is also the only means to exhibit positive growth. The increased variety in the means of suicide is in accordance with the fact that members of the younger generation have relatively greater access to internet chat rooms and discussion forums, and to information therein pertaining to suicide and means of suicide.[22] The variety of means also adds to the evidence of migration of suicide from the middle-aged to the younger generation.

---

[21]Note the difference in the growth rate, compared to that in Table 5; this is because the data in Table 5 exclude cases of unknown age or gender.

[22]For more background on this discussion, refer to a recent survey by Chen et al. (2012a). A recent event in Japan underscores the change in the means of suicide. In early 2008, the "recipe" for creating the means of suicide by inhaling hydrogen sulfide (created by mixing an ordinary household laundry detergent with a cleanser) became widely known through internet discussion forums. On April 23, 2008, a 14-year-old girl gassed herself to death by following a method learned from the internet, releasing in the process fumes that sickened 90 people in her apartment building (April 25, 2008, Japan Times). Press reports indicated that during the first six months of 2008, more than 500 people in Japan had killed themselves by inhaling hydrogen sulfide (September 26, 2008, New York State Office of Homeland Security).

Table 8 Decomposition of the 1999–2006 cumulative suicide growth rate, by employment status (Unit: %)

Suicide growth rate (A). (A) = (B) + (C) + (D) + (E) + (F) + (G)	Employed (B)	Housewife or husband (C)	Self-employed (D)	Student (E)	Supervisory (F)	Unemployed (G)
–1.177	1.074	–0.04	–2.224	0.192	–0.299	0.119

Note The sample does not include suicides of unknown employment status
Source Annual Report on Suicide, Japan National Police Agency

Table 9 Decomposition of the 1998–2007 cumulative suicide growth rate, by gender and means of suicide (Unit: %)

Means	Sum of the degree of contribution (A).(A) = (B) + (C)	Male (B)	Female (C)
Drowning	–1.275	–0.583	–0.692
Drug overdose	–1.077	–0.769	–0.308
Gas poisoning	5.002	4.15	0.852
Hanging	–1.568	–0.740	–0.828
Jumping (towards a moving object such as a train)	–0.417	–0.276	–0.141
Jumping (others)	–1.18	–1.036	–0.144
Others	–1.819	–1.354	–0.465
Total	–2.334	–0.608	–1.751

Source Vital Statistics, Japan Ministry of Health, Labour, and Welfare

4.4 The Link Between Economic Hardship and Suicide

Let us further analyze the characteristics of suicide in Japan, i.e., the sharp increase in the total number, the consistency in the subsequent numbers, and the increase in younger suicide victims. As a means to examine how the credit crunch occurred, because this is considered to be the characteristic feature of the financial crisis from 1997 to 1998 in Japan, it is effective to utilize the Short-Term Economic Survey of Enterprises in Japan (*Tankan*), a statistical survey of enterprises conducted and published quarterly by the Bank of Japan. Figure 2 shows the results obtained, based on the *Tankan* survey, by subtracting the contribution ratios (%) of enterprises responding that financial institutions' lending attitudes were "severe" from the contribution ratios (%) of enterprises responding that they were "accommodative." Lower figures indicate severer attitudes on the part of financial institutions. In the first quarter of 1998, the index showed a dramatic drop, which is considered to reflect the occurrence of the credit crunch and credit withdrawal. Similar tendencies can be observed in the DI relating to target enterprises' financial positions.

The rise in the suicide rate in Japan since 1998 has come in tandem not only with the rise in the unemployment rate as shown in Fig. 3, but also with the deterioration of debt problems caused by the credit crunch and credit withdrawal, as shown in Fig. 2. In March 1998, in particular, the number of male suicide victims increased significantly along with the increase in unemployment and corporate bankruptcies around the close of the fiscal year. Careful analysis is further required to conclude whether the credit crunch and credit withdrawal actually had a *causal connection* with the increase in suicides of small and medium-sized business owners and self-employed workers at the beginning of 1998 and the increase in suicides among the jobless, which had increased due to corporate downsizing, but there is clearly a strong *correlation* among these variables.

Therefore, let us proceed to clarify the correlation between the suicide rate and the unemployment rate. Indeed, unemployment has become one of the most serious issues in Japan's current labor market. The overall unemployment rate in postwar Japan had maintained an extremely low level compared with that of other OECD countries, but as shown in Fig. 3, it showed a sharp rise from 1997 to 1999, in particular. During the economic slowdown in 2001 and 2002, the unemployment rate began to rise again, and following the subsequent decline, it started to rise at the end of 2008, reaching 5.6% in July 2009. Although the rate slightly declined to 4.9% in January 2010, it has remained at a relatively high level. By age group, for both men and women, the overall unemployment rates among those aged between 15 and 24 and those aged between 25 and 34 continued to rise from 1990 to 2003,

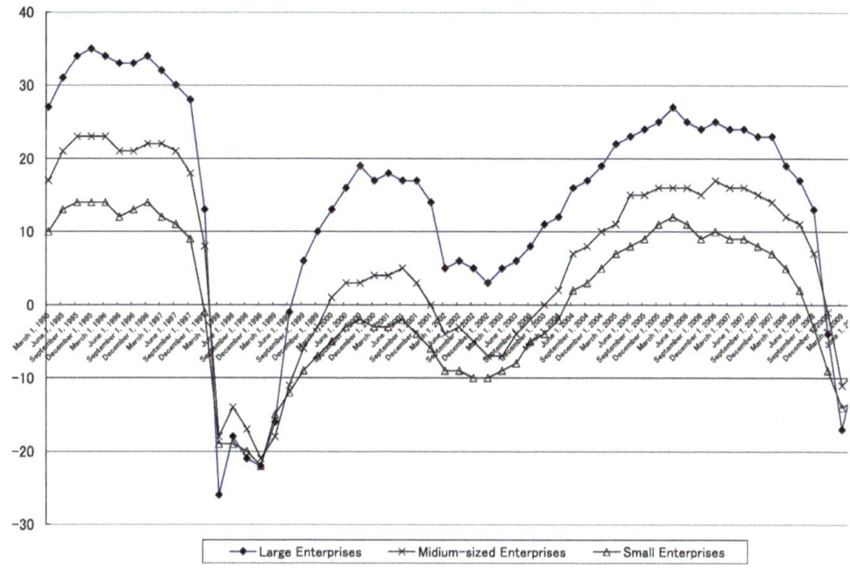

Fig. 2 DI of the Lending Attitudes of Financial Institutions *Source*: Short-Term Economic Survey of Enterprises in Japan (Bank of Japan)

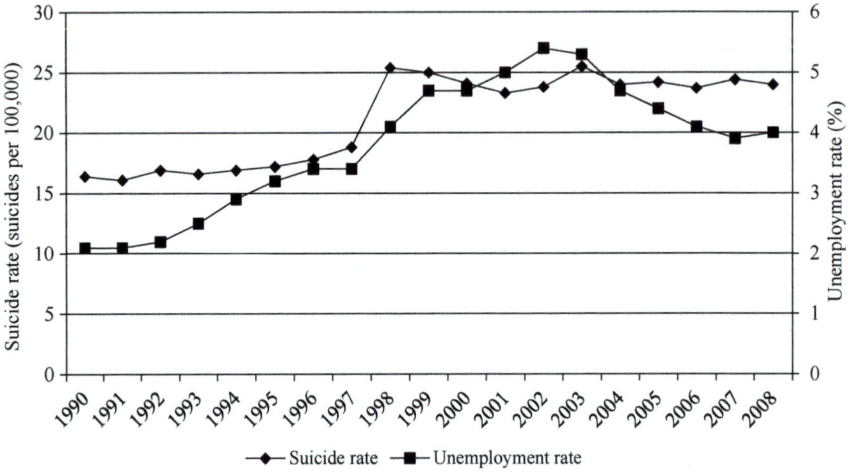

Fig. 3 Changes in Suicide Rates and Unemployment Rates in Japan *Source*: Suicide rates show the number of suicide victims (among 100,000 people), obtained from *Vital Statistics of Japan* by the Ministry of Health, Labour and Welfare. Unemployment rates show overall, nationwide unemployment rates for people aged 15 or over in all industries, and were obtained from the *Labor Force Survey* by the Ministry of Internal Affairs and Communications

and reached 10.1% and 7.1%, respectively, in July 2009. The jobs-to-applicants ratio also has declined sharply since 2008, with a rapid expansion of employment adjustments, including the termination of dispatched and non-regular employees' employment contracts.

Under such circumstances, empirical studies from the point of view of theoretical economics have progressed significantly with regard to determinants for employment and unemployment in Japan (Genda et al. 2010). These are of importance as research aiming to empirically clarify structures of the Japanese labor market that faced rapid changes in the 1990s, such as increases in the unemployment rate and the number of young people without jobs, expansion of temporary and other non-regular employment, and decreases in self-employed workers and small and medium-sized enterprises. However, empirical studies into various costs of unemployment incurred by individuals, households, and society as a whole have not necessarily been sufficient, due to a lack of available individual data in Japan. If unemployment insurance or other public safety nets, or various private safety nets including support against unemployment offered by individuals, households, or organizations are functioning well, the costs of unemployment incurred by individuals who have lost their jobs should not be too large. On the other hand, if such public or private safety nets are not functioning well enough, the costs of unemployment are likely to become intensively focused on individuals, often in excess of their capacity. Such intensive imposition of the costs of unemployment may lead to disastrous results, such as suicide.

Based on Hamermesh and Soss's (1974) conception of rational suicide, a higher unemployment rate is expected to increase suicides since unemployment not only causes difficulties in the short-term living environment but also increases uncertainties over income that preclude a clear future forecast and creates a decline in lifetime income. Furthermore, unemployment is often associated with mental or physical disorders, which increases the risk of suicide in a complex and serious manner. In reality, many empirical studies have demonstrated a correlation between high unemployment rates and high suicide rates (Platt 1984; Chen et al. 2012b).[23] As can be observed in Fig. 3, the correlation between the unemployment rate and the suicide rate is especially strong in Japan. Furthermore, Chen et al. (2009) indicate that this correlation is larger in Japan than in other OECD countries.

4.5 Regression Analysis

The decomposition results show that males aged 40–59 who suffered from financial problems contributed the most to the upsurge of suicides in 1998. In addition, the self-employed had been seriously affected by the 1997 credit crunch. On the other hand, the persistently high suicide rate after 1998 has been attributed to young men aged 20–39; in terms of employment status, the suicides of the employed account most for the persistently high level of suicide after 1998. In periods following 1998, a considerable proportion of suicides among the employed were due to financial problems. These results point to a link in Japan between economic hardship and suicide. In this section, we use prefecture-level panel regressions to examine this link and, in particular, the presumption that bankruptcies and unemployment following the 1997 credit crunch played an influential role in both the 1998 suicide upsurge and the persistence of suicide afterwards. The focus will be on male suicides: middle-aged men aged 40–59, and young men aged 20–39.

Regression Model of Choi et al. (2012b, 2015)

For our purpose, we adopted the following regression model for suicide of Choi et al. (2012b, 2015):

$$Suicide\,Rate_{i,t} = \beta_1 Unemp_{i,t} + \beta_2 Fbankrupt_{i,t} + \beta_3 Ibankrupt_{i,t} + \alpha_i + \alpha_t + \varepsilon_{i,t}, \quad (5)$$

with i and t being the indexing prefectures and years, respectively. The dependent variable, *Suicide Rate*, is the suicide rate of all men: middle-aged men aged 40–59, or young men aged 20–39. The independent variables included economic variables such as

[23] See Chen et al. (2012a) for an extensive survey of economic studies on suicide.

unemployment rate (*Unemp*), firm bankruptcy rate (*Fbankrupt*), and individual bankruptcy rate (*Ibankrupt*). Previous literature suggests that unemployment and bankruptcies diminish the present value of expected lifetime utility and result in a greater number of suicides.[24] We included prefecture fixed effects, α_i, and year effects, α_t.

To address a potential endogeneity problem in the estimation equation, we introduced another regression equation for unemployment and bankruptcies, using as an instrument the diffusion index (DI) from the Short-Term Economic Survey of Enterprises in Japan (*Tankan*), conducted by the Bank of Japan (BOJ). We explain the instruments in greater detail in the section below; for now, however, it is noteworthy that changes in the instruments have no effects on changes in the suicide rates, except through their association with changes in the unemployment rate, firm-bankruptcy rate, and individual-bankruptcy rate.

Data

The dataset covered 47 Japanese prefectures for the period of 1997–2005. Table 10 lists the definitions and sources of the variables; summary descriptive statistics are shown in Table 11. The number of suicides and population figures by age and gender were obtained from the MHLW *Vital Statistics*. Suicide rates (per 100,000 members of the population) for specific gender–age groups were calculated via the ratio of the number of suicides to the population of a specific gender–age group. Unemployment rates were taken from the Annual Report on the Labour Force Survey, from the Ministry of Internal Affairs and Communications. The number of firm bankruptcies was obtained from Japan's Enterprise Bankruptcy Survey Annual Report, from the Organization for Small and Medium Enterprises and Regional Innovation. We calculated the firm-bankruptcy rate as the number of firm bankruptcies per 1,000 persons. The number of individual bankruptcies was obtained from the Annual Report of Judicial Statistics, from the Supreme Court of Japan. We calculated the individual-bankruptcy rate as the number of individual bankruptcies per 100 people.

For the instrument variables, we used two sets of variables: the lending attitude of the financial institution DI and the financial position DI. Each BOJ branch issues quarterly data with respect to each of these two DIs.[25] To match them up with annual variables, we used averages to convert quarterly DIs to annual data. The lending attitude of financial institution DI indicates businesses' judgment of financial institutions' attitudes towards lending.[26] The financial position DI

---

[24]See, for example, Hamermesh and Soss (1974). For a recent survey of the literature of unemployment and suicide, we refer the readers to Chen et al. (2012a).

[25]The BOJ has 37 branches. In general, there is one branch for each prefecture, but some branches serve more than one prefecture.

[26]Respondent companies chose one of three options: "Accommodative," "Not so severe," or "Severe." The lending attitude of financial institutions DI is the percentage of companies that responded "Accommodative" minus the percentage of companies that responded "Severe".

Table 10 Variable definitions and data sources

Variable		Variable definition	Source
Suicide rate		Rate per 100,000 persons	Demographic statistics; ministry of health, labour, and welfare
Age group-specific male suicide rate		Aged 00–19, 20–39, 40–59, 60–79, and 80 and above.	
Total population		Per 1,000	
Unemployment rate		Percentage of total labor force	Labor force survey, ministry of internal affairs and communication
Firm-bankruptcy rate		*N* of firm bankruptcies per 1,000 persons	Enterprise bankruptcy survey annual report, organization for small and medium enterprises and regional innovation
Individual-bankruptcy rate		*N* of personal bankruptcies per person *100	Annual report of judicial statistics, supreme court
DI	Lending attitude of financial institution DI (LEND_DI)	Percentage of firms responding with "Accommodative," minus the percentage responding with "Severe"	Short-term economic survey of enterprises in Japan (*Tankan*), Bank of Japan
	Financial position DI (FIN_DI)	Percentage of firms responding with "Easy," minus the percentage responding with "Tight"	
Interaction term of DI	LEND_FINANCIAL_DI	Interaction term of LEND_DI and FIN_DI	
Cube of DI	LEND_DI3	Cube of lending attitude of financial institution DI	
	FIN_DI3	Cube of financial position DI	
DI by categorization	LEND_DI_verylow	=1 if lending attitude of financial institution DI < –15	
	LEND_DI_low	=1 if –15 < lending attitude of financial institution DI < –5	
	LEND_DI_mid	=1 if –5 < lending attitude of financial institution DI < 5	
	LEND_DI_high	=1 if 5 < lending attitude of financial institution DI	
	FIN_DI_verylow	=1 if financial position DI < –15	
	FIN_DI_low	=1 if –15 < financial position DI < –5	
	FIN_DI_mid	=1 if –5 < financial position DI < 5	
	FIN_DI_high	=1 if 5 < financial position DI	

Table 11 Summary descriptive statistics of key variables

Variable	# of obs.	Mean	Std. Dev.	Min	Max
Suicide rate of all males	423	0.416	0.092	0.173	0.760
Suicide rate of men aged 20–39	423	0.290	0.075	0.123	0.583
Suicide rate of men aged 40–59	423	0.572	0.143	0.167	1.117
Unemployment rate	423	4.262	1.155	1.700	8.400
Firm-bankruptcy rate	422	0.122	0.120	0.041	2.400
Individual-bankruptcy rate	423	0.131	0.060	0.031	0.323
Lending attitude of financial institutions DI	364	–0.887	10.233	–30.750	23.250
Financial position DI	364	–9.371	8.558	–29.750	17.250
LEND_FINANCIAL_DI	364	80.5	133.3	–137.6	630.4
LEND_DI3	364	–193	3519	–29076	12568
FIN_DI3	364	–2661	4122	–26331	5133
LEND_DI_verylow	364	0.080	0.271	0	1
LEND_DI_low	364	0.288	0.454	0	1
LEND_DI_mid	364	0.346	0.476	0	1
LEND_DI_high	364	0.286	0.452	0	1
FIN_DI_verylow	364	0.275	0.447	0	1
FIN_DI_low	364	0.440	0.497	0	1
FIN_DI_mid	364	0.225	0.418	0	1
FIN_DI_high	364	0.060	0.239	0	1

indicates businesses' judgment of their financial (cash) status.[27] Therefore, the DIs represent the subjective financial prospects of businesses covered in the BOJ survey. During the first quarter in 1998, these two DIs dropped sharply.

After the collapse of the Bubble economy in Japan, financial institutions encountered non-performing loan problems. Revealing the huge amount of non-performing loans[28] and experiencing the bankruptcy of several financial institutions such as the Cosmo credit union, the government passed the financial-related bills for the stabilization of the financial system.[29] Then, in January 1997, the government also announced that it would introduce the prompt corrective

[27]Respondent companies chose one of three options: "Easy," "Not so tight," or "Tight" Financial position DI is the percentage of companies that responded "Easy" minus the percentage of companies that responded "Tight".

[28]The Ministry of Finance (MOF) in Japan disclosed the amount of non-performing loans, which was 8 trillion JPY in April 1992 for the first time. Since MOF changed the coverage of financial institutions and the definition of bad loans, the amount turned out to be about 40 trillion JPY in 1995.

[29]For details about a credit crunch in 1997, see Yoshikawa (2007).

action program in April 1998. This program mandates business improvement administrative order to banks that fail to fulfill the capital adequacy ratio based on the international risk management guideline Based Capital Accord. In March 1997, it issued an official notice of the valuation standard for banks to make self-assessments of their own assets. In 1997, some big financial institutions including Yamaichi Securities went bankrupt and stock market price declined significantly. Triggered by these situations, most of the financial institutions tightened their credit supplies to firms, particularly to small and medium enterprises in 1997, because financial institutions should maintain the proper capital adequacy ratio by screening out risky borrowers. This situation is called a "credit crunch", as is pointed in the White Chapter on Small and Medium Enterprises in Japan 2000 (hereafter, the SME white chapter 2000). Reflecting the situation, the lending attitude of financial DI and financial position DI indices dropped sharply in the first quarter in 1998.

A decline in bank loans is generally caused by two effects, demand and supply of loans. When firms' demand for loans declines because of an economic downturn or a business slump, the demand curve shifts downward and amount of lending decrease.[30] On the other hand, if banks with bad loans are reluctant to grant new loans while the interest rate remains unchanged, the supply curve shifts upward.[31] Many studies have pointed out that the decline in bank loans in 1997 was driven by a supply-side factor[32] (Sawada et al. 2011). Especially, the SME white chapter 2000 states that financial institutions with high ratios of non-performing loans tended to severely tighten credit supply to small and medium enterprises.

In a credit market, Stiglitz and Weiss (1981) show the existence of excess demand equilibria, that is, credit rationing is in equilibrium if there is asymmetric information between banks and borrowers. They examine the question of whether, if there are borrowers who are good and bad risks, market equilibrium could be characterized by an interest rate at or below the market clearing level, r*. In a rationing equilibrium, a shock to the supply curve will affect not the interest rate, but rather the availability of loans. Responding to Based Capital Accord and the introduction of a prompt corrective action program, banks started to tighten lending in 1997, and the supply curve shifted to the left. While the demand curve remained constant. Also, it was difficult to find alternative funds for borrowers. Because SME, compared to large firms, have limited access to direct finance and alternative funds, if banks limit their lending to them, they immediately face a tight financial position. Therefore, a credit crunch caused by the supply side expanded excess demand and some firms were limited in borrowing money, that is, they faced

[30]Yoshikawa (2007) found that the decline in bank loan in 1991 was accompanied by the decrease in the growth rate of the amount of the lending and interest rate. Therefore, the decline in loans in 1991 was caused by the demand factor.

[31]In 1998, banks suddenly increased having government bonds instead of loans. It means that banks avoided risk taking and were reluctant to supply loans at that time.

[32]Some maintain that the decline in bank loans was caused by adjustment for over-borrowing in the Bubble periods or because of a demand-side factor.

credit rationing. These firms would go bankrupt and the unemployment rate would increase. When a credit crunch is driven by the supply side, it is orthogonal to the error term of the suicide rate. The lending attitude of the financial DI and financial position DI reflects the credit crunch in 1997, and these could be instrumental variables.

Estimation Results of Choi et al. (2012b, 2015)

Table 12 shows the results of the multiple regression analysis on the effects of unemployment and bankruptcies on male suicide rates. Both the ordinary least squares (OLS) regressions and panel (FE) regressions with prefecture and year fixed effects were conducted. Tables 13, 14, and 15 show, respectively, the instrumental variable (IV) estimation results for the overall male suicide rate, the male suicide rate for those aged 20–39, and the male suicide rate for those aged 40–59. In fact, there were three IV settings: IV(a) used both DIs, the cubes of these two DIs, and their interaction terms; IV(b) used the categorized DIs; and IV(c) used categorized DIs, the cubes of both DIs, and their interactions.[33] For more details on variable names and definitions, see Table 10. For each IV setting, there were two specifications; the first included only year fixed effects, while the other included both year and prefecture fixed effects.

For all men, those aged 20–39 and those aged 40–59, the OLS regressions suggested that the individual bankruptcy rate was positively associated with the suicide rate, while the unemployment rate was insignificant. The firm-bankruptcy rate was found to have a negative impact on the suicide rate. However, the fixed-effect estimations showed that both the unemployment rate and the individual-bankruptcy rate were positively associated with the suicide rate, while the firm-bankruptcy rate became insignificant. Controlling for possible endogeneity, the IV estimation results in Tables 13 resemble the FE estimation results, suggesting that for men overall, both the unemployment rate and the individual-bankruptcy rate were positively associated with the suicide rate. This result is consistent with Hamermesh and Soss's (1974) hypothesis vis-à-vis the positive impact of unemployment on suicide rate. Moreover, this finding is in line with the decomposition analysis, which showed that unemployed individuals experienced a high suicide growth rate and that financial problems not only constituted one of the major reasons for suicide, but that it has also been a main contributor to the high suicide growth rate since 1998.

Separate IV regressions results for men aged 20–39 and men aged 40–59 are shown in Tables 14 and 15, respectively. As with the results in Tables 12 and 13, the individual-bankruptcy rate was positively associated with the suicide rate. Nonetheless, the magnitude was stronger for men aged 40–59 than for men aged 20–39. Meanwhile, unemployment was positively associated with the suicide rate

[33]The validity of the instrumental variables was tested using Sargan's over-identification test.

Table 12 OLS and fixed-effect regression results

Dependent variables	Total male suicide rate		Men aged 20–39 suicide rate		Men aged 40–59 suicide rate	
	OLS	FE	OLS	FE	OLS	FE
Unemployment rate	–0.002 [0.003]	0.030*** [0.006]	0.003 [0.004]	0.027*** [0.008]	0.007 [0.006]	0.040*** [0.012]
Firm-bankruptcy rate	–0.097*** [0.036]	–0.008 [0.016]	–0.097* [0.056]	0 [0.024]	–0.146*** [0.047]	–0.01 [0.032]
Individual-bankruptcy rate	0.729*** [0.068]	0.228** [0.104]	0.448*** [0.071]	0.113 [0.155]	1.183*** [0.106]	0.395* [0.212]
Constant	0.341*** [0.015]	0.211*** [0.017]	0.300*** [0.015]	0.130*** [0.026]	0.407*** [0.023]	0.270*** [0.035]
Year fixed effect	NO	YES	NO	YES	NO	YES
Prefecture fixed effect	NO	YES	NO	YES	NO	YES
Observations	422	422	422	422	422	422
Number of prefectures		47		47		47

Notes
(1) Robust standard errors are in brackets
(2) *** Significance at 1%; ** Significance at 5%; * Significance at 10%

in only one specification, and the firm-bankruptcy rate was not significant. There is a possible interpretation regarding the reason why the firm-bankruptcy rate shows little effect on suicide: self-employed persons can close their businesses before assuming a large debt load, because of limited liability; in contrast, in Japan, individual loans function as *de facto* unlimited liability contracts (Chen et al. 2010). As a matter of fact, we do have the decomposition result from Table 8 that suicides by self-employed persons contributed to a reduction in suicides in the periods after 1998. However, our estimation results should be interpreted with caution; although we have separate regressions for different age groups, economic variables are aggregated variables that are applied to all groups, not just those that are age group-specific.

In conclusion, the regression results support the hypothesis that the economic recession following the 1997 credit crunch played an influential role on the abrupt increase in and persistence of suicide since 1998. Especially, unemployment and individual bankruptcies had strong impacts on the suicide rate.

5 Recent Decline

While the number and rate of suicides in Japan are still high among OECD countries, the annual suicide rate and suicide number in Japan have shown continuous decline in the last several years since 2010. In 2012, the total number of suicides fell below the 30,000 level to 27,736 for the first time in the previous 15 years. Since the Basic Law on Suicide Countermeasures was enacted in 2006, the central as well as local

Table 13 IV estimation result: total male suicide rate

	IV(a)		IV(b)		IV(c)	
Unemployment rate	–0.026 [0.038]	0.006 [0.087]	–0.005 [0.025]	0.0512** [0.023]	–0.018 [0.017]	0.06334*** [0.022]
Firm-bankruptcy rate	–0.057 [2.461]	–3.131 [4.126]	–1.2 [1.284]	0.675 [0.862]	–0.798 [0.868]	0.46902 [0.736]
Individual-bankruptcy rate	2.956*** [1.018]	1.129 [1.257]	2.082*** [0.594]	0.041 [0.532]	2.200*** [0.408]	–0.2007 [0.519]
Constant	0.218 [0.252]		0.347*** [0.130]		0.33120*** [0.093]	
Year dummy	YES	YES	YES	YES	YES	YES
Prefecture-fixed effect	NO	YES	NO	YES	NO	YES
Observations	363	363	363	363	363	363
Number of prefectures		42		42		42
First stage for the null hypothesis of joint significance of the excluded IVs						
F-stat	F(5, 349)	F(5, 308)	F(6, 348)	F(6, 307)	F(9, 345)	F(9, 304)
Unemployment rate [P-val]	18.89 [0.000]	5.51 [0.000]	9.89 [0.000]	8.71 [0.000]	8.07 [0.000]	6.26 [0.000]
Firm-bankruptcy rate [P-val]	4.42 [0.001]	0.41 [0.840]	3.43 [0.003]	1.02 [0.415]	2.76 [0.000]	1.1 [0.363]
Individual-bankruptcy rate [P-val]	7.47 [0.000]	6.58 [0.000]	7.86 [0.000]	5.34 [0.000]	6 [0.000]	3.64 [0.000]
Sargan statistic [P-val]	3.808 [0.149]	0.583 [0.747]	4.305 [0.230]	0.837 [0.841]	10.772 [0.096]	3.122 [0.793]

Notes
(1) IV(a) uses two DIs, cubes of two DIs and interaction terms of two DIs; IV(b) uses all the segmented DIs; and IV(c) uses all the segmented DIs, cubes of two DIs, and the interaction of two DIs. In IV(a)–(c), the results in the first column include only year -ixed effects, while the results in the second column include both year- and prefecture-fixed effects
(2) Robust standard errors are in brackets
(3) *** Significance at 1%; ** Significance at 5%; * Significance at 10%

governments have continued suicide-prevention measures at all levels in collaboration with public health and medical institutions and non-profit organizations. Public frameworks such as the General Principles of Suicide Prevention Policy combined with appropriate public funding schemes by the Emergency Reinforcement Fund for Suicide Prevention in Local Areas enabled different stakeholders to adopt effective suicide countermeasures (see Chap. 9 for details). For example, local governments started establishing customized policies by age, occupation, and problem, to provide counseling services by experts on legal issues, labor problems, and mental care for people with high suicidal risks such as those who have attempted suicide as well as the bereaved families of suicide victims.

Yet, we should also note that the number of suicides among the young remained stable in spite of the recent overall decline in suicides. Chapter 5 investigates issues related to youth suicide.

Table 14 IV estimation result: suicide rate of men aged 20–39

	IV(a)		IV(b)		IV(c)	
Unemployment rate	−0.01 [0.028]	−0.044 [0.151]	0.006 [0.020]	0.059 [0.037]	−0.007 [0.014]	0.079** [0.037]
Firm-bankruptcy rate	−0.939 [1.821]	−5.752 [7.128]	−1.656 [1.028]	0.505 [1.386]	−1.243* [0.690]	0.367 [1.230]
Individual-bankruptcy rate	1.929** [0.753]	1.264 [2.172]	1.229*** [0.476]	−0.811 [0.855]	1.401*** [0.324]	−1.2781 [0.866]
Constant	0.244 [0.187]		0.329*** [0.104]		0.307*** [0.074]	
Year dummy	YES	YES	YES	YES	YES	YES
Prefecture fixed effect	NO	YES	NO	YES	NO	YES
Observations	363	363	363	363	363	363
Number of prefectures		42		42		42
First stage for the null hypothesis of joint significance of the excluded IVs						
F-stat	F(5, 349)	F(5, 308)	F(6, 348)	F(6, 307)	F(9, 345)	F(9, 304)
Unemployment rate [P-val]	18.89 [0.000]	5.51 [0.000]	9.89 [0.000]	8.71 [0.000]	8.07 [0.000]	6.26 [0.000]
Firm-bankruptcy rate [P-val]	4.42 [0.001]	0.41 [0.840]	3.43 [0.003]	1.02 [0.415]	2.76 [0.000]	1.1 [0.363]
Individual-bankruptcy rate [P-val]	7.47 [0.000]	6.58 [0.000]	7.86 [0.000]	5.34 [0.000]	6 [0.000]	3.64 [0.000]
Sargan statistic [P-val]	4.358 [0.113]	0.237 [0.888]	5.09 [0.165]	1.488 [0.685]	10.772 [0.096]	3.122 [0.793]

Note see the notes in Table 13

6 Concluding Remarks

The number of suicides in present-day Japan is at an all-time high. The dauntingly high level of suicide began in 1998 with an abrupt 35.16% increase in the suicide rate. We used a generalized decomposition formula, and the results showed that the suicide upsurge in 1998 was primarily caused by suicide among middle-aged men aged 40–59 who had suffered from financial problems. Moreover, a disproportionate increase in suicide among self-employed male workers was also uncovered. These results are consistent with the suggestion that the upsurge in the number of suicides in 1998 was largely due to the severe credit crunch in late 1997.

However, a new problem has arisen, given that the number of suicides each year after 1998 has shown no sign of dropping, despite there being some economic recovery in 2003 and 2004. The decomposition of cumulative changes from 1998 to 2007 pointed to an aspect of age-profile migration in suicides—namely, the growth in suicides among the younger generation (i.e., those aged 20–39). Naturally, one wonders about the reasons underlying the growing number of suicides among members of the younger Japanese generation. Our decomposition analysis shows that four different reasons strongly contributed to suicide among that subset of the population: health,

Table 15 IV estimation result: suicide rate of males aged 40–59

	IV(a)		IV(b)		IV(c)	
Unemployment rate	–0.015 [0.055]	0.025 [0.131]	0.01 [0.037]	0.072 [0.047]	–0.006 [0.026]	0.091** [0.045]
Firm-bankruptcy rate	–0.737 [3.556]	–3.681 [6.203]	–1.915 [1.923]	1.115 [1.757]	–1.6 [1.274]	0.91 [1.487]
Individual-bankruptcy rate	4.483*** [1.470]	1.969 [1.890]	3.321*** [0.890]	0.522 [1.084]	3.360*** [0.598]	0.182 [1.047]
Constant	0.272 [0.365]		0.413** [0.195]		0.418*** [0.136]	
Year dummy	YES	YES	YES	YES	YES	YES
Prefecture fixed effect	NO	YES	NO	YES	NO	YES
Observations	363	363	363	363	363	363
Number of prefectures		42		42		42
First stage for the null hypothesis of joint significance of the excluded IVs						
F-stat	F(5, 349)	F(5, 308)	F(6, 348)	F(6, 307)	F(9, 345)	F(9, 304)
Unemployment rate [P-val]	18.89 [0.000]	5.51 [0.0001]	9.89 [0.000]	8.71 [0.000]	8.07 [0.000]	6.26 [0.000]
Firm-bankruptcy rate [P-val]	4.42 [0.0006]	0.41 [0.8402]	3.43 [0.0027]	1.02 [0.4147]	2.76 [0.000]	1.1 [0.363]
Individual-bankruptcy rate [P-val]	7.47 [0.000]	6.58 [0.000]	7.86 [0.000]	5.34 [0.000]	6 [0.000]	3.64 [0.000]
Sargan statistic [P-val]	4.358 [0.113]	0.237 [0.888]	5.09 [0.165]	1.488 [0.685]	10.772 [0.096]	3.122 [0.793]

Notes see the notes in Table 13

finances, family, and work-related problems. Our data do not allow for further exploration; from both academic and policy-making perspectives, future research is needed to identify the factors that drive suicide among young Japanese people today.

One hypothesis attributes the rise in suicide among young people in Japan to structural changes in the Japanese labor market. Since the late 1990s, the number of unskilled, non-regular workers in the Japanese labor market has been increasing at an alarming rate (Asano et al. 2011). Compared to regular workers, most of these workers are relatively young; also, their jobs are typically low-paying, and the employees are not provided with enough job security or appropriate benefits. This institutional structure may have played a role in increasing suicide risk among the younger generation in recent years. This hypothesis should be carefully investigated in future research.

Our results also indicate that the aging of the population is another phenomenon that has caused a rise in the overall number of suicides. As shown in psychiatric studies, depressive illness is more prevalent among older suicide victims.[34] This indicates another policy direction in combating suicide: one that involves the detection and treatment of depressive illness among older people, especially as their conditions are less likely to be correctly diagnosed and treated.

[34]See, for example, Conwell and Brent (1995).

References

Asano, H., Ito, T., & Kawaguchi, D. (2011). Why has the fraction of contingent workers increased? A case study of Japan. RIETI Discussion Chapter Series 11-E-021.

Bank of Japan. The Short-Term Economic Survey of Enterprises in Japan (TANKAN), various years.

Chen, J., Choi, Y., & Sawada, Y. (2008). Suicide and life insurance. CIRJE Discussion Chapter Series CIRJE-F-558. Tokyo: University of Tokyo.

Chen, J., Choi, Y., & Sawada, Y. (2009). How is suicide different in Japan? *Japan and the World Economy, 21*(2), 140–150.

Chen, J., Choi, Y., & Sawada, Y. (2010). Joint liability borrowing and suicide: the case of Japan. *Economic Letters, 109*(2), 69–71.

Chen, J., Choi, Y., Sawada, Y., Mori, K., & Sugano, S. (2012a). Socio-economic studies on suicide: a survey. *Journal of Economic Surveys, 26*(2), 271–396.

Chen, J., Choi, Y., Mori, K., Sawada, Y., & Sugano, S. (2012b). Recession, Unemployment, and Suicide in Japan. *Japan Labor Review 9*(2), 75–92.

Chen, J., Choi, Y. J., Mori, K., Sawada, Y., & Sugano, S. (2015). An Analysis of Suicides in Japan, 1997–2007: Changes in Incidence, Persistence, and Age Profiles. *Social Indicators Research, 121*(1), 253–272.

Conwell, Y., & Brent, D. (1995). Suicide and aging I: Patterns of psychiatric diagnosis. *International Psychogeriatrics, 7*(2), 149–164.

Genda, Y., Kondo, A., & Ohta, S. (2010). Long-term effects of a recession at labor market entry in Japan and the United States. *Journal of Human Resources 45*(1), 157–196.

Hamermesh, D. S., & Soss, N. M. (1974). An economic theory of suicide. *Journal of Political Economy, 82*(1), 83–98.

Japan National Police Agency. (2009). *Annual report on suicide*. Tokyo: Japan National Police Agency.

Kohara, M. (2010). The response of Japanese wives' labor supply to husbands' job loss, *Journal of Population Economics 23*, 1133–1149.

Mann, J. J., Apter, A., Bertolote, J., Beautrais, A., Currier, D., Haas, A., et al. (2005). Suicide prevention strategies: a systematic review. *Journal of the American Medical Association, 294*, 2064–2074.

Ministry of Health, Labour, and Welfare of Japan. (1997–2007). *Vital statistics*. Tokyo: Statistics and Information Department, Ministry of Health, Labor, and Welfare.

Ministry of Health, Labour, and Welfare of Japan. (2004). *Special report of vital statistics*. Tokyo: Statistics and Information Department, Ministry of Health, Labor, and Welfare.

Ministry of Internal Affairs and Communications of Japan. (1997–2007). *Annual report on current population estimates*. Tokyo: Statistical Bureau of Ministry of Internal Affairs and Communications.

Ministry of Internal Affairs and Communications of Japan. (2008). *Annual report on the labour force survey, 2008*. Tokyo: Statistics Bureau, Ministry of Internal Affairs and Communications.

Mori, K., Sugano, S., Chen, J., Choi, Y., & Sawada, Y., (2012). A note on decomposition technique of variables. *Economics Bulletin* EB-12-00317.

Organization for Small and Medium Enterprises and Regional Innovation. Enterprise Bankruptcy Survey Annual Report. http://www.smrj.go.jp/keiei/chosa/tosanchosa/007564.html.

Platt, S. (1984). Unemployment and suicidal behaviour: a review of the literature. *Social science & medicine, 19*(2), 93–115.

Sawada, Y., Nawata, K., Ii,M., & Lee, M. (2011). Did the financial crisis in Japan affect household welfare seriously? *Journal of Money, Credit, and Banking 43*(2–3), 297–324.

Stiglitz, J. E., & Weiss, A. (1981). Credit rationing in markets with imperfect information. *The American economic review, 71*(3), 393–410.

Suicide Investigation Team. (2008, in Japanese). Jisatsu Jittai Hakusho 2008 (White Chapter on Suicide Reality 2008). Tokyo: Suicide Investigation Team.

Supreme Court of Japan. Annual Report of Judicial Statistics, various years.
Yoshikawa, H. (2007). Japan's lost decade: What have we learned and where are we heading? *Asian Economic Policy Review 2*, 186–203.
World Health Organization. (2006). *World Health Organization Mortality Database, 2006*. Geneva: World Health Organization.

Chapter 4
Natural Disasters and Suicide

1 Introduction

Hundreds of natural disasters hit a variety of regions around the world every year (Guha-sapir et al. 2015), causing upheavals, death, and pain. The recent examples of massive natural disasters causing more than 10,000 deaths include Cyclone Nargis in Myanmar and the Sichuan Earthquake in China in 2008, the Haiti Earthquake, drought in Somalia, the heat wave in Russia in 2010, and the Great East Japan Earthquake in 2011.[1] Natural disasters not only took many lives, but also deprived countless survivors of their houses and jobs and forced some to evacuate from their hometowns. Such natural disasters often cause post-traumatic stress and depression among survivors in their aftermath (Norris et al. 2002; Gelea et al. 2005). Moreover, survivors suffer from physical, mental, and economic distress even after they recover from the initial damages.

Given that mental distress and economic hardship are well-known risk factors of suicide (Lönnqvist 2009; Chen et al. 2012), one might expect that suicide rates increase after natural disasters. Several studies have found that this is indeed the case; studies on the consequences of the 1999 earthquake in Taiwan found that suicide rates increased after the earthquake (Chou et al. 2003; Yang et al. 2005; Chuang and Huang 2006; Liaw et al. 2008; Yip 2009, but see also Chen et al. 2016). Controlling for the effects of demographic factors, Chou et al. (2003) found earthquake victims are 1.46 times more likely to die by suicide compared with non-victims. Similarly, Yang et al. (2005) compared the mean monthly suicide rates before and after the Taiwanese earthquake and found that suicide rates in the severely affected areas increased by 42% after the quake, while the rates exhibited no change in the unaffected areas.

The content of this chapter was based on the published article: "Natural Disasters and Suicides: Evidence from Japan." Social Science & Medicine 82: 126-33."

[1]The list is based on EM-DAT The International Disaster Database at http://www.emdat.be/.

Y. Sawada et al., *Economic Analysis of Suicide Prevention*, Creating a Society for All, DOI 10.1007/978-981-10-1500-7_4

In contrast to these findings, other studies found that natural disasters are followed by a *decrease* in suicide rates. Shioiri et al. (1999) and Nishio et al. (2009) compared the suicide rates in Kobe City, Japan, before and after the January 1995 Great Hanshin-Awaji (Kobe) Earthquake, and found a significant reduction in the rates following the quake. For example, Nishio et al. found that the suicide rate in Kobe City decreased for 2 years after the earthquake. Moreover, using data from Los Angeles County in California, Shoaf et al. (2004) reported that the suicide rate was lower in the 3 years following the Northridge earthquake in 1994. However, they note that the decrease may have merely reflected a continuous downward trend in suicide rates in Los Angeles County.

Another group of scholars found that disasters have no statistically significant impact on suicide rates. Krug et al. (1999) report that no discernible change in suicide rates was detected after natural disasters in the United States. Although the focus was on human-made disasters, Mezuk et al. (2009) and Pridemore et al. (2009) found no increase in suicide rates after terrorist attacks, including the September 11 attacks in 2001 and the Oklahoma City bombing in 1995. Similarly, no change was reported in suicide rates following the 2004 tsunami in Sri Lanka, which is known for its highest suicide rate among developing countries (Rodrigo et al. 2009).

Thus, the effects of natural disasters on suicide mortality are inconclusive (Kõlves et al. 2013). This chapter seeks to reconcile these conflicting findings on the association between natural disasters and suicide rates and ultimately contribute to our understanding of the health consequences of natural disasters. Because natural disasters tend to cause serious psychological stress in the damaged areas, one might expect that suicide rates increase after disasters occur. On the other hand, if natural disasters enhance social connectedness among people in the damaged areas as proposed by some researchers (Gordon et al. 2011), we can expect suicide rates to decrease in the post-disaster period. Using extensive data from Japan, this study aims to investigate which hypothesis is more closely aligned with the empirical pattern.

Our analysis improves upon past studies in three major ways. First, we analyzed the effect of numerous natural disasters on suicide rates, covering wide geographical areas and a long period of time. This is in contrast to typical past research in which the effects of a single natural disaster were studied over a short period of time, so that these research findings are hard to generalize from or compare. The natural disasters considered in our study range from hydrometeorological disasters such as floods and storms to geological disasters such as earthquakes, tsunamis, and volcanic eruptions. The study covered the period 1982–2010, and our estimation exploits variations over time and across subnational jurisdictions, namely, the 47 prefectures of Japan. We examined whether prefectures damaged by natural disasters, regardless of the type, experience a significant change in suicide rates in the following years.

Second, we used the number of deaths and people affected by natural disasters (as defined in the next section) as a measure of the damages, allowing for a possibility that the effects of natural disasters on suicide rates vary according to the severity of the damages. The past studies did not take into account the severity of damages in their analysis. Natural disasters were denoted by an indicator variable, or a single disaster was typically subjected to a before-and-after comparison. Therefore, our understanding of how the level of damages is related to the prevalence of suicide following disasters is limited. In this study, we hypothesize that the magnitude of damages caused by natural disasters (measured by the number of deaths and affected people) is linearly associated with subsequent suicide rates.

Third, we closely examined a varying lagged effect of natural disasters on suicidal acts. Studies that assessed the prevalence of post-traumatic stress disorder (PTSD) after natural disasters found various PTSD patterns, including delayed-onset and an increase of PTSD over time (Norris et al. 2002; Galea et al. 2005). Given the close association between PTSD and suicidal acts (e.g., Oquendo et al. 2005), the results of such studies suggest that the effects of natural disasters on suicide rates can also vary over the post-disaster period. In addition, if natural disasters enhance social connectedness among residents in the damaged areas, which in turn might decrease suicide rates, it is plausible that disasters have a lagged effect because social connectedness is likely to evolve incrementally in the period of post-disaster recovery. Accordingly, we hypothesized that the effects of natural disasters on suicide rates change over the post-disaster period.

During our study period from 1982 to 2010, Japan experienced large variations in the incidence of natural disasters and suicide rates, both over time and across subnational units. Such variations are crucial for obtaining reliable estimates of the effects of natural disasters on suicide rates. Japan is vulnerable to a wide variety of natural disasters such as earthquakes, tsunamis, volcanic eruptions, typhoons, floods, landslides, and avalanches (Skidmore 2001). In fact, more than 20% of the world's largest earthquakes, with a magnitude of more than 6, have occurred in and around Japan (Cabinet Office 2007). In addition, suicide rates in Japan have shown large variations during the period of our study. Since the early 1990s, when the bubble in the domestic asset market burst, Japan has been suffering slow and even negative growth, accompanied by price deflation. While this did not have any immediate effect on the number of suicides, things changed dramatically in 1998 when a 35.16% jump in the number of suicides shocked the nation. Since then, more than 30,000 people have died from suicidal acts each year, for 14 consecutive years, in a country with a total population of 120 million (Chen et al. 2012). Our data did not include the tremendous damages by the Great East Japan Earthquake (GEJE) in 2011, but we tried to extend our findings between 1982 and 2010 to suicide in the region affected by GEJE in the fifth section.

2 Methodology and Data

To examine the association between natural disasters and suicide, we estimated the following regression model by assuming that suicide rates in each prefecture are determined as a linear function of the number of people who died or were affected by natural disasters. Our main model is written as:

$$S_{jt} = \beta_0 D_{jt} + \beta_1 D_{jt-1} + \beta_2 D_{jt-2} + \beta_3 D_{jt-3} + \beta_4 D_{jt-4} + \beta_5 D_{jt-5} + \lambda_0 V_{jt} + \lambda_1 V_{jt-1} + \lambda_2 V_{jt-2} + \lambda_3 V_{jt-3} + \lambda_4 V_{jt-4} + \lambda_5 V_{jt-5} + \gamma_j + \varphi_t + \rho_j + \varepsilon_{jt}, \tag{1}$$

where S_{jt} denotes the suicide rate in prefecture j in year t. D_{jt} equals the number of people who died as a result of a natural disaster in prefecture j in year t, while V_{jt} equals the number of people who were directly affected (e.g., injured or losing a house) by a natural disaster. We explain the details of these variables below. Because natural disasters can have long-term consequences on the affected region, we also included lagged values of D in the estimation. D_{jt-s} and V_{jt-s} in Eq. (1) denote the number of disaster deaths and victims lagged at $t-s$ in prefecture j, with $s = 1, \ldots, 5$. In our model, we set the maximum value of s at 5, which means that the impact of natural disasters on suicide rates was measured over the subsequent 5 years. Changing the number of lags from $s = 5$ to $s = 3, 4, 6$, or 7 did not change our substantive results. In Eq. (1), ρ_j represents prefecture-specific fixed effects, and φ_t indicates year-specific effects. Moreover, ε_{jt} is a prefecture–year-specific error term. The year effect captures the effects of economic depression and any other major events in Japan in a particular year. The prefecture-specific fixed effects were expected to capture the effects of time-invariant unobserved factors that could be related to suicide rates. They could include the culture and norms embedded in each prefecture, stable socioeconomic conditions, and geographical characteristics. Because Eq. (1) includes the fixed effects for each prefecture, our estimation exploited the variation within each prefecture over time. Finally, we also included the prefecture-specific time trend, $\gamma_j T$, in the model to mitigate a potential spurious relationship between the number of people exposed to natural disasters and the number of suicides arising from a common time trend.

For this study, we developed a 29-year panel dataset on the 47 prefectures of Japan from 1982 to 2010. The total number of observations was 1,363 prefecture-years. The population size of the prefectures ranged from around 600,000 (Tottori Prefecture in 2010) to 13,159,000 (Tokyo Prefecture in 2010). Note that any impact associated with the geographical characteristics of prefectures was accounted for by the inclusion of prefecture-specific fixed effects.

The suicide rate, S_{jt}, equals the number of suicides per 100,000 persons in prefecture j in year t. We computed suicide rates for the entire population and for two age groups (under 65 years of age and age 65 and above) of both men and women. We used age- and gender-specific rates because the impact of natural disasters might differ across demographic groups. For example, women are known to be more likely to have PTSD in the aftermath of natural disasters than are men (Galea et al. 2005). Data on suicide rates are obtained from *Jinko Dotai Toukei* (Vital Statistics of Japan, various years), published by the Ministry of Health, Labour, and Welfare.

Figure 1 plots the temporal changes in suicide rates by age in the 47 prefectures between 1982 and 2010. The suicide rates are represented by the line for population under 64 years of age and by the solid dashed line for population over age 65 years

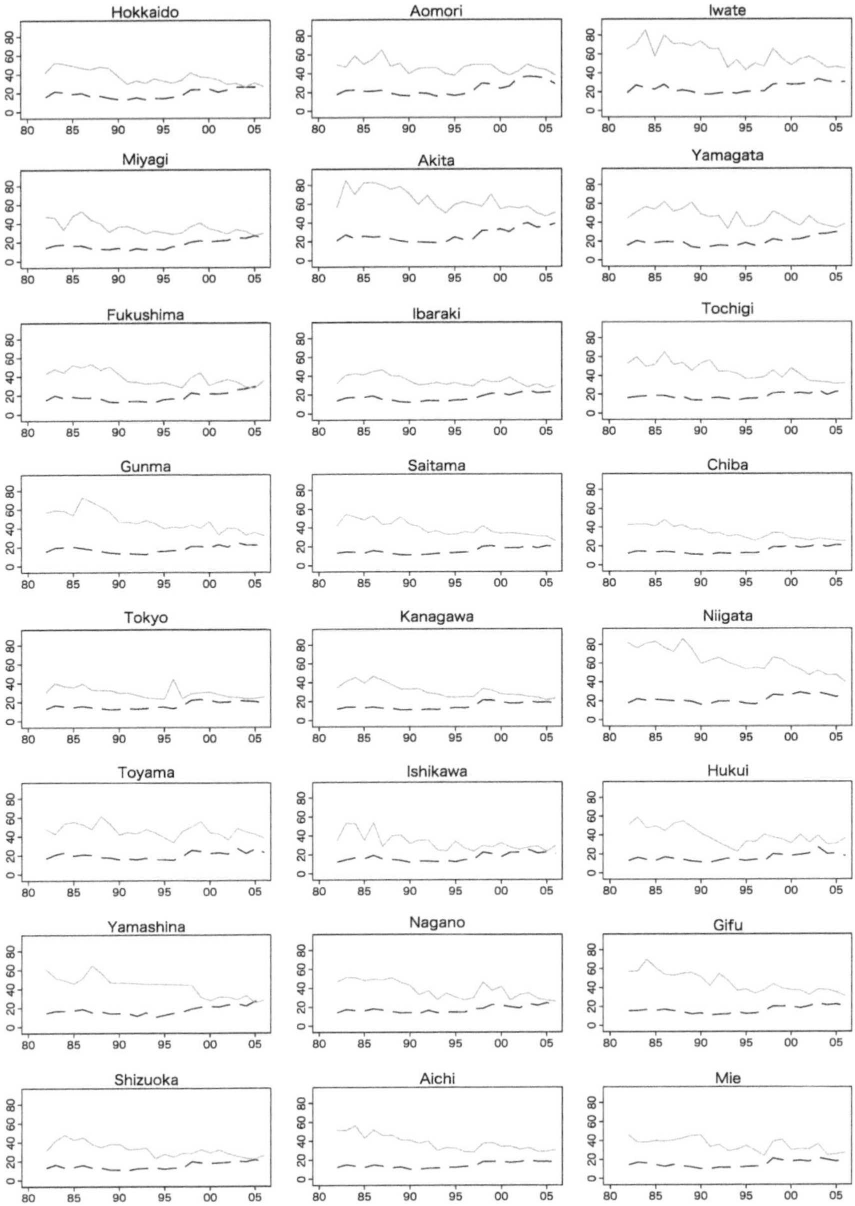

Fig. 1 Temporal changes in suicide rates in 47 prefectures

and above. The suicide rates during our study period in Japan differed greatly across prefectures and time. The suicide rates were higher among the senior population, especially in Iwate, Akita, Niigata, and Miyazaki prefectures during the 1980s and 1990s. The highest average suicide rates during the study period were found in

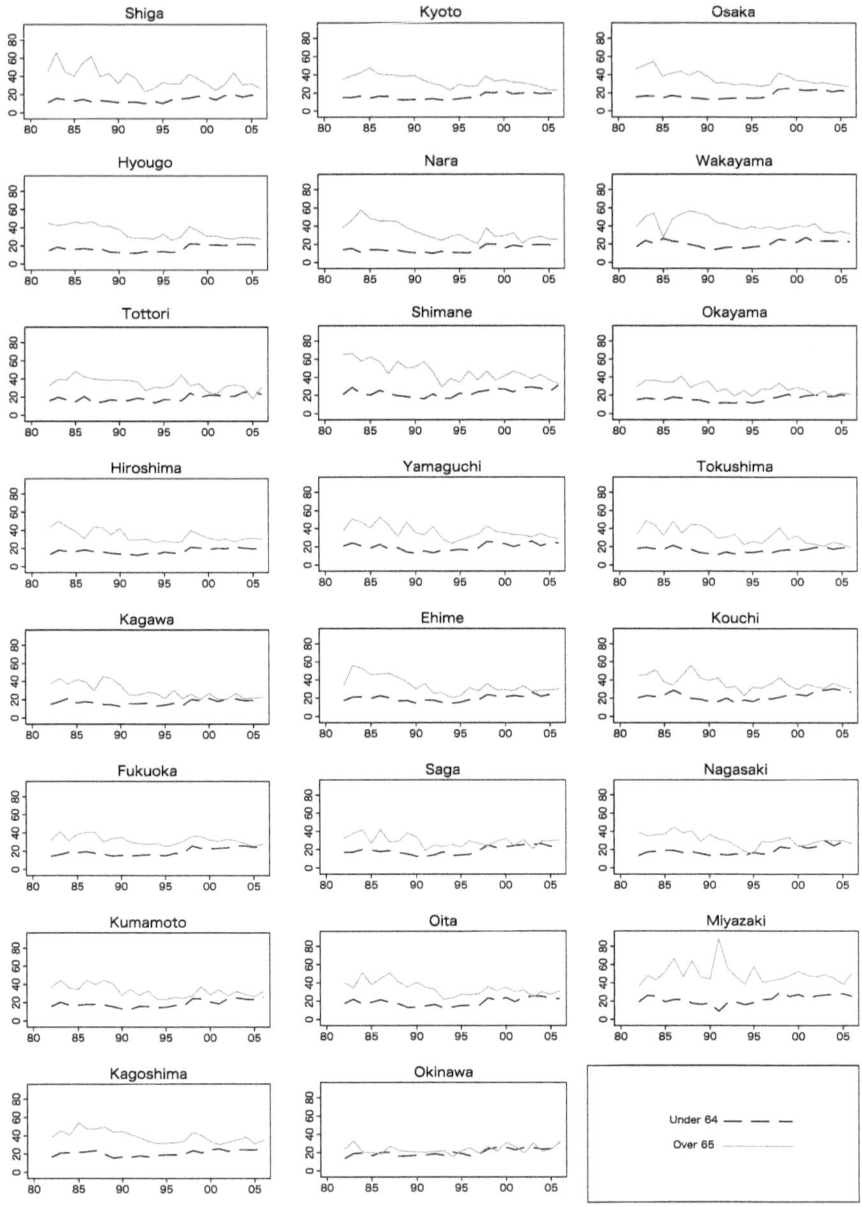

Fig. 1 (continued)

Akita Prefecture (= 28 below age 64 years and 62 for age 65 years and above). Summary statistics of the suicide rates for the entire population and subgroups are presented in Table 1.

Table 1 Summary statistics

Variable	Mean	SD	Min	Max
Total suicide rate	21.839	5.019	11.924	44.473
Male suicide rate under 64	28.442	8.744	12.690	64.920
Female suicide rate under 64	9.780	1.917	2.544	18.579
Male suicide rate over 65	48.098	13.035	15.763	130.882
Female suicide rate over 65	29.736	12.797	4.000	91.429
Number of deaths by disasters (per 100)	0.077	1.703	0000	62.810
Number of affected people (per 10,000)	0.211	3.276	0.000	119.911
Number of blood donors (per 10,000)	552.685	141.350	279.354	1235.953

Note The total number of observations is 1,363 for the period of 1982 and 2010. The data on the number of blood donors are available only for the period of 1982 and 2008. The suicide rates are measured per 100,000 persons

Data on the number of disaster victims by natural disasters were taken from *Shobo Hakusho* (White Paper on Fire Service), published annually by the Fire and Disaster Management Agency. The white paper aggregated the number of persons who died or were affected by all natural disasters in each prefecture in a given year. Natural disasters in the dataset included storm, heavy rain, flood, tide, earthquake, tsunami, volcanic eruption, and other unusual natural disorders. The number of deaths included those who were missing after disasters. Victims affected by natural disasters were defined as *risaisya* in the white paper, i.e., who were injured as a direct result of natural disasters or those whose houses were destroyed or damaged by natural disasters.

Tables 2 and 3 present the list of 10 natural disasters with the largest number of deaths and people affected by natural disasters between 1982 and 2010. During the study period, the average annual number of deaths was 7.677 with the standard deviation 170. This means that 7 or 8 people died or were missing as a result of natural disasters per year in each prefecture. The average of deaths was 3.071 after we excluded the Great Hanshin-Awaji Earthquake in 1995 in which 6,281 people

Table 2 Ten disasters with the largest number of deaths between 1982 and 2010

Victims	Prefecture	Year	Major disaster
6,281	Hyogo	1995	Earthquake
299	Nagasaki	1982	Rain
232	Hokkaido	1993	Earthquake
121	Kagoshima	1993	Rain
107	Shimane	1983	Rain
86	Akita	1983	Earthquake
70	Niigata	2004	Earthquake
49	Nagasaki	1991	Volcanic eruption
49	Niigata	1984	Snow
43	Niigata	1985	Snow

Note Of the total 1,363 observations (i.e., prefecture-years), 725 reported more than zero deaths

Table 3 Ten disasters with the largest number of affected people between 1982 and 2010

Victims	Prefecture	Year	Major disaster
1,199,109	Hyogo	1995	Earthquake
74,133	Niigata	2004	Earthquake
67,045	Aichi	2000	Rain
64,103	Nagasaki	1982	Rain
43,947	Osaka	1995	Earthquake
38,978	Miyagi	1986	Rain
35,583	Kagoshima	1993	Rain
33,595	Kochi	1998	Rain
32,299	Osaka	1982	Explosion
32,042	Shimane	1983	Rain

Note Of the total 1,363 observations (i.e., prefecture-years), 1,140 reported more than zero disaster victims. "Explosion" was caused by an accident at an industrial plant, but *Shobo Hakusho* (White Paper on Fire Service) included this type of industrial disaster as a natural disaster in their report

lost their lives. The annual average number of people affected by natural disasters was 2,110, a standard deviation of about 33,000. Thus, about 2,000 people in Japan were affected by natural disasters every year. The average of deaths was 1,240 after the Great Hanshin-Awaji Earthquake was excluded. Of the total 1,363 observations (i.e., prefecture-years), 725 reported more than zero disaster deaths and 1,140 reported more than zero affected people. In the regression analysis reported in the next section, the number of deaths was measured per 100, while the number of affected population was measured per 10,000.

We expected that the numbers of deaths and affected victims captured different aspects of damages caused by natural disasters. The number of deaths was expected to measure the direct damage of disasters to individual victims and their families, while the number of affected people was expected to measure the broad damage to the region and community. Thus, these two measures of natural disasters might have a different impact on the suicide rates. Note that the correlation between them was strong; the coefficient is close to 0.99 if the Great Hanshin Awaji Earthquake was included and 0.5 if excluded. Some disasters were characterized by the large number of deaths and the small number of affected people, while other disasters showed the opposite pattern. In our analysis, we assumed that as the severity of the damages increased, the number of deaths or affected people increased.

Our identification strategy exploited the basic characteristics of natural disasters: they were assigned exogenously to each prefecture every year. The natural disasters should be completely random occurrences, and we have limited control over their influence on our lives. Thus, the number of people affected by natural disasters in a particular area was unlikely to be correlated with any attributes of the area, such as its socioeconomic and political characteristics. The random nature of natural disasters allowed the use of a simple estimation model [Eq. (1)) that included only the measures of natural disasters and the fixed effects. We conducted a supplementary analysis in order to check the validity of this assumption by regressing the size of deaths and affected population on a set of time-varying political and socioeconomic variables. None of the estimated coefficients was statistically significant, suggesting that the natural disasters and the associated human damage were exogenous.

3 Findings

We began with estimating Eq. (1) with the suicide rate of the total population as the dependent variable. Column (1) of Table 4 reports the estimation result. “Victims” include those who did not lose their lives but were affected by the disaster. The

Table 4 Natural disasters and suicide rates (all prefectures), 1982–2010

	(1)	(2)	(3)	(4)	(5)
	Total	Male	Female	Male	Female
		Under 65	Under 64	Over 64	Over 65
N of deaths at *t*	0.065 (0.159)	0.271 (0.258)	0.049 (0.112)	−0.306 (1.036)	−0.353 (0.564)
N of deaths at *t*−*1*	0.446*** (0.136)	1.019*** (0.226)	0.215 (0.187)	−0.886 (0.934)	0.245 (0.496)
N of deaths at *t*−2	0.292** (0.122)	0.632** (0.302)	−0.079 (0.153)	−0.581 (0.854)	0.581 (0.443)
N of deaths at *t*−*3*	0.162 (0.170)	0.558* (0.285)	0.007 (0.178)	−0.555 (0.474)	−0.383 (0.391)
N of deaths at *t*−*4*	0.214 (0.157)	0.190 (0.258)	0.011 (0.161)	0.939** (0.397)	0.300 (0.418)
N of deaths at *t*−*5*	0.195** (0.077)	0.201 (0.220)	0.191 (0.164)	−0.551 (0.684)	0.244 (0.254)
N of victims at *t*	−0.028 (0.083)	−0.134 (0.135)	−0.029 (0.059)	0.209 (0.544)	0.216 (0.295)
N of victims at *t*−*1*	−0.251*** (0.071)	−0.551*** (0.118)	−0.123 (0.099)	0.461 (0.485)	−0.174 (0.260)
N of victims at *t*−2	−0.160** (0.064)	−0.335** (0.158)	0.033 (0.081)	0.301 (0.451)	−0.302 (0.231)
N of victims at *t*−*3*	−0.070 (0.088)	−0.269* (0.147)	−0.003 (0.093)	0.292 (0.252)	0.271 (0.206)
N of victims at *t*−*4*	−0.101 (0.082)	−0.078 (0.135)	−0.004 (0.085)	−0.491** (0.208)	−0.125 (0.222)
N of victims at *t*−*5*	−0.097** (0.041)	−0.086 (0.115)	−0.101 (0.087)	0.251 (0.359)	−0.119 (0.136)
Year fixed effect	Yes	Yes	Yes	Yes	Yes
Prefecture fixed effect	Yes	Yes	Yes	Yes	Yes
Prefecture-specific trend	Yes	Yes	Yes	Yes	Yes

Note Table entries are regression coefficients with robust standard errors in parentheses. Standard errors are estimated by Driscoll and Kraay’s (1998) covariance matrix estimator. The dependent variable is the suicide rate per 100,000. The number of disaster victims is measured per 10,000. The number of observations is 1,363. * $p < 0.10$, ** $p < 0.05$, *** $p < 0.01$ (two-tailed tests)

year- and prefecture-specific fixed effects, and prefecture-specific time trends were always included in the following estimations, but the estimates are not reported in the tables. In order to address the potential heterogeneity and autocorrelation in the error terms within each prefecture and contemporaneous correlations across prefectures, standard errors were estimated by using Driscoll and Kraay's (1998) covariance matrix estimator.

Column (1) of Table 4 shows that the number of deaths by the disaster has no association with the suicide rates in the year of the disaster. The coefficient at year t is not statistically significant at the conventional level. Note that the positive effects of natural disasters on suicide rates are likely to be *underestimated*. This is because we treated natural disasters that happened in January and December of a particular (calendar) year on the same footing; while the former's effects on suicide rates were evaluated for all the remaining months of the year, the latter's effects were analyzed for only less than a month. Thus, estimating the average effect of the disasters in a particular calendar year yields an absolute value of the estimates considerably less than it would be were the effects of these disasters estimated over 12 months after each incident.

Importantly, column (1) shows a lagged effect of the natural disaster on the suicide rate of the total population. The number of deaths was positively associated with the suicide rates in the next 2 years of the natural disaster. The estimated coefficients are 0.45 and 0.30, which are statistically significant at $p = 0.05$. The total suicide rate increased by about 0.5 as the number of deaths by the natural disaster increases by 100. Given that the average suicide rate of the total population was 22, the substantive impact of natural disasters on the total suicide rate was nontrivial. In the case of severe disasters causing large numbers of deaths, suicide became a serious concern in the next few years for the affected region. The similar positive relationship is also found at $t-5$, yet its coefficient is smaller than those at $t-2$ and $t-3$.

When turning to the coefficients associated with the number of victims in column (1) of Table 4, we found that the damages caused by natural disasters had an opposite lagged impact on the suicide rate of the total population. In the next 2 years after a disaster, the number of affected population was negatively associated with the suicide rate. The coefficient at $t-2$ indicates that the total suicide rate decreased by 0.25 as the number of disaster victims who were injured or lost their house increased by 10,000. The negative relationship became weaker as time progresses. Because we found a negative and statistically significant coefficient at $t-2$, $t-3$, and $t-5$, the increase in suicide rates by the disaster deaths in these years was offset by the decline of disaster victims.

In sum, the estimation result in column (1) of Table 4 suggests that the relationship between natural disasters and the total suicide rates was complicated. The areas with large numbers of deaths by natural disasters experienced a temporary increase in suicide rates in the few years after the disaster, while the areas with the larger number of affected population experienced a temporary decrease in the rates over the next 2 years.

The complicated pattern found in column (1) might be due to combined heterogeneities across different age and gender groups. For a further examination of the complex pattern, columns (2)–(5) of Table 4 report estimation results when age- and gender-specific suicide rates are used as outcome variables. The results suggest the male working-age population [column (2)) was more likely to be affected by exposure to natural disasters; their suicide rates tended to follow the same pattern found in column (1). The sizes of the estimated coefficients at $t-1$ and $t-2$ for both the number of deaths and victims in column (2) are twice as large as those in column (1). In contrast, the coefficients are smaller or statistically insignificant in columns (3)–(5). These findings indicate that the effects of natural disasters on suicide rates varied considerably across demographic groups and that males under 64 years of age were more sensitive to the impact of natural disasters than others.

Next, we conducted the same analysis excluding an outlier in our dataset, the massive 1995 Great Hanshin-Awaji Earthquake, which primarily affected Hyogo Prefecture leaving a death toll of 6,281. Because the magnitude of the Hanshin earthquake was considerably larger than the other disasters in our dataset (see Tables 2 and 3), it is possible that the results in Table 4 were strongly influenced by this particular earthquake. In order to check this possibility, we re-estimated Eq. (1) by excluding Hyogo Prefecture from our data. The estimation results are reported in Table 5.

According to column (1) of Table 5, in which the total suicide rate was used as the dependent variable, the suicide rates tended to decrease in the first and second years after the disasters as the number of affected people increased. This is consistent with the finding reported in Table 4. However, the positive association between suicide rates and the level of damage measured by deaths is no longer found once the most severe natural disaster was excluded from the dataset. This suggests that powerful natural disasters tended to increase suicide rates in their aftermath, but less severe natural disasters tended to *decrease* suicide rates in the affected areas. An analysis with age- and gender-specific suicide rates (columns (2)–(5) of Table 5) indicates that column (1) of Table 5 largely reflects the suicide rate patterns of working-age males, as shown in Table 4.

Taken together, the results reported in Tables 4 and 5 suggest that when the damage caused by natural disasters was extremely large, as in the case of the Hanshin-Awaji earthquake, suicide rates tended to increase in the immediate aftermath of the disaster and several years later. However, when the damage by natural disasters was less severe, suicide rates tended to *decrease* after the disasters, especially 1 or 2 years later. Thus, natural disasters affected the suicide rates of affected populations in a complicated way, depending on the severity of damages as well as on how many years have passed since the disaster.

Table 5 Natural disasters and suicide rates (excluding Hyogo Prefecture), 1982–2010

	(1)	(2)	(3)	(4)	(5)
	Total	Male	Female	Male	Female
		Under 64	Under 64	Over 65	Over 65
N of deaths at *t*	−0.000 (0.401)	0.422 (0.708)	−0.326 (0.265)	0.129 (2.235)	1.463 (0.908)
N of deaths at *t−1*	−0.245 (0.372)	0.029 (0.439)	−0.097 (0.156)	−2.246 (2.842)	0.598 (0.715)
N of deaths at *t−2*	−0.015 (0.237)	0.385 (0.581)	−0.385* (0.205)	1.024 (0.908)	0.030 (0.932)
N of deaths at *t−3*	0.393 (0.365)	1.307* (0.700)	0.097 (0.320)	−2.068* (1.178)	0.292 (1.027)
N of deaths at *t−4*	0.233 (0.254)	0.449 (0.501)	−0.160 (0.140)	1.127 (1.416)	1.459** (0.638)
N of deaths at *t−5*	−0.019 (0.208)	0.282 (0.325)	−0.393 (0.298)	−0.581 (2.293)	0.698 (0.842)
N of victims at *t*	−0.036 (0.086)	−0.141 (0.140)	−0.042 (0.057)	0.198 (0.527)	0.231 (0.336)
N of victims at *t−1*	−0.257*** (0.077)	−0.555*** (0.112)	−0.137 (0.099)	0.483 (0.521)	−0.135 (0.261)
N of victims at *t−2*	−0.152** (0.064)	−0.312* (0.166)	0.028 (0.081)	0.301 (0.430)	−0.283 (0.235)
N of victims at *t−3*	−0.076 (0.091)	−0.281* (0.162)	−0.006 (0.093)	0.314 (0.271)	0.274 (0.213)
N of victims at *t−4*	−0.094 (0.083)	−0.062 (0.142)	0.002 (0.080)	−0.516** (0.227)	−0.092 (0.231)
N of victims at *t−5*	−0.095** (0.039)	−0.084 (0.118)	−0.097 (0.090)	0.248 (0.367)	−0.098 (0.133)
Year fixed effect	Yes	Yes	Yes	Yes	Yes
Prefecture fixed effect	Yes	Yes	Yes	Yes	Yes
Prefecture-specific trend	Yes	Yes	Yes	Yes	Yes

Note Table entries are regression coefficients with robust standard errors in parentheses. Standard errors are estimated by Driscoll and Kraay's (1998) covariance matrix estimator. The dependent variable is the suicide rate per 100,000. The number of disaster victims is measured per 10,000. The number of observations is 1,334. * $p < 0.10$, ** $p < 0.05$, *** $p < 0.01$ (two-tailed tests)

4 Why Do Natural Disasters Reduce Suicide?

How can we explain this complicated pattern of suicide rates in the aftermath of natural disasters? When natural disasters cause extraordinary disruption and damage, as in the case of the 1995 Hanshin-Awaji earthquake, they can leave both immediate and long-lasting adverse consequences on people's lives and mental health. For example, many evacuees of Hurricane Katrina had high levels of mental distress in the immediate aftermath of the hurricane (e.g., Brodie et al. 2006; Mills et al. 2007), and the prevalence of post-traumatic stress and psychological distress remained high several years after the disaster (Paxson et al. 2012). Depression, somatic complaints, and PTSD were also reported among the 1995 Hanshin earthquake victims and a high prevalence of PTSD among elderly and school-age victims was found even seven years later (Shinfuku 2006, Ministry of Internal Affairs and Communications 2012). In general, past research suggests severe natural disasters are associated with a high prevalence of PTSD and other adverse mental health outcomes (Norris et al. 2002), which are known risk factors of suicide (Lönnqvist 2009).

Highly destructive natural disasters produce not only immediate and long-term psychological disturbance but can also cause long-term disruption in victims' social and economic lives through the destruction of properties, local businesses, and community structures. The consequences of such losses often hit disaster victims hard several years later, when the initial shock and relief efforts have subsided. For example, about 50% of small business owners reported financial hardship (their income became less than half compared to the pre-disaster level) 2 years after the Hanshin earthquake, but the number increased to about 70% in a survey taken 3 years after the initial survey (*Kobe Shimbun* Jan. 15, 2004). The number of "isolated deaths" (referring to people who die alone at home and are not immediately found) in Kobe City has sharply increased several years after the Hanshin-Awaji earthquake, which is attributed to eroding social ties due to prolonged evacuation and relocations of affected populations (Tanaka et al. 2009). In sum, devastating natural disasters can cause major economic and social hardship among disaster victims, which can increase the risk of self-destructive behaviors and suicide.

In contrast, the impact of natural disasters on people's lives and mental health is likely to be limited when the severity of natural disasters is not as high. Such disasters are likely to be less traumatic, and small-scale natural disasters are unlikely to force affected populations to relocate or evacuate for a long period. Thus, the long-term adverse consequences of natural disasters are also unlikely to be present. Therefore, different levels of damages caused by natural disasters are one potential factor that explains differences in the patterns found between Tables 4 and 5.

At the same time, natural disasters can enhance social connectedness in the post-disaster period, which can mitigate psychological stress. Eventually, greater social connectedness might reduce the overall risk of suicidal acts. Several past studies have shown that individuals or areas with greater social capital are quicker to recover from natural disasters (Weil et al. 2012; Aldrich 2012; See also Hikichi et al. (2016), Sone et al. (2016), and Matsuyama et al. (2016) in the case of GEJE), suggesting that social capital works as a protective factor against adverse events. In addition, other scholars claim that the common experience of tragedy and the subsequent recovery effort following natural disasters can enhance social integration, which can also be protective against suicide risk (Gordon et al. 2011; see also Joiner 2005).

To empirically check the protective features of social connectedness, we tested the relationship between the degree of social connectedness and the level of damages caused by natural disasters. The model that we estimated was essentially the same as Eq. (1), but the outcome variable was the level of social connectedness in each prefecture in a given year. We measured social connectedness by the number of people donating blood, which has been used as a measure of social capital in the past (MacIntyer and Ellaway 2003; Mohan et al. 2005; Buonanno et al. 2009; Kuroki 2011). Because donating blood is largely an altruistic act with no significant material payoffs, we can view it as a measure of connectedness between people. We used the number of blood donors per 10,000 people as the dependent variable in the analysis, based on data from 1982 to 2008, collected from the Ministry of Health, Labour, and Welfare. If natural disasters increased social connectedness in the damaged areas, we should be able to find a positive association between the size of affected people and the number of blood donors.

The results are reported in Table 6. The estimation results using data from all prefectures [column (1)) indicate that the number of blood donors was negatively associated with the number of deaths after the occurrence of natural disasters, while it was positively associated with the number of victims. With the removal of Hyogo Prefecture from the dataset to exclude the effect of the Hanshin earthquake [column (2)), the negative association between the number of blood donors and the number of deaths became statistically insignificant, while the positive association between the number of blood donors and the number of victims remained to be significant and positive. Column (2) suggests that the damages caused by natural disasters increased blood donation for about 4 years after the disaster. This suggests that people are more likely to donate blood when natural disasters hit their prefectures. It is possible that a shortage of blood caused by natural disasters partly explains the increase in the number of blood donors in the immediate aftermath of the disasters, but it is unlikely that the shortage lasts more than a couple of years. Thus, the finding in Table 6 suggests that people were more willing to engage in an altruistic act that signifies their support to other members of the society after natural disasters. Note that natural disasters were completely exogenous to area characteristics, and thus the association found in Table 6 solely reflects the impact of natural disasters on people's willingness to help others.

The remaining question is whether the higher level of social connectedness in the post-disaster period explains the observed post-disaster decrease in suicide rates in Tables 4 and 5. A full exploration of this question is beyond the scope of this chapter, but our preliminary analysis reveals that the number of blood donors was indeed negatively associated with suicide rates, suggesting that social connectedness is a protective factor against suicide. Table 7 reports the estimation results when prefecture-level suicide rates were regressed on the number of blood donors. Because the distribution of blood donors was not random, our analysis also controlled for the effects of other socioeconomic confounding factors, such as population size, the percentages of population under 15 and 65 years of age and above, unemployment rate, and mean personal income, on suicide rates. According to column (1) of Table 7, prefectures with more blood donors tended to have fewer suicides of the total population. This pattern is confirmed for males under 64 years old and females over 65 years old. The results suggest that the observed decrease in

Table 6 Natural disasters and blood donation, 1982–2008

	(1) All	(2) Excluding Hyogo
N of deaths at *t*	−10.719* (6.202)	5.258 (9.542)
N of deaths at *t−1*	−14.501** (6.926)	0.835 (11.728)
N of deaths at *t−2*	−13.789* (6.998)	−5.771 (6.246)
N of deaths at *t−3*	−12.774** (6.083)	−4.147 (6.389)
N of deaths at *t−4*	−13.152** (5.244)	−2.765 (5.800)
N of deaths at *t−5*	−8.757 (5.353)	−6.920 (6.712)
N of victims at *t*	5.372 (3.265)	5.598* (3.172)
N of victims at *t−1*	7.910** (3.650)	8.318** (3.811)
N of victims at *t−2*	7.534* (3.699)	7.912* (3.880)
N of victims at *t−3*	6.783** (3.218)	7.099** (3.317)
N of victims at *t−4*	6.131** (2.778)	6.208** (2.870)
N of victims at *t−5*	4.498 (2.811)	4.594 (2.809)
Year fixed effect	Yes	Yes
Prefecture fixed effect	Yes	Yes
Prefecture-specific trend	Yes	Yes

Note: Table entries are regression coefficients with robust standard errors in parentheses. Standard errors are estimated by Driscoll and Kraay's (1998) covariance matrix estimator. The dependent variable is the number of people donating blood per 100,000. The number of disaster victims is measured per 10,000. The number of observations is 1,269. * $p < 0.10$, ** $p < 0.05$, *** $p < 0.01$ (two-tailed tests)

suicide rates can partly be explained by the higher level of social connectedness caused by natural disasters.

Taken together, the results in Tables 6 and 7 suggest that natural disasters can increase social connectedness, which may offset some of the adverse consequences of natural disasters. However, our findings also suggest that when natural disasters are highly destructive and disruptive, the protective feature of social connectedness is unlikely to be enough to compensate for the severe negative impact of disasters on population health.

Table 7 Blood donation and suicide rates, 1982–2008

	(1)	(2)	(3)	(4)	(5)
	Total	Male	Female	Male	Female
		Under 64	Under 64	Over 65	Over 65
Blood donation	−0.003*** (0.001)	−0.004** (0.002)	−0.001 (0.001)	−0.003 (0.003)	−0.009*** (0.003)
Log population size	4.583 (9.222)	7.705 (18.459)	−2.433 (5.407)	−12.051 (25.877)	8.972 (20.759)
Percent population under 15	−0.083 (0.148)	−0.966*** (0.343)	0.019 (0.115)	1.535** (0.683)	1.046* (0.578)
Percent population over 65	−0.088 (0.308)	−0.121 (0.650)	0.017 (0.231)	−1.904*** (0.498)	−0.658 (0.708)
Log mean income	−5.111** (2.159)	−9.035 (5.326)	−1.397 (1.960)	−2.847 (8.659)	−12.679** (5.638)
Unemployment rate	1.280*** (0.393)	2.651*** (0.757)	0.170 (0.234)	1.743 (1.043)	−0.101 (0.649)
Year fixed effect	Yes	Yes	Yes	Yes	Yes
Prefecture fixed effect	Yes	Yes	Yes	Yes	Yes
Prefecture-specific trend	Yes	Yes	Yes	Yes	Yes

Note Table entries are regression coefficients with robust standard errors in parentheses. Standard errors are estimated by Driscoll and Kraay's (1998) covariance matrix estimator. The dependent variable is the suicide rate per 100,000. The number of observations is 1,222. * $p < 0.10$, ** $p < 0.05$, *** $p < 0.01$ (two-tailed tests)

5 Great East Japan Earthquake and Suicide

Our findings in the previous sections should be able to speak to a suicide trend after the Great East Japan Earthquake (GEJE), an unprecedented earthquake that hit the northeastern region Japan in March 11, 2011. Collapsing buildings, the tsunami, and other incidents caused by the earthquake took a total of 19,475 lives and left 2,587 people's missing. The earthquake not only took away lives, but also had a detrimental effect on the well-being of survivors. More than 400,000 homes were damaged or destroyed, traffic networks torn apart, fields, harbors, and industrial facilities demolished; and due to the massive loss of private property and assets, the domestic and international supply chain had been adversely scarred. Moreover, the earthquake and tsunami caused the explosion and meltdown of the Fukushima Daiichi Nuclear Power Plant operated by Tokyo Electric Power Company, resulting in the mandatory evacuation of about 100,000 people from the affected area. The GEJE is one of the most destructive and disruptive natural disasters in the history of Japan and its damage was significantly larger than that of the Hanshin-Awaji earthquake in 1995. Given our findings that suicide rates tend to increase in the aftermath of a highly destructive disaster, we might find that the number of suicides in the heavily affected regions, such as Iwate, Miyagi, and Fukushima prefectures, increased after the earthquake and the nuclear disaster.

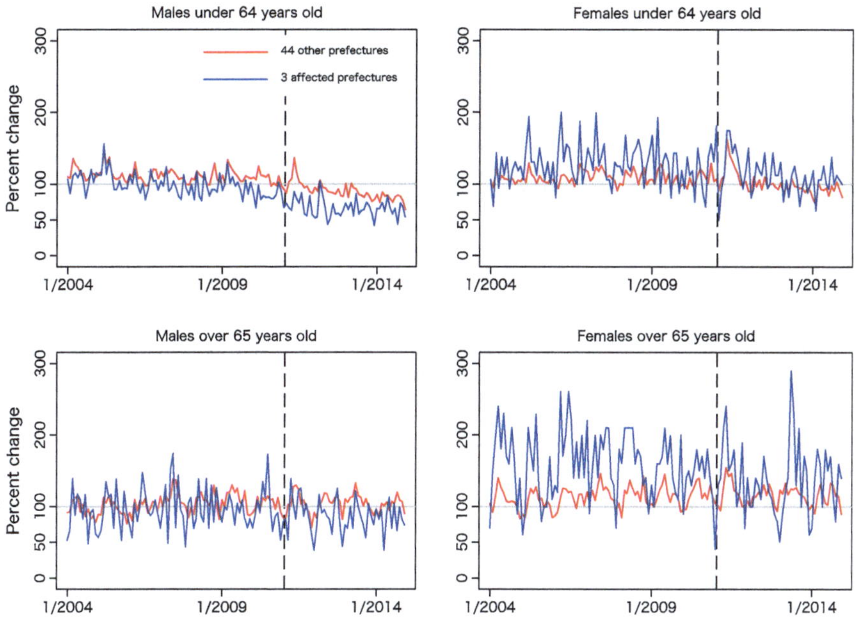

Fig. 2 Percent changes in suicide counts before and after GEJE

Alternatively, if the GEJE, despite its disastrous impact, increased social connectedness among the affected population, we might be able to see a decline in the number of suicides in those three prefectures.

To evaluate the suicide trend after GHJE, we compared a monthly change in the number of suicides in the three heavily damaged prefectures and 44 other prefectures. We set the baseline to be the number of suicides in February 2011, a month before the GEJE hit, and computed the percent change relative to the baseline. Our analysis covered the period from January 2004 to December 2014. Figure 2 presents four plots on the percent change in the number of suicides by (1) male population under 64 years old, (2) female population under 64 years old, (3) male population aged 65 and older, and (4) female population aged 65 and older. The horizontal gray line denotes the baseline value, while the vertical dashed line separates the study period before and after the GEJE. The top left panel indicates that the number of suicides among males under 64 years old did not systematically deviate from the one during the baseline period before February 2011, while it has declined steadily after March 2011. Importantly, the decline began earlier and was more obvious in Iwate, Miyagi, and Fukushima than in the other 44 prefectures. In contrast to panel (1) of Fig. 1, panels (2)–(4) show no visible difference in the trend after March 2011 between the three affected and 44 other prefectures. This implies that the suicide counts by the senior male population and female population were not strongly affected by the disaster (See the similar findings by Orui et al. 2015).

Table 8 Number of suicides associated with GEJE

	Iwate	Miyagi	Fukushima	Total
2011	17	22	10	49
2012	8	3	13	24
2013	4	10	23	37
2014	3	4	15	22
2015	3	1	19	23
Total	35	40	80	155

Source 2015 White Paper on Suicide Prevention, Cabinet Office of Japan

The above analysis does not mean that the GEJE did not heighten suicidal risks in the affected region. A review article by Harada et al. (2015) reports that the substantial number of people in the affected region experienced mental distress including posttraumatic stress disorder, depression, and anxiety symptoms. Surveys conducted in the disaster-affected areas revealed that about 43% of disaster survivors have moderate to severe mental health problems, which makes the prevalence of mental health problems among survivors 1.5 times greater than that of the general population (Yokoyama et al. 2014). Using the panel survey before and after the disaster, Tsuboya et al. (2016) shows that a depressive symptom is more evident among those who lost their houses than others, although it does not differ between those who lost their family members and friends and those who did not after 3 years of the disaster.

The heightened mental distress could lead to an increase in the suicidal risks. In fact, Table 8 summarizes the number of suicides between 2011 and 2015 that were determined to be directly related to the GEJE by the police agency. The police declares one's suicide as GEJE-related if one of the following five criteria is met; (1) the victim's body was found at a charnel house of earthquake or tsunami victims or in temporary housing, (2) the victim was known to reside in temporary housing, (3) the victim was known to be an evacuee from the disaster-affected region, (4) the victim's house or workplace was seriously damaged, or (5) the motive of the victim is judged to have a direct association with GEJE. Between 2011 and 2015, a total of 155 suicide deaths in Iwate, Miyagi, and Fukushima were determined to be directly related to the disaster. Note that 4,240 suicides occurred in these three prefectures between 2011 and 2015, and some of these suicides could be indirectly associated with the tremendous adverse effects of GEJE.

A part of the decline in the number of suicides in Iwate, Miyagi, and Fukushima, as shown in Fig. 2, can be explained by enhanced social connectedness after the disaster. Several studies that documented mental consequences of GEJE in the affected region emphasize the importance of social relationships in reducing mental distress. Hikichi et al. (2016) and Matsuyama et al. (2016) report that higher levels of social cohesion and support at the community level before the disaster are associated with low levels of mental distress after the disaster. Sone et al. (2016) show that becoming connected with others after the disaster is associated with lower levels of distress. Other studies that documented the relationship between social trust and subjective well-being after GEJE also present important findings. Hommerich (2012) shows that the personal experience of having been affected by the disaster is associated with higher levels of social trust and a stronger local identity among those aged at 20–39 and that social trust is then positively associated with happiness. Yamaura et al. (2015) found that the positive relationship between social trust and subjective well-being was strengthened for people in the region affected by GEJE, suggesting that social trust mitigated the mental shock of the disaster. Thus, if the disaster results in the enhancement of social cohesion in the affected region, this might help to protect mental health and offset some of the adverse consequences of the disaster.

6 Discussion

This chapter provided systematic evidence on the relationship between natural disasters and suicide rates. Using extensive Japanese data on natural disasters and suicide rates for the period 1982–2010, we estimated lagged and complicated effects of natural disasters on the suicide rates of various demographic groups. Our estimation results indicate that working-age men are particularly at risk of suicidal behaviors in the aftermath of natural disasters. However, the impact of natural disasters depends on their magnitude. When natural disasters cause highly destructive damages to local communities, as in the case of the 1995 Hanshin-Awaji earthquake in Hyogo Prefecture, the number of deaths attributed to the disaster show an increase in suicide rates in the subsequent years among men under 64 years of age. Thus, for natural disasters of extraordinary magnitude, suicide rates in the affected areas with a large number of deaths heighten the risks of suicide. However, if we excluded the 1995 Hanshin-Awaji earthquake and focus on less disruptive disasters, we found that suicide rates have no association with the number of deaths but tend to decrease as the number of affected population increases.

We then explored the underlying mechanism of why the number of affected population is negatively associated with suicide rate. We hypothesized that natural disasters enhance people's willingness to help others in society, an effect that may work as a protective factor against disaster victims' suicidal risks. Our analysis showed that social connectedness, measured by the number of blood donors, tends to increase after natural disasters. We also found some evidence of the negative association between social connectedness and suicide risks. In the case of GEJE, a large portion of the population experiencing damages was likely to suffer mental distress, which might increase the risk of suicide especially among the most vulnerable people. Yet, several studies offer suggestive evidence that enhanced social cohesion and trust might mitigate the adverse effect of GEJE on mental health, which might result in the decline in the number of suicides among men under 64 years of age in the affected region.

In summary, our findings suggest that social connectedness in affected areas can increase in the post-disaster period, which may mitigate some of the adverse effects of natural disasters on mental health. This in turn may explain the observed decrease in suicide rates in affected areas. However, our findings also indicate that the protective role of social connectedness is unlikely to be powerful enough to offset the impact of extremely severe natural disasters, as in the case of the Hanshin-Awaji earthquake.

We conducted two robustness checks of our findings. First, we estimated the same model with a different measure of damages inflicted by natural disasters. As an alternative measure, we used the estimated amount of economic and material damages from natural disasters. This variable, also obtained from *Shobo Hakusho,* is highly correlated with the number of disaster victims. The amount of economic and material damages is adjusted for inflation. Our substantive findings remained the same with this alternative measure. The results are available upon request.

Second, we checked the validity of our assumption that natural disasters are randomly assigned to the observations. We did so by regressing the number of disaster victims by natural disasters on several time-varying political and socioeconomic variables. If our assumption is valid, the number of victims should be uncorrelated with any of the explanatory variables included in the regression model. The model includes the following variables: government expenditures for public investment, number of fire service personnel, per capita income, unemployment rate, logged population size, logged population density, and proportions of the population under 15 and over 65 years of age and older, and in urban areas. Our regression analysis found no statistically significant results for any of these independent variables. This suggests that the number of disaster victims is indeed a random occurrence. In addition, the main results reported in Tables 4 and 5 hold even when these political and socioeconomic variables are included in Eq. (1).

Our findings are consistent with the previous studies that documented an increase in suicide rates following the 1999 earthquake in Taiwan (Chou et al. 2003; Yang et al. 2005; Chuang and Huang 2006; Liaw et al. 2008). This earthquake also caused severe damages including more than 2,400 deaths and the collapse of more than 100,000 homes. While these studies did not report a subsequent decrease in suicide rates in the following 2 years, it is likely this is due to the fact that they examined suicide rates for a short period of time after the disaster. Had they monitored the suicide rates in the severely damaged areas for a long enough period of time following the disaster, they might have found a complicated trajectory of suicide rates reported in this study. Similarly, the findings of this study suggest a need for a reevaluation of the conclusion reached by Rodrigo et al. (2009) that found no discernible change in suicide rates in the aftermath of another highly severe disaster, the 2004 tsunami in Sri Lanka, as they tracked the area's suicide rate only for 1 year after the disaster.

Our findings about the influence of the Hanshin-Awaji earthquake on suicides appear to be somewhat at odds with previous studies that found the suicide rate in Kobe City declined after the disaster (Shioiri et al. 1999; Nishio et al. 2009). However, these two studies only examined the suicide rate of an affected municipality and not that of an entire prefecture. They did not consider the possibility that the population data may not have reflected the number of people who actually lived in the municipality after the catastrophe, although thousands of people were estimated to have fled their hometown in the chaotic post-disaster period without informing their local governments (Cabinet Office 2006). Therefore, the number of actual residents in Kobe City might have been lower than the official population count (tallied annually by local governments based on relocation reports by residents), in which case the reported suicide rates are likely to be lower than the actual rates. While this potential undercount of local residents could apply to our study as well, the effect on our results should be less because our unit of analysis is a much larger geographical area.

Our study made several important contributions. First, we have shown that suicide risks in areas affected by highly destructive and disruptive natural disasters tend to increase and that the impact of natural disasters on suicide rates can vary depending on the severity of disasters. Such complex patterns after natural disasters were entirely overlooked in the prior literature. Second, this study reconciled the conflicting findings of prior studies by closely examining the long-term and heterogeneous effects of disasters. Our findings suggest that the previous literature could not reach a consensus on the impact of natural disasters on suicides partly because these complicated lagged and heterogeneous effects of disasters were often ignored. Third, we provided evidence on the potential role of social ties in reducing suicide risks. Despite growing evidence that social capital is associated with various health outcomes, robust evidence of a relationship between social capital and suicide was surprisingly limited, although Durkheim's classic theory on suicide and social connectedness is often considered the first study that linked social ties with population health. Our study highlights the importance of further exploration of this topic.

We believe our findings have important policymaking implications. In order to reduce the risk of suicidal acts after massive natural disasters, a prevention program targeting age and gender groups should be in place for at least 5–6 years after a major natural disaster. Policymakers should understand that suicide rates might eventually increase following massive natural disasters, even if they initially decrease. In addition, they should make every effort to preserve existing social ties and community structures when they devise a plan for the recovery and reconstruction of affected areas. For example, disaster victims should be relocated to a temporary housing unit together with their neighbors, instead of allocating housing units based on lotteries, as in the case of the Hanshin-Awaji earthquake (Cabinet Office 2006; Sawada 2011).

Our analysis has several potential limitations. First, our dataset did not allow us to test the possibility that natural disasters can have different influences on suicide rates depending on the type of disaster, such as earthquake or flood. This is because the data source only reported total damages from all natural disasters in each prefecture in a given year, and we had no easy method to disentangle the data. Second, this study treated the Hanshin-Awako earthquake as the only "severe" natural disaster in our dataset based on the number of deaths and the size of population affected (see Tables 2 and 3), but other researchers might well categorize other disasters in the same period as highly destructive. Future studies should define what constitutes severe or highly destructive natural disasters in a more precise manner, so that we can understand when disaster victims are at a high risk of suicide after natural disasters.

References

Aldrich, D.P. (2012). *Building resilience: social capital in post-disaster recovery*. Chicago: University of Chicago Press.

Buonanno, P., Montolio, D., & Vanin, P. (2009). Does Social Capital Reduce Crime?. *Journal of Law and Economics, 52*(1), 145–170.

Brodie, M., Weltzien, E., Altman, D., et al. (2006). Experiences of Hurricane Katrina evacuees in Houston shelters: Implications for future planning. *American Journal of Public Health, 96*(8), 1402–1408.

Cabinet Office, the Government of Japan. (2007). *White Paper on Disaster Management*.

Cabinet Office, the Government of Japan. (2006). Lessons learned from the great Hanshin-Awaji earthquake. Retrieved September 1, 2012, from http://www.bousai.go.jp/1info/kyoukun/hanshin_awaji/about/index.html.

Chen, J., Choi, Y. J., Mori, K., et al. (2012). Socio-economic studies on suicide: A survey. *Journal of Economic Surveys, 206*(2), 271–306.

Chen, S. L. S., Lee, C. S., Yen, A. M. F., et al. (2016). A 10-year follow-up study on suicidal mortality after 1999 Taiwan earthquake. *Journal of Psychiatric Research, 79,* 42–49.

Chou, Y.-J., Huang, N., Lee, C.-H., et al. (2003). Suicides after the 1999 Taiwan earthquake. *International Journal of Epidemiology, 32*(6), 1007–1014.

Chuang, H.-L., & Huang, W.-C. (2006). A re-examination of the suicide rates in Taiwan. *Social Indicators Research, 83*(3), 465–485.

Driscoll, J. C., & Kraay, A. C. (1998). Consistent covariance matrix estimation with spatially dependent panel data. *Review of Economics and Statistics, 80*(4), 549–560.

Fire and Disaster Management Agency, the Government of Japan. (Various years). *Shobo Hakusho*.

Galea, S., Nandi, A., & Viahov, D. (2005). The epidemiology of post-traumatic stress disorder after disasters. *Epidemiologic Reviews, 27,* 78–91.

Gordon, K. H., Bresin, K., Dombeck, J., Routledge, C., & Wonderlich, J. A. (2011). The impact of the 2009 red river flood on interpersonal risk factors for suicide. *Crisis, 32*(1), 52–55.

Guha-Sapir, D., Hoyois, P., & Below, R. (2015). *Annual Disaster Statistical Review 2014*. Bangkok: Centre for Research on the Epidemiology of Disasters.

Harada, N., Shigemura, J., Tanichi M., Kawaida, K., Takahashi, S., & Yasukata, F. (2015). Mental health and psychological impacts from the 2011 Great East Japan Earthquake Disaster: a systematic literature review. *Disaster and Military Medicine*, 1–17.

Hikichi, H., Aida, J., Tsuboya, T., Kondo, K., & Kawachi, I. (2016). Can community social cohesion prevent posttraumatic stress disorder in the aftermath of a disaster? A natural experiment from the 2011 Tohoku earthquake and tsunami. *American Journal of Epidemiology, 183*(10), 902–910.

Hommerich, C. (2012). Trust and subjective well-being after the Great East Japan earthquake, tsunami and nuclear meltdown: Preliminary results. *International Journal of Japanese Sociology, 21*(1), 46–64.

Joiner, T. (2005). *Why people die by suicide*. Cambridge, MA: Harvard University Press.

Kõlves, K., Kõlves, K., & De Leo, D. (2013). Natural disasters and suicidal behaviors: A systematic literature review. *Journal of Affective Disorders, 146,* 1–14.

Krug, E. G., Kresnow, M., Peddicord, J. P., et al. (1999). Retraction: suicide after natural disasters. *New England Journal of Medicine, 340*(2), 148–149.
Kuroki, M. (2011). Does social trust increase individual happiness in Japan?. *Japanese Economic Review, 62*(4), 444–459.
Liaw, Y.-P., Wang, P.-W., Huang, C.-C., Chang, C.-M., & Lee, W.-C. (2008). The suicide mortality rates between 1997-1998 and 2000-2001 in Nantou County of Taiwan following the earthquake of September 21 in 1999. *Journal of Forensic Sciences, 53*(1), 199–202.
Lönnqvist, J. (2009). Major psychiatric disorders in suicide and suicide attempters. In D. Wasserman & C. Wasserman (Eds.), *Suicidology and suicide prevention: A global perspective*. Oxford: Oxford University Press.
Macintyre, S., & Ellaway, A. (2003). Neighborhoods and health: Overview. In I. Kawachi & L. Berkman (Eds.), *Neighbourhoods and health*. Oxford: Oxford University Press.
Matsuyama, Y., Aida, J., Hase, A., Sato, Y., Koyama, S., Tsuboya, T., et al. (2016). Do community- and individual-level social relationships contribute to the mental health of disaster survivors? A multilevel prospective study after the Great East Japan Earthquake. *Social Science and Medicine, 151,* 187–195.
Mezuk, B., Larkin, G. L., Prescott, M. R., et al. (2009). The influence of a major disaster on suicide risk in the population. *Journal of Traumatic Stress, 22*(6), 481–488.
Mills, M. A., Edmondson, D., & Park, C. L. (2007). Trauma and stress response among Hurricane Katrina evacuees. *American Journal of Public Health, 97*(Suppl 1), S116–S123.
Mohan, J., Twigg, L., Barnard, S., et al. (2005). Social capital, geography and health: a small-area analysis for England. *Social Science and Medicine, 60*(6), 1267–1283.
Nishio, A., Akazawa, K., Shibuya, F., et al. (2009). Influence on the suicide rate two years after a devastating disaster: A report from the 1995 Great Hanshin-Awaji earthquake. *Psychiatry and Clinical Neurosciences, 63*(2), 247–250.
Norris, F. H., Friedman, M., Watson, P., et al. (2002). 60,000 Disaster victims speak: part I. An empirical review of the empirical literature, 1981–2001. *Psychiatry, 65*(3), 207–239.
Oquendo, M., Brent, D. A., Birmaher, B., et al. (2005). Posttraumatic stress disorder comorbid with major depression: Factors mediating the association with suicidal behavior. *American Journal of Psychiatry, 162*(3), 560–566.
Orui M., Sato Y., Tazaki, K., Kawamura I., Harada S., & Hayashi M. (2015). Delayed Increase in Male Suicide Rates in Tsunami Disaster- Stricken Areas following the Great East Japan Earthquake: A Three-Year Follow-Up Study in Miyagi Prefecture. Tohoku *Journal of Experimental Medicine,235*, 215–222.
Paxson, C., Fussell, E., Rhodes, J., et al. (2012). Five years later: Recovery from post traumatic stress and psychological distress among low-income mothers affected by Hurricane Katrina. *Social Science and Medicine, 74*(2), 150–157.
Pridemore, W. A., Trahan, A., & Chamlin, M. B. (2009). No evidence of suicide increase following terrorist attacks in the United States: An interrupted time-series analysis of September 11 and Oklahoma City. *Suicide and Life-threatening Behavior, 39*(6), 659–670.
Rodrigo, A., McQuillin, A., & Pimm, J. (2009). Effect of the 2004 tsunami on suicide rates in Sri Lanka. *Psychiatric Bulletin, 33*(5), 179–180.
Sawada, Y. (2011). *Are there any lessons from the past natural disasters? Economic recovery and livelihood rehabilitation from the Great East Japan earthquake*. Tokyo: The Research Institute of Economy, Trade, and Industry (RIETI).
Shinfuku, N. (2006). Long-term health consequences among victims of the Great Hanshin-Awaji Earthquake. *Clinical Psychiatry, 48*(3), 247–254.
Shioiri, T., Nishimura, A., et al. (1999). The Kobe earthquake and reduced suicide rate in Japanese males. *Archives of General Psychiatry, 56*(3), 282–283.
Shoaf, K., Sauter, C., Bourque, L. B., Giangreco, C., & Weiss, B. (2004). Suicides in Los Angeles County in relation to the Northridge earthquake: Correspondence. *Prehospital and Disaster Medicine, 19*(4), 307–310.
Skidmore, M. (2001). Risk, natural disasters, and household saving in a life cycle model. *Japan and the World Economy, 13*, 15–34.

Sone, T., Nakaya, N., Sugawara, Y., Tomata, Y., Watanabe, T., & Tsuji, I. (2016). Longitudinal association between time-varying social isolation and psychological distress after the Great East Japan Earthquake. *Social Science and Medicine, 152,* 96–101.

Tanaka, M., Takahashi, C., & Ueno, Y. (2009). The relationship between the actual conditions of "isolated death" occurrences and residential environments in disaster restoration public housing. *Journal of Architecture and Planning, 74*(642), 1813–1820.

The Ministry of Internal Affairs and Communications, Government of Japan. (2012, in Japanese). *Report on suicide prevention policies.*

Weil, F., Lee, M. R., & Shihadeh, E. S. (2012). The burdens of social capital: How socially-involved people dealt with stress after Hurricane Katrina. *Social Science Research, 41* (1), 110–119.

Yamamura, E., Tsutsui, Y., Yamane, C., Yamane, S., & Powdthavee, N. (2015). Trust and happiness: Comparative study before and after the Great East Japan earthquake. *Social Indicators Research, 123,* 919–935.

Yang, C.-H., Xirasagar, S., Chung, H.-C., Huang, Y.-T., & Lin, H.-C. (2005). Suicide trends following the Taiwan earthquake of 1999: Empirical evidence and policy implications. *Acta Psychiatrica Scandinavica, 112*(6), 442–448.

Yip, P. (2009). Effects of an earthquake on suicide rates in Nantou. *Taiwan. British Journal of Psychiatry, 194,* 190.

Yokoyama Y., Otsuka, K., Kawakami, N., Kobayashi S., Ogawa, A., Tannno K., Onoda, T., Yaegashi, Y., & Sakata, K. (2014). Mental Health and Related Factors after the Great East Japan Earthquake and Tsunami. *Public library of Science, 9*(7), 1–10.

Chapter 5
Suicide Among Adolescents and Young Individuals

1 Introduction

Suicide among adolescents and young adults constitutes a serious global public health problem. Suicide is one of the leading causes of death for young individuals in many countries, and prevalence of attempted suicides by young individuals, especially among females, is also high (White Paper on Suicide Prevention, 2016). Because previous suicide attempts are a strong risk factor for a subsequent completion of suicide Owens, et al. (2002), these young suicide attempters can become a major high-risk group later in their lives.

Although the number of suicides by young individuals is relatively small compared to the number of suicide deaths by the elderly population, completed and attempted suicides by young individuals have large consequences to society. Young individuals had long potential years to live had they not died prematurely, and the years of potential life lost are concentrated heavily among adolescents and young individuals. As seen in Chap. 2, the estimated total Potential Years of Life Lost (PYLL) due to suicide deaths in Japan (as of 2010) is 852976 years, out of which 385735 years are attributable to suicide deaths by individuals aged less than 39 years. In addition, suicide deaths by young individuals result in substantial lost productivity because they tend to have higher levels of earnings compared to older generations.

This chapter provides a more detailed account of suicides by adolescents and young adults in Japan. Suicide among adolescents and young individuals aged 15–24 is a major problem in Japan. Figure 1 displays the mortality rate of suicide by young males aged 15–24 in five countries: Japan, South Korea, USA, France, and Australia. These nations were chosen because of their similar economic development from four different regions. Figure 1 suggests that the suicide rate of young males has stayed low in France and South Korea, while it was high but has been declining in Australia. Most importantly, the suicide rate in Japan used to be low in the 1990s but has continued to rise in the 2000s. Japan now shows the highest rate

Y. Sawada et al., *Economic Analysis of Suicide Prevention*, Creating a Society for All, DOI 10.1007/978-981-10-1500-7_5

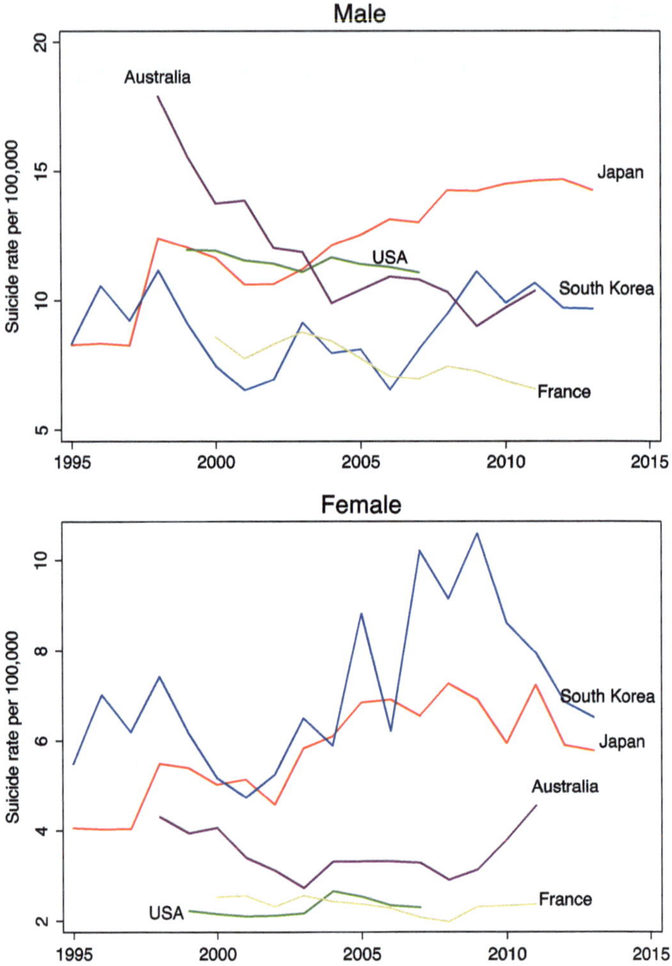

Fig. 1 Suicide rates in five countries *Source* WHO Mortality Database

among these five nations. When looking at the suicide rate of young females aged 15–24 as shown in Fig. 2, the suicide rate of young females in Japan shows a similar increasing trend between 1995 and 2013 and is one of the highest. Japan is also one of the few developed countries where adolescents and young individuals aged 15–34 die more by suicide than by any other cause (White Paper on Suicide Prevention, 2016). Because a majority of adolescent suicide victims is students, we examine the effects of school-related risk factors on the timing and rates of suicide among young individuals. Although the findings of these analyses are based on data from Japan, their implications should be applicable to young individuals in any country.

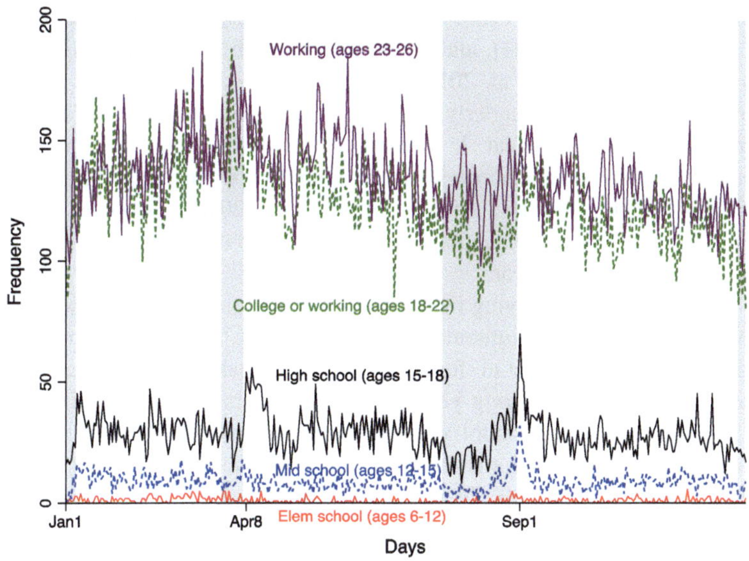

Fig. 2 Daily frequencies of suicide by five age/grade groups. *Note* The number of suicide deaths by grade groups and age groups is plotted against the calendar dates. February 29th is excluded. The sample includes individuals who died by suicide at 6–26 years of age between 1974 and 2014 in Japan. The total number of suicide deaths is 108968 *Source* Death records, Vital Statistics of Japan

2 School Calendar and the Timing of Suicide

Numerous studies have examined seasonality in suicide, a cyclical change in the frequency of suicide across seasons. Empirical support for the seasonal pattern has been found across various countries, including Belgium, Finland, France, Germany, Greece, Greenland, Hong Kong, Ireland, Italy, Japan, Norway, Slovenia, South Africa, Spain, Switzerland, Taiwan, the United Kingdom, and the United States (Ajdacic-Gross et al. 2010; Altamura et al. 1999; Chew and McCleary 1995). The frequency typically increases in the spring and early summer months, but the pattern varies across regions, times, and methods (Ajdacic-Gross et al. 2010)

When focusing on seasonality in youth suicide, however, the literature remains inconclusive. For example, using data from the United States, McCleary et al. reported unimodal seasonality in the fall and winter among male youth aged under 16, while Frank and Lester and Hoberman and Garfinkel found no such pattern among those aged between 15 and 24 and under 20, respectively (McCleary et al. 1991; Frank and Lester 1998; Hoberman and Garfinkel 1988). Similar heterogeneous results were also found in other European nations such as England and Wales (Yip et al. 2000), Lecomte and Fornes 1998; Souêtre et al. 1987) Germany

(Massing and Angermeyer 1985; Schmidt et al. 2002), and Italy (Altamura et al. 1999; Preti and Miotto 1998), and Asian nations such as Singapore (Parker et al. 2001) and China (Zhang et al. 2011).

Further, the mechanism underlying the cyclical pattern in youth suicide, if such a pattern exists, remains unclear. In general, seasonal variations are associated with psychiatric and physical disorders, the availability of suicide methods, and the intensity of social activities (Ajdacic-Gross et al. 2010). However, it remains uncertain whether these explanations can be applied to the cyclical change in youth suicide within any given year.

To account for an underlying mechanism of seasonality in youth suicide, several previous studies offered arguments and evidence that highlight the importance of the school calendar. Lahti et al. found a significant peak in the number of suicides from August to October among youths below 18 years in northern Finland (Lahti et al. 2007). Because the school year begins in the middle of August in Finland, they argued that a stressful environment at school increases suicidal risk among vulnerable students. Similarly, Näyhä attributed a significant rise in suicide in the fall among youths aged between 15 and 24 in Finland to an intensity in school life (Nayha 1982). McCleary et al., Chew and McCleary, and Hansen and Lang all studied suicide among students in the United States and found that the number of suicides increases when the academic year starts but tends to be low during school breaks (McCleary et al. 1991; Chew and McCleary 1994; Hansen and Lang 2011). In addition, a recent report by Japan's Cabinet Office showed a sharp spike in suicide by young individuals aged 16 or younger on the dates when schools start a new semester in the spring and fall (White Paper on Suicide Prevention, 2015). All these findings suggest that the number of youth suicides increases at the beginning of the academic year or after a long break because vulnerable students may be exposed to school-related problems, including violence, bullying, interpersonal issues, dissatisfaction with school, and academic performance, which can become a cause of suicide (Gould et al. 2003; Brunstein Klomek et al. 2010; Serafini et al. 2015). They also suggest that students are less likely to die by suicide during school breaks because they are detached from the potential stress associated with school life or from bullies at school.

We seek to offer additional evidence for the role of the school calendar in youth suicide by using national mortality data from Japan. It improves upon previous studies in two major ways. First, we used daily records of suicide frequencies over a period of about 30 years, which allowed us to identify the exact timing of suicide in relation to the school calendar. Most previous studies used monthly data to examine the association between the school calendar and the timing of suicide deaths. Second, regional and temporal variations in the school calendar have been small in Japan, which enabled us to design a nationwide analysis for a long period of time, including about 15,000 cases of suicides by young individuals below 18 years of age.

Using the mortality data from the Vital Statistics of Japan between 1974 and 2014, we compiled the daily frequency of suicides across the calendar among young individuals of ages 6 to 26. We then examined whether the frequency of suicides by students increases around the dates when the school session begins in

January, April, and September. We also investigated whether suicides among students tend to decrease when school is not in session. We used the data of individuals aged 19 and older as a comparison group, under the assumption that they are less likely to be affected by the typical Japanese school calendar.

2.1 Methods

The mortality data in our analysis came from the death records in the Vital Statistics of Japan, compiled by the Ministry of Health, Labour and Welfare. The Vital Statistics data were collected for administrative purposes and anonymized by the Ministry prior to analysis. The data in the Vital Statistics are based on death certificates issued by physicians that are subsequently reported to the local government by a family member of the deceased. The local government then transfers the information to the Ministry of Health, Labour and Welfare. The Ministry assigns an International Classification of Diseases (ICD) code to each case using the information reported in the death certificate. If it is not clear if a particular death is intentional (suicide), unintentional (accident), or homicide, it will not be treated as suicide. Thus, it is possible that the number of suicides reported in the Vital Statistics is lower than the actual number of suicides. The quality of the Vital Statistic is likely to be high throughout our study period because only physicians are legally allowed to issue a death certificate, and a false report is subject to criminal penalty. The records cover all reported deaths in Japan and include the date of birth, the date of death, the place of death, marital status, and the underlying cause of death based on the ICD-8/9 standard (until 1994) and the ICD-10 standard (1995 to the present).

Our analysis focused on deaths by suicide (ICD-8/9: E950-E959, ICD-10: X60-X84) among young individuals who died at ages 6–26. We categorized the individuals into five groups: elementary school students (ages 6–12), middle school students (ages 12–15), high school students (ages 15–18), college students and working individuals (18–22), and graduate students and working individuals (ages 23–26). In Japan, education is compulsory until the end of middle school, and almost all students (97%) attend high school. The first three groups follow a similar school calendar, as discussed below. The last two groups were included for the purpose of comparison because their behavior is likely to be affected by different calendars, such as the Japanese fiscal year, which starts on April 1.

We excluded death records on the basis of several criteria. First, we focused on Japanese citizens who were in Japan at the time of their death because those outside Japan were likely to follow a different school calendar. Second, we excluded records without any information on the dates of birth or death because this information is vital for calculating the person's exact age and the timing of suicide. Third, we excluded records with no information on the place of death because an unknown place of death was likely to indicate that the authorities had no personal information about the deceased or could not specify the exact date of death.

Using individual suicide records, we counted the frequencies of suicides on each calendar date from January 1 to December 31 for each of the five age groups defined above. To simplify our analysis, we excluded the data of those who died on February 29. Accordingly, the number of observations was 365.

In Japan, an academic year begins in April and ends in March. Our survey of public elementary and middle schools in the 150 most populated municipalities and public high schools in 46 out of 47 prefectures revealed that the following school calendar is typical across regions. The first (spring) semester begins around April 8 and ends around July 20. It is immediately followed by the summer break, which ends around August 31. The second (fall) semester begins typically on September 1 and continues until December 25. The winter break follows and ends around January 7. The third (winter) semester is in session between January 8 and March 25, followed by the spring break. This typical academic calendar, as summarized in Table 1, applies to students in the majority of elementary, middle, and high schools.

However, there is a slight variation in the school calendar across regions. According to our survey, about 30% of the surveyed municipalities start the fall semester up to 10 days earlier than September 1. These early starts are concentrated in the northern part of Japan which tends to have harsh winter conditions.

We examined the relationship between the school calendar and the frequency of suicides in two different ways. First, we plotted the frequencies of suicides against the school calendar dates by the five age groups. If the school calendar affects suicidal risks among young individuals who are vulnerable to a stressful situation around the start date of the school, we should be able to find a spike in the frequencies of suicides around April 8, September 1, and January 8, when the semesters begin. In contrast, the frequencies of suicide were expected to decrease during the spring, summer, and winter breaks. Those aged 18–26 were expected to show no spike on these dates because they are affected by different calendars.

Second, we estimated a Poisson regression model where the frequency of suicides on each calendar date was regressed on 52 dummy variables. These dummy variables were coded 1 if a particular calendar date was included in one of the 52 weeks of the year and zero otherwise. For example, the dates between January 1 and January 7 were set to one for the Week 1 dummy, while all other dates were set to be zero. The dates between January 8 and 14 were set to one for the Week 2 dummy, etc. The baseline week excluded from the regression model was set to be Week 26, from June 25 to July 1, that is, the middle of the year. Using these dummy variables, we examined whether a particular week of the year was associated with higher frequencies of suicides among young individuals in school. More specifically, we expected that the weeks in which most schools begin a session (i.e., Week 2, January 8–14; Week 35, April 3–10; and August 27 to September 2) were

Table 1 A typical school calendar in Japan

1st semester	Summer break	2nd semester	Winter break	3rd semester	Spring break
Apr 8–Jul 20	Jul 21–Aug 31	Sep 1–Dec 25	Dec 26–Jan 7	Jan 8–Mar 24	Mar 25–Apr 7

associated with higher frequencies, while those weeks in which school is in break were associated with lower frequencies. To facilitate the interpretation of the Poisson regression results, we visually depicted the incidence rate ratios (IRR) for each dummy variable in the regression model.

2.2 Results

Our analysis included 108,968 suicides by young individuals who died at 6–26 years of age between 1974 and 2014 in Japan. Among those, the number of suicides by elementary school students (ages 6–12) was 459. Further, 3,274 suicides were by middle school students (ages 12–15), and 10,388 suicides were by high school students (ages 15–18). These groups are likely to be affected by the Japanese school calendar. In our control group, which is not likely to be affected by the school calendar, 45,312 individuals died by suicide at ages 18–22, and 49,535 died at ages 23–26. Table 2 contains the summary statistics for the frequency of suicides per calendar day by age groups.

The frequencies of suicides are plotted against the calendar dates by five age groups in Fig. 2. The shaded regions indicate the typical period of school break in spring (March 26 to April 7), summer (July 21 to August 31), and winter (December 26 to January 7). Accordingly, the right end of the shaded regions indicates the beginning of the school session. The figure shows the frequency of suicides by elementary school students in red, middle school students in blue, high school students in black, college students and working individuals 18–22 years old in green, and working individuals 23–26 years old in purple.

We found several notable patterns in Fig. 2. First, the frequencies of suicides by middle school students and high school students show large spikes when the school starts, around January 8, April 8, and September 1. No such pattern is found for elementary school students, but this could be due to the small number of suicides in this age group. Second, the frequencies of suicides among school-age children and adolescents tend to decrease during the breaks. Most evidently, the beginning of the summer break is associated with a large reduction in suicides. The frequencies,

Table 2 Summary statistics of daily suicide frequencies by age categories

	Mean	SD	Min	Max	Total count
Elementary school students, ages 6–12	1.258	1.229	0.000	6.000	459
Middle school students, ages 12–15	8.970	3.842	0.000	32.000	3,274
High school students, ages 16–18	28.460	8.333	8.000	70.000	10,388
College students and working individuals, ages 19–22	124.142	17.093	79.000	188.000	45,312
Working individuals, ages 23–26	135.712	16.306	96.000	187.000	49,535
N					

Note Total count indicates the total number of suicides by each grade/age group between 1974 and 2014 in Japan. *Source* Death records, Vital Statistics of Japan

however, tend to increase as the summer break approaches the end, resulting in the highest frequency on September 1.

Third, and most importantly, Fig. 2 shows no similar pattern in suicides by those aged 18–22 and 22–26 around April 7 and September 1, because these cohorts are unaffected by the typical Japanese school calendar. The number of suicides in such individuals tends to increase toward early April, but the timing seems to coincide more with the beginning of the Japanese fiscal year. We speculate that this is because colleges and companies typically start the new school or fiscal year around April 1.

The Poisson regression results are presented in Fig. 3. We used the frequencies of suicide by middle and high school students and those at ages 18–22 as the outcome variables. We excluded elementary school children from this part of the analysis because of the insufficient number of observations. The x-axis in Fig. 2 indicates the 52 weeks in the school calendar: Week 1 (January 1 to January 7) to Week 52 (December 24 to December 31). The baseline category was set to be Week 26 (June 25 to July 1). The y-axis shows the estimated influences of the corresponding weeks on suicide counts. The height indicates the percent increase in the number of suicides from the baseline period.

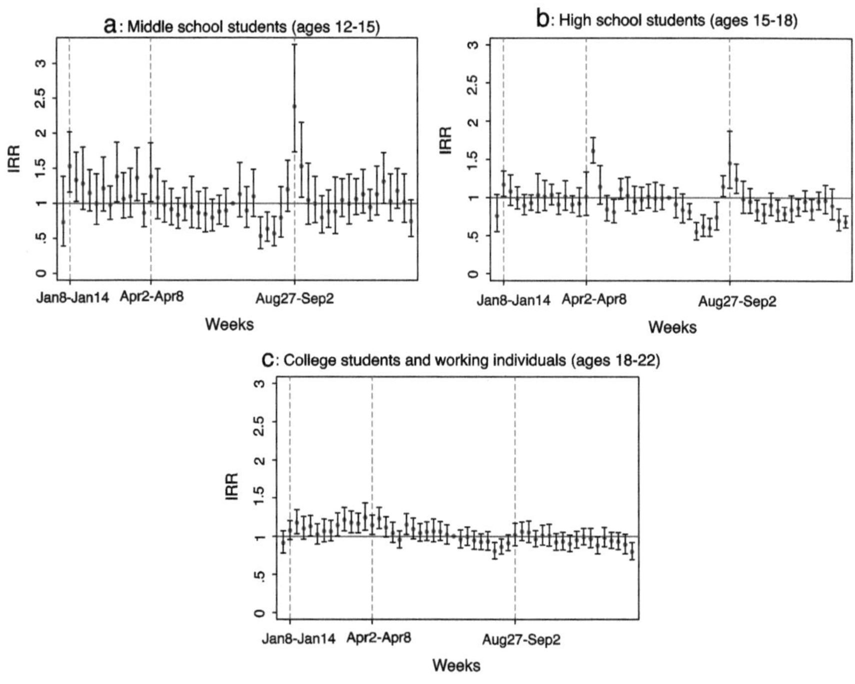

Fig. 3 Poisson regression estimation results by age/grade groups. Note: The estimated incidence rate ratios (IRRs) are shown with 95% confidence intervals (*vertical lines*). The baseline week is June 25 to July 1. All estimates are based on Poisson regressions using the frequency of suicides per calendar day. The data include individuals who were middle school students (a), high school students (b) at the time of death, and individuals who died by suicide at ages 18–22 years (c) *Source* Death records (1974–2014), Vital Statistics of Japan

Figure 3a shows that the frequency of suicides among middle school students increases dramatically in the week of August 27 to September 2 (Week 35). The IRR is 2.383 (95% CI: 1.735, 3.272), meaning that the incidence rate of suicide doubled around the dates when the summer break ends and the second semester begins. Similarly, the incidence rate also increases by approximately 40–50% in the weeks of April 2–8 and January 8–14 when the first and third semester begins. In contrast, the incidence rate decreases by half during the period of Week 30 to Week 32 (July 23 to August 12), which corresponds to the summer break.

Figure 3b shows a similar pattern for high school students. The frequency of suicides among high school students significantly increases in the weeks of January 8–14 with the IRR 1.117 (CI: 1.102, 1.346), April 9–15 with the IRR 1.610 (CI: 1.453, 1.785), and August 27 to September 2 with the IRR 1.451 (CI: 1.125, 1.871). The incidence rate is smaller just before these weeks when school is in the summer or winter break, as compared to the baseline category.

Finally, Fig. 3c shows a quite different pattern for young individuals between ages 18 and 22. Most of them are either in college or in the labor market and thus follow a different calendar from those below 18 years old. While we found a statistically significant increase in suicides in the spring, no spike was found in the weeks of April 2–8 and April 9–15. Those at ages 18–22 were more likely to die by suicide around the dates when the new fiscal year begins. Further, the incidence rate of suicide shows no increase in the week of August 27 to September 2.

2.3 Discussion

Using the daily frequencies of suicides by the youth in Japan between 1974 and 2014, we found that middle school students at ages 12–15 and high school students at ages 15–18 had the highest frequency of suicide around April 8 and September 1. These dates correspond to the beginning of the school session. Conversely, lowest frequency of suicide was observed in late July and early August, when they were not in school. Importantly, no such pattern existed for those who died at age 18–26, who were unaffected by the school calendar. This implies that the timing of suicide is clearly related to the school calendar for middle and high school students, and, their decision to take their own lives is therefore likely to be associated with school-related issues. Our results are also consistent with a so-called “broken promise” effect (Gabennesch 1988); because students are free from school-related issues when school is in break, vulnerable students may increase their hope that their troubled situation may improve once a new academic year or semester starts. If these expectations are not met, however, their hopelessness could have been enhanced, which may contribute to their decision to die by suicide.

Our findings make two important contributions to the literature. First, we used an extensive dataset of suicides by young individuals, which offers strong evidence regarding the seasonality of suicide among youth. The bimodal peak, as shown in Figs. 2 and 3, is consistent with the findings by Näyhä in Finland (Nayha 1982) and

Souêtre et al. in France (Souêtre et al. 1987), while the peak in the fall is consistent with studies conducted in Finland (Lahti et al. 2007), in the United States (McCleary et al. 1991), and in Canada (Thompson 1987).

Second, in contrast to the monthly data typically used in previous studies, the daily records of suicide in our analysis allowed us to compare the school calendar and the exact timing of suicides. Our findings uncover a part of the underlying mechanism of seasonality in youth suicide because the cyclical pattern corresponds to the school calendar; thus, it is plausible that stressful environments and the "broken promise" at the beginning of school sessions affect suicidal risk among vulnerable students.

Our analysis has several limitations. First, the present study could not provide direct evidence that these school-aged individuals died by suicide for school-related reasons. Future studies should investigate whether students tend to experience a higher level of stress when school starts or resumes and whether those who died by suicide in April and September had school-related problems. Second, our findings are based on the data from a single country. A cross-national analysis would improve our understanding of the extent to which school calendars account for the seasonality in youth suicide.

The findings here have crucial policy implications for designing a prevention strategy for youth suicide. Previous studies on youth suicidal behavior suggest that school-related problems, such as violence, bullying, interpersonal issues, dissatisfaction with school, and academic performance, are significant risk factors (Brunstein et al. 2010; Serafini et al. 2015; Gabennesch 1988). These risk factors may have a larger effect on suicidal behavior among youth particularly when a semester begins. Thus, our analysis suggests that any intervention effort to reduce these risk factors should be implemented not only when school is in session but also before school resumes from breaks. Potential school-based prevention strategies include suicide awareness programs and skill training that facilitate help-seeking behavior, self-reports, or individual interviews to identify vulnerable students, and gatekeeper training to improve the skills of school personnel to screen at-risk students (Gould et al. 2003). These strategies should be implemented during the semesters so that vulnerable students can seek help or be contacted and treated by school personnel before a new semester begins. In conclusion, our findings offer additional evidence that the school calendar plays an important role in accounting for the seasonality in youth suicide. The suicide prevention effort in the school community setting should take this seasonality into account to prevent an increase in suicides when the semester begins.

3 Relative Age and Suicide

A growing body of literature has examined the relationship between children's relative age in a grade and their academic performance. Evidence collected in many parts of the world suggests that, compared to older students, students who are relatively younger at school entry tend to perform worse on achievement tests (Bedard and Dhuey 2006; Elder and Lubotsky 2009; Kawaguchi 2011) are more likely to be held back a grade in elementary school (Elder and Lubotsky 2009), and are less likely to attend college (Bedard and Dhuey 2006). Some studies reported that such "relative age effects" can have long-term consequences, affecting the level of income in adulthood (Fredriksson and Öckert 2014; Kawaguchi 2011) whereas others found no long-term wage effects (Dobkin and Ferreira 2010; Black et al. 2011).

This study extends the findings of these past studies and examines how relative age in a grade affects suicide mortality rates of adolescents and young adults between 15 and 25 years of age. We focus on mortality by suicide because it is likely to be associated with the mental health of adolescents and young adults, who can be affected by their experiences at school and academic achievement. It is known that academically struggling students are more likely than peers who succeed in academics to suffer from depression (Bandura et al. 1999; Fröjd et al. 2008; Quiroga et al. 2013), one of the major factors associated with suicide. Studies also document a direct link between low academic performance and suicidal behaviors (Martin et al. 2005; Madge et al. 2011; Taliaferro and Muehlenkamp 2014).

Not only can academic disadvantage be a risk factor for students while at school, it can also have long-term negative consequences, which could elevate a risk for suicide (Beautrais et al. 1996; Goodman 1999; Qin et al. 2000). Kawaguchi (2011) found that the difference in the years of education at ages 30-34 between those with a relative age disadvantage and those with an advantage was 0.13 and 0.08 for male and female workers, respectively. He also reported that men who were born between January and March earn 3.9% less than those with a relative age advantage (born in April-June), although he found no difference in wage for women (Kawaguchi 2011).

To our knowledge, almost no previous studies have examined the association between children's relative ages within a cohort and their mortality rates. The only exception is a Canadian study in the late 1990s that examined suicides by individuals less than 20 years of age in Alberta (Thompson et al. 1999). They found that individuals who had completed suicide were more likely to have been relatively younger than their classmates when they were at school. However, they could not precisely assign individuals to more than 150 school districts in Alberta, where each local authority can set its school entry cutoff date, because they obtained only the addresses of individuals at the time of death. Moreover, the authors could not rule out the possibility that these individuals had received education outside Alberta, making their calculation of relative age even more imprecise. Thus, more accurate estimation is needed in order to fully understand whether children's birth dates are related to their mortality rates.

In this study, we use data from Japan to compare suicide mortality rates among young individuals who were born right before and after the school entry cutoff date. We investigate whether those who were born right before the school cutoff day and thus youngest in their cohort have higher mortality rates by suicide, as compared to their peers who were born right after the cutoff date and thus older.

Japan is uniquely suited to studying the relative age effect on suicide for three reasons. First, the school entry cutoff date, April 2nd, does not vary by region, and the cutoff date has not changed since 1947. Second, the length of mandatory schooling does not vary by the date of birth, and only the age at which children start school varies by the date of birth. In Japan, children are expected to stay in school until they finish junior high school after 9 years of education, typically at 15 years of age.

Third, most importantly, the Japanese education system allows us to implement a Regression Discontinuity (RD) approach to examine the causal effect of relative age on suicide. In contrast to other countries, late entry to primary school is not allowed in Japan. The School Education Law, enacted in 1947, specifies that the parents of the Japanese citizens shall send their children to elementary school once they turn 6 years of age. The only exceptions are cases of severe illness and underdevelopment, but such exclusions are rarely allowed. The fact that parental discretion is not permitted means that selection at school entry is not a concern because the timing of school entry is almost randomly determined by the birth date. This randomization mechanism around the school cutoff date allows us to utilize the RD approach where we isolate the causal effect of relative age on suicide by assuming that individuals who were born right before the school entry cutoff date are unlikely to differ in their baseline characteristics from those who were born immediately after the cutoff date.

3.1 Data and Method

The individual-level mortality data in this study come from the death records in the Vital Statistics of Japan, compiled by the Ministry of Health, Labour and Welfare. The Vital Statistics data used in this study were collected by the Ministry for administrative purposes and were anonymized and de-identified by the Ministry prior to analysis. The use of the Vital Statistics data for this study has been approved by the Ministry of Health, Labour and Welfare. Informed consent was not obtained from the individuals in the data because the individual records were anonymized before the data were released for public use.

The data in the Vital Statistics are based on death certificates issued by physicians that are subsequently reported to the local government by a family member of the deceased. The records cover all reported deaths in Japan. The information in the death records includes the date of birth, the date of death, age at time of death, occupation groups (in years that end in 0 and 5), marital status, and the underlying cause of death based on the ICD-9 standard (until 1994) and the ICD-10 standard (1995–present). We limit our sample to Japanese citizens because it is possible that the non-Japanese went to school under a different education system outside of Japan. Additionally, we focus on death records from 1989 to 2010 for the reason described below.

Using the individual death records from the Vital Statistics, we compared the mortality rates by suicide among adolescents and young adults who were born just before and after the school entry cutoff date in Japan. More specifically, we estimated the following simple model:

$$Rate_{dob} = \alpha + \beta After_{dob} + \varepsilon_{dob}$$

where $Rate_{dob}$ denotes the suicide rates of adolescents and young adults whose birth date is *dob*, and $After_{dob}$ is a dummy variable that takes a value of 1 if *dob* is on or after April 2 in the calendar year and 0 otherwise. We expected that the suicide rates would be higher among those who were born just before April 2nd (i.e., right before the cutoff date) than those who were born just after this date. Thus, β was expected to be negative.

We chose to use the simple linear model for three reasons. First, the calendar dates, except for the cutoff date, were unlikely to affect the suicide rates. It was difficult to imagine that the suicide rates were linearly or nonlinearly related to the calendar date (for example, those born on April 10th are not more likely to die by suicide than those born on April 20th). In fact, a local regression line, as shown later, detected no nonlinear relationship between the calendar dates and the suicide rates. Second, our estimation relied on a very small window around the cutoff date and thus a complicated relationship between the forcing variable and the suicide rate would unlikely to exist. Third, using AIC, we confirmed that the linear model was the best fit.

The suicide rates on each date of birth were calculated in the following way:

$$Rate_{dob} = \frac{\sum death_{[dob,t]}}{\sum birth_{[dob,t]}} * 100$$

where $[dob, t]$ denotes the date of birth in year t. Because our main focus was on the comparison of the suicide rates by the date of birth of the deceased, we summed up the number of suicides by young individuals with a given date of birth, regardless of their birth year. This created 365 observations from January 1 to December 31 for each external cause of death. We excluded data on February 29 in leap years from our study. We then divided the total number of suicides for each *dob* by the total number of births on the same calendar day multiplied by 100, creating the rate of suicides for each date of birth. The data on the number of births were also obtained from the Vital Statistics of Japan. Our analysis included deaths coded as E950–E959 under the ICD-9 standard (1989–1994) and X60–X84 under the ICD-10 standard (1995–2010).

Note that $death_{dob}$ is not the number of suicides on a particular day; rather, it is the number of suicides by young individuals whose birthday is *dob*. We calculated $Rate_{dob}$ for adolescents and young adults who died between 15 and 25 years of age because the relative age effect is most likely to appear around the end of compulsory education (at age 15 in Japan) or while students are still in school and to be less influential after young adults leave school and enter the labor market. It is also because deaths by intentional injury are rare for individuals aged less than 15 years. During our study period, the number of suicides among those below 15 years old was about 70 per year.

We analyzed individuals who were born during the period of 1974 to 1985 and died at ages 15–25 between 1989–2010. This is because individual birth records are available from 1974 and the latest death records available at the time of this study were from 2010. Table 1 presents descriptive statistics of the mortality rates by suicide.

Our empirical strategy rests on the assumption that the timing of births around the school entry cutoff date was randomly determined and therefore that individuals who were born just before and after the cutoff date had similar baseline characteristics. This is a reasonable assumption because, as mentioned previously, parental discretion is minimized by the strict enforcement of the school entry rule. Thus, we took advantage of the school entry cutoff date to implement a RD design. To ensure that our assumption was valid, we fitted the above linear regression model within small windows of data centered at the school entry cutoff date. In the discussion section, we consider the possibility that the timing of birth was manipulated around the school entry cutoff date by parents who were aware of the relative age effects.

3.2 Results

We began by graphically examining the patterns of deaths by the date of birth. Figure 4 presents the rates of mortality by suicide plotted against the date of birth. The thick vertical line denotes the school entry cutoff date in Japan, i.e., April 2nd. The thick gray line represents a locally weighted regression line fitted separately before and after the cutoff date.

Figure 4 reveals a clear, discrete break in the suicide rate of young individuals at the school entry cutoff date; those who were born in late March or on the 1st of April were more likely to have died by suicide compared to those who were born on or right after the 2nd of April.

Next, in order to understand the effects of the school entry cutoff more precisely, we turned to the results of our regression Table 3 analysis. Table 4 displays the estimated coefficients of β in Eq. (1). The sizes of bandwidth are 7, 14, 21, and 28 days around April 2nd. The results strongly suggest that adolescents and young individuals who were born immediately before the school entry cutoff date were more likely to have died by suicide, as compared to those who were born on or right after that date. According to Column (1) of Table 4, the mortality rate for individuals who were born between March 26th and April 1st was higher by 0.034 than that for those who were born between April 2nd and April 8th. Given that the baseline mortality rate for suicide is 0.126, this is not a trivial difference. The magnitude of the difference decreases as the size of the window widens, but Column (4) suggests that there is a statistically meaningful difference between the

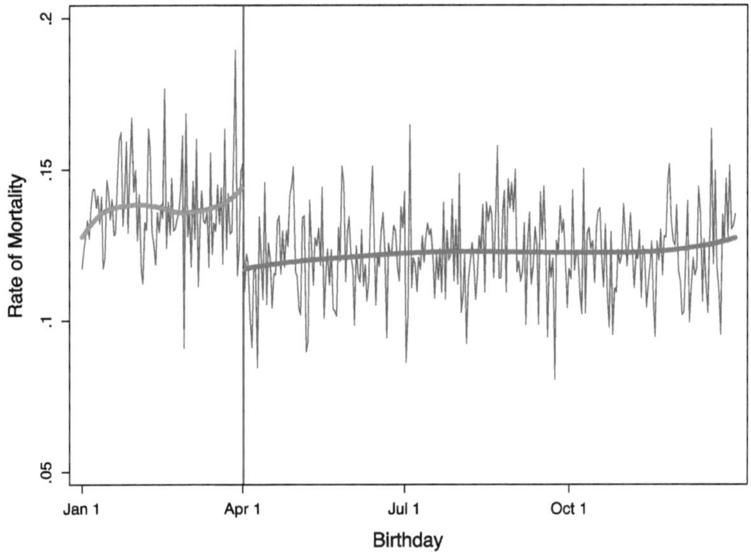

Fig. 4 Rate of suicide by date of birth The rate of suicide is plotted against the date of birth. The red line denotes the school entry cutoff date (i.e., April 2nd) in Japan. The thick gray line represents a locally weighted regression line fitted separately before and after the cutoff date. The data include individuals aged between 15 and 25 at the time of death that occurred between 1989 and 2010.*Source* Birth records (1974–1985) and death records (1989–2010), Vital Statistics of Japan.}

Table 3 Descriptive statistics on the rate of mortality by suicide

	Mean	SD	Min	Max
Suicide	0.126	0.016	0.081	0.190

The sample includes individuals aged between 15 and 25 at the time of death that occurred between 1989 and 2010. The rate of suicide is calculated as the number of suicides divided by the number of total births for each date of birth, multiplied by 100. The number of observations is 365.

Source Birth records (1974–1985) and death records (1989–2010), Vital Statistics of Japan

groups of individuals who were the oldest and the youngest in class, even when the size of the bandwidth is 28 days.

The results presented in Table 5 may mask informative patterns across different demographic groups or birth cohorts. Table 5 shows estimation results by gender, by age groups at the time of death, and by birth cohorts. Both male and female individuals who were relatively old in class were less likely to have died by suicide than the youngest ones in class. In addition, the difference between the oldest and the youngest individuals in class was most pronounced among those who died by suicide between ages 19 and 21. We did not see a strong difference in suicide mortality rates based on the date of birth when individuals were younger than

Table 4 Estimated effects of school entry cutoff date on the rate of suicide.

	Bandwidth			
	(1)	(2)	(3)	(4)
	±7	±14	±21	±28
Suicide	−0.034*** (0.010)	−0.026*** (0.007)	−0.022*** (0.005)	−0.017*** (0.004)
N	14	28	42	56

All estimates are based on linear regressions using data within ± 7-day, ± 14-day, ± 21-day, ± 28-day windows centered at the school entry cutoff date (April 2). The outcome variable is the rate of mortality by suicide. The mortality rate is calculated as the number of suicides divided by the number of total births on each date of birth, multiplied by 100. The data include individuals aged between 15 and 25 at the time of death that occurred between 1989 and 2010

*** $p < 0.01$ (two-tailed tests)

Source Birth records (1974–1985) and death records (1989–2010), Vital Statistics of Japan

Table 5 Estimated effects of school entry cutoff date on the rate of suicide by subgroups

	Bandwidth			
	(1)	(2)	(3)	(4)
	±7	±14	±21	±28
Male	−0.037** (0.012)	−0.030*** (0.009)	−0.026*** (0.007)	−0.019*** (0.007)
Female	−0.033* (0.015)	−0.023** (0.009)	−0.019** (0.007)	−0.015** (0.006)
Age ≦ 18	−0.005* (0.003)	−0.002 (0.002)	−0.002 (0.002)	−0.001 (0.002)
19 ≦ Age ≦ 21	−0.016*** (0.004)	−0.016*** (0.003)	−0.012*** (0.002)	−0.009*** (0.002)
Age ≧ 22	−0.013 (0.008)	−0.008 (0.006)	−0.008* (0.004)	−0.007* (0.003)
Born in 1974–1980	−0.030** (0.013)	−0.028*** (0.009)	−0.025*** (0.007)	−0.015** (0.006)
Born in 1981–1985	−0.041** (0.016)	−0.024** (0.011)	−0.018** (0.009)	−0.020** (0.008)
N	14	28	42	56

All estimates are based on linear regressions using data within ±7-day, ±14-day, ±21-day, ±28-day windows centered at the school entry cutoff date (April 2). The outcome variable is the rate of mortality by suicide. The mortality rate is calculated as the number of suicides divided by the number of total births by each subgroup on each date of birth, multiplied by 100. The data include individuals aged between 15 and 25 at the time of death that occurred between 1989 and 2010

*** $p < 0.01$

** $p < 0.05$

* $p < 0.10$ (two-tailed tests)

Source Birth records (1974–1985) and death records (1989–2010), Vital Statistics of Japan

19 years old or older than 21 years old. Finally, the magnitude of the relative age effect did not vary by cohort.

3.3 Discussion

Using individual data of death by adolescents and young adults in Japan from 1989 to 2010, we estimated the effect of relative age within a grade on suicide mortality rates. We exploited the school entry cutoff date, which is April 2nd in Japan, to implement a regression discontinuity design, assuming that the timing of births around the school entry cutoff date was randomly determined and therefore that individuals who were born just before and after the cutoff date have similar baseline characteristics. Our analysis showed that those who were born right before the school cutoff day and thus youngest in their cohort had higher suicide rates at ages between 15 and 25 years old, compared to their peers who were born right after the cutoff date and thus relatively older.

We conducted three robustness checks of our main findings. First, we verified the assumption that individuals who were born before and after the school entry cutoff were comparable in their baseline characteristics. Our findings were unaffected by selection at school entry because, as explained above, delayed entry to school is not allowed in Japan except for serious medical conditions. However, the timing of birth, rather than the timing of school entry, might be manipulated by parents, which could result in the correlation between parents' characteristics and their children's relative age in class. For example, parents with high socioeconomic status might be more likely to be aware of the relative age effect, and might therefore be more likely to ensure that their children were the oldest in class. In other words, individuals who were born right before the cutoff date tended to have parents with low socioeconomic status, while those who were born right after the cutoff date tended to have parents with high socioeconomic status. Because low socioeconomic status is a known risk factor for suicide (Beautrais et al. 1996; Goodman 1999; Qin et al. 2000), a part of the observed effects might be explained by the gap in parents' socioeconomic status. In contrast, if such shifts are observed uniformly across different socioeconomic statuses, our main results are attributable to the relative age effect as a result of the school entry cutoff.

To address the possibility that parents with high socioeconomic status were more likely to manipulate the timing of birth, we examined whether parents with certain occupations were more likely to shift the timing of birth using occupation data in the Vital Statistics. We used information on the father's occupation because the occupation of a child's father is more likely to be indicative of a family's socioeconomic status for the birth cohorts in our study. Our supplementary analysis showed no compelling evidence that only parents with certain occupations systematically shifted the timing of birth to ensure that their children were the oldest in class (results available upon request).

Second, we examined the possibility that the sizes of bandwidth we chose (i.e., 7, 14, 21, and 28 days around April 2nd) drove our main findings. We estimated Eq. (1) by varying the sizes of bandwidth from ±2 days to ±91 days around April 2nd. The estimation with the smallest bandwidth of ±2 includes 4 observations from March 31 to April 3rd, while the estimation with the largest bandwidth of ±91 includes 182 observations from January 1st to July 1st. We found that our main findings held regardless of the selection of the sizes of the bandwidths.

Third, we investigated whether alternative cutoffs other than April 2nd in the calendar year have a similar effect on the suicide risk of young individuals. If suicide risks change significantly before and after any other calendar date that is not related to school entry, the observed effects in this study are likely to be explained by other potential mechanisms. To check the possibility that other calendar dates make a difference in the suicidal risks, we estimated Eq. (1) by including a dummy variable as *After* that equals 1 if *dob* is on or after each day of the calendar year and 0 otherwise. In other words, we compared the mortality rate by suicide before and after all calendar days from January 8th to December 25. Because we set the bandwidth as 7 days before and after the cutoff, our analysis could not use the calendar days from January 1 to January 7 and from December 26 to December 31 as cutoffs. All cutoff dates other than April 2nd can be viewed as a placebo. Our analysis indicated that April 2nd was the only date that created a major gap in the rate of suicides, confirming that the school entry cutoff changed the suicidal risks of young adults between 15 and 25 years old.

While our analysis highlighted the importance of relative age within a grade as a risk factor of youth suicide, the underlying mechanism remains unclear. As discussed in the introduction, one explanation is that children who were among the youngest in class suffered academically during school years and that such academic disadvantage affected their future career choices.

Our supplementary analyses provided further evidence that those who are relatively young in a grade tend to have a lower educational attainment and a different career path than the relatively older ones in the same grade. We compared educational attainment and employment status of all individuals between ages 16 and 25 using the Population Census of Japan in 2000. We used the data of those who were born in March and April because the decennial census contains the information on people's birth year and month but not the date.

We found that the percent of high school students at ages 16–18 is greater among those born in April than in March by 0.44 point, and the percent of college students or graduates at ages 19–22 and 23–25 is also greater by about 2.0 points. Thus those who were born before and after the cutoff seem to pursue a different career path, where the latter looks for higher educational attainment than the former.

We also compared the employment statuses and the types of jobs between those who were born in March and April. Our analysis here was restricted to those who were in the labor market, and thus not in school at the time of data collection. When focusing on those at ages 16–18, the percent of those who were unemployed is larger among those born in March, while the percent of those with a full-time job is larger among those born in April. A similar pattern is present for those at ages

19–22 and 23–25, but the difference is smaller. When comparing the types of industry, those born in March are more likely to work in the primary and secondary industries, while those born in April are more likely to work in the service industry. Our analysis using the 2010 Census showed very similar results.

The above evidence suggests that those with relative age disadvantage tend to follow a different career path than those with relative age advantage. The former are less likely to attend high school or college, and are more likely to have blue-collar jobs. This implies that the relative age disadvantage translates into academic disadvantage, which may ultimately affect socioeconomic status. Individuals with a low socioeconomic status have higher odds for suicidal behavior and completed suicides.

Our study has two major limitations. First, our analysis examined only individuals who died at ages between 15 and 25 years because the individual-level birth data before 1974 are not available for researchers. It is possible that we would have obtained different results if we had studied older individuals. Second, the observed relationship between relative age and suicide rates may exist only in Japan and possibly other East Asian countries, where academic pressure is generally high. It is an important future research agenda to replicate our findings with data from other countries.

The empirical results of this study suggest that relative age effects have broader consequences than previously assumed. This study showed that the relative age at school entry affects mortality rates by suicide, not just academic performance and economic outcomes as the previous research has demonstrated. This study highlighted the importance of policy intervention that alleviates the relative age effect. Given that education at an early stage of life plays an important role in people's future well-being, the arbitrary cutoff of school entry will generate a lifetime disadvantage by the timing of birth for a non-trivial number of people. In the case of Japan, those who were born in February and March will be strongly affected by the current cutoff of April 2nd. To alleviate the negative consequences of the arbitrary cutoff, the government has a few policy options, such as allowing late entry to primary school or special assistance to those born just before the cutoff at the early stage of primary education.

References

Ajdacic-Gross, V., et al. (2010). Seasonality in suicide–A review and search of new concepts for explaining the heterogeneous phenomena. *Social Science and Medicine, 71*(4), 657–666.

Altamura, C., et al. (1999). Seasonal and circadian rhythms in suicide in Cagliari Italy. *Journal of Affective Disorders, 53*(1), 77–85.

Bandura, A., et al. (1999). Self-efficacy pathways to childhood depression. *Journal of Personality and Social Psychology, 76*(2), 258–269.

Beautrais, a L., Joyce, P.R. & Mulder, R.T., 1996. Risk factors for serious suicide attempts among youths aged 13 through 24 years. *Journal of the American Academy of Child and Adolescent Psychiatry, 35*(9), 1174–1182.

Bedard, K., & Dhuey, E. (2006). The persistence of early childhood maturity: International evidence of long-run age effects. *The Quarterly Journal of Economics, 121*(4), 1437–1472.

Black, S. E., Devereux, P. J., & Salvanes, K. G. (2011). Too young to leave the nest? The effects of school starting age. *Review of Economics and Statistics, 93*(2), 455–467.

Brunstein K. A, Sourander, A., & Gould, M. (2010). The Association of Suicide and Bullying in Childhood Longitudinal Research Findings. *The Canadian Journal of Psychiatry*, *55*(5), 282–288.

Chew, K.S.Y. & McCleary, R., (1994). A Life Course Theory of Suicide Risk. *Suicide and Life-Threatening Behavior*, *24*(3), 234–244.

Chew, K. S. Y., & McCleary, R. (1995). The spring peak in suicides: A cross-national analysis. *Social Science and Medicine, 40*(2), 223–230.

Dobkin, C., & Ferreira, F. (2010). Do school entry laws affect educational attainment and labor market outcomes? *Economics of Education Review, 29*(1), 40–54.

Elder, T. E., & Lubotsky, D. H. (2009). Kindergarten entrance age and children's achievement: Impacts of state policies, family background, and peers. *Journal of Human Resources, 44*(3), 641–683.

Frank, M. L., & Lester, D. (1998). Geophysical variables and behavior: LI. Temporal variation of suicide in teens and young adults. *Perceptual and Motor Skills, 67*(2), 586.

Fredriksson, P., & Öckert, B. (2014). Life-cycle effects of age at school start. *Economic Journal, 124*(579), 977–1004.

Fröjd, S. A., et al. (2008). Depression and school performance in middle adolescent boys and girls. *Journal of Adolescence, 31*(4), 485–498.

Gabennesch, H. (1988). When promises fail: A theory of temporal fluctuations in suicide. *Social Forces, 67*(1), 129–145.

Goodman, E. (1999). The role of socioeconomic status gradients in explaining differences in US adolescents' health. *American Journal of Public Health, 89*(10), 1522–1528.

Gould, M. S., et al. (2003). Youth suicide risk and preventive interventions: A review of the past 10 years. *Journal of the American Academy of Child and Adolescent Psychiatry, 42*(4), 386–405.

Hansen, B., & Lang, M. (2011). Back to school blues: Seasonality of youth suicide and the academic calendar. *Economics of Education Review, 30*(5), 850–861.

Hoberman, H. M., & Garfinkel, B. D. (1988). Completed suicide in children and adolescents. *Journal of the American Academy of Child and Adolescent Psychiatry, 27*(6), 689–695.

Kawaguchi, D. (2011). Actual age at school entry, educational outcomes, and earnings. *Journal of the Japanese and International Economies, 25*(2), 64–80.

Lahti, A., et al. (2007). Autumn peak in shooting suicides of children and adolescents from Northern Finland. *Neuropsychobiology, 54*(2), 140–146.

Lecomte, D., & Fornes, P. (1998). Suicide among youth and young adults, 15 through 24 years of age. A report of 392 cases from Paris, 1989-1996. *Journal of Forensic Sciences, 43*(5), 964–968.

Madge, N., et al. (2011). Psychological characteristics, stressful life events and deliberate self-harm: Findings from the child and adolescent self-harm in Europe (CASE) study. *European Child and Adolescent Psychiatry, 20*(10), 499–508.

Martin, G., et al. (2005). Perceived academic performance, self-esteem and locus of control as indicators of need for assessment of adolescent suicide risk: Implications for teachers. *Journal of Adolescence, 28*(1), 75–87.

Massing, W., & Angermeyer, M. C. (1985). The monthly and weekly distribution of suicide. *Social Science and Medicine, 21*(4), 433–441.

McCleary, R., et al. (1991). Age–and sex-specific cycles in United States suicides, 1973 to 1985. *American Journal of Public Health, 81*(11), 1494–1497.

Nayha, S. (1982). Autumn incidence of suicides re-examined: data from Finland by sex. *British Journal of Psychiatry, 141,* 512–517.

Owens D., Horrocks J., & House A. (2002). Fatal and non-fatal repetition of self-harm: systematic review. *British Journal of Psychiatry*, *181*, 193–199.

Parker, G., Gao, F., & Machin, D. (2001). Seasonality of suicide in Singapore: data from the equator. *Psychological Medicine, 31*(3), 549–553.

Preti, A., & Miotto, P. (1998). Seasonality in suicides: The influence of suicide method, gender and age on suicide distribution in Italy. *Psychiatry Research, 81*(2), 219–231.

Qin, P., et al. (2000). Gender differences in risk factors for suicide in Denmark. *The British Journal of Psychiatry: The Journal of Mental science, 177,* 546–550.

Quiroga, C. V., et al. (2013). Early adolescent depression symptoms and school dropout: mediating processes involving self-reported academic competence and achievement. *Journal of Educational Psychology, 105*(2), 552–560.

Schmidt, P., et al. (2002). Suicide in children, adolescents and young adults. *Forensic Science International, 127*(3), 161–167.

Serafini, G., et al. (2015). Life adversities and suicidal behavior in young individuals: a systematic review. *European Child and Adolescent Psychiatry, 24*(12), 1423–1446.

Souêtre, E., et al. (1987). Seasonality of suicides: environmental, sociological and biological covariations. *Journal of Affective Disorders, 13*(3), 215–225.

Taliaferro, L. A., & Muehlenkamp, J. J. (2014). Risk and protective factors that distinguish adolescents who attempt suicide from those who only consider suicide in the past year. *Suicide and Life-Threatening Behavior, 44*(1), 6–22.

Thompson, A. H., Barnsley, R. H., & Dyck, R. J. (1999). A new factor in youth suicide: The relative age effect. *Canadian Journal of Psychiatry, 44*(1), 82–85.

Thompson, T. R. (1987). Childhood and adolescent suicide in Manitoba: a demographic study. *Canadian Journal of Psychology, 32,* 264–269.

White Paper on Suicide Prevention, various years, Tokyo: Cabinet Office.

Yip, P.S.F., Chao, A., & Chiu, C.W.F. (2000). Seasonal variation in suicides: Diminished or vanished. experience from England and Wales, 1982–1996. *British Journal of Psychiatry, 177* (OCT.), 366–369.

Zhang, J., Gao, Q., & Jia, C. (2011). Seasonality of Chinese rural young suicide and its correlates. *Journal of Affective Disorders, 134*(1–3), 356–364.

Chapter 6
Railway Suicide in Japan

1 Introduction

Railway and subway suicides constitute a major problem in many parts of the world (Mishara 2007). Suicides at train stations and on railroads pose a serious challenge to transportation safety and inflict severe economic losses by causing suspension and delays in train operations. The costs associated with railway suicides can be extremely high in places where trains are a major method of transportation for commuters and students, as in many metropolitan areas of the world.

This chapter focuses on the problems of railway suicides in Japan where the public transportation system has been highly developed. Japan is ranked third in the world when we compare the amount of transportation by railways (World Development Indicators 2016). As of 2016, 211 operators offer railway transportation (Ministry of Land, Infrastructure, Transport and Tourism 2016) and the total route length of the railway network is about 27,000 km (CIA Fact Book 2016). These railway operators transported more than 60 million passengers per day in 2015 (Ministry of Land, Infrastructure, Transport and Tourism 2016).

The next section presents descriptive data of railway suicides in Japan, including the annual frequencies, demographic characteristics of the deceased, and the timing of occurrence. The third section discusses the economic costs imposed by railway suicides. The fourth section presents an overview of our previous studies that used data from Japan to examine the effectiveness of railway suicide prevention strategies, such as blue light-emitting-diode (LED) lamps on platforms and platform screen doors (PSD).

The content of this chapter was based on the published article: "Railway suicides in Japan: facts and prevention strategies." Japanese Journal of Psychiatric Treatment 30(3): 381–386, 2015.

Y. Sawada et al., *Economic Analysis of Suicide Prevention*, Creating a Society for All, DOI 10.1007/978-981-10-1500-7_6

2 Descriptive Data of Railway Suicides in Japan

We begin by summarizing the frequencies of railway suicides at stations and crossings. Our analysis relied on two databases. The first database was obtained from death records in the Vital Statistics of Japan. The Vital Statistics data were collected for administrative purposes and were anonymized and de-identified by the Ministry prior to analysis. Individual death records were made available for research purposes under the approval of the Ministry. Using the Vital Statistics, we counted the annual frequencies of deaths by "intentional self-harm by jumping or lying in front of motor vehicle" that corresponds to X81 in ICD-10 standard. We limited the analysis to the period of 1995–2014 when ICD-10 was applied.

Figure 1 presents the frequencies of deaths coded as X81 between 1995 and 2014 by a dashed line. Until the early 2000 s, more than 700 people died by jumping or lying in front of moving objects, but the number declined to 500 in 2013 and 2014. Note that X81 includes all deaths by jumping or lying in front of moving objects including cars and trucks, while our interest lies in the deaths by moving trains. Accordingly, the frequencies reported in Fig. 1 might be overestimated and should be viewed as the upper limit of the number of railway suicides.

Given the limitation in the Vital Statistics to evaluate the frequencies of railway suicides, we used the second database that allowed us to examine the number of railway accidents as a result of attempted and completed suicide. The Railway Safety Database, operated by the Railway Technology Promotion Center, archives the details of all railway accidents that are reported by each operator to the Ministry of Land, Infrastructure, Transport and Tourism. Note that this dataset included

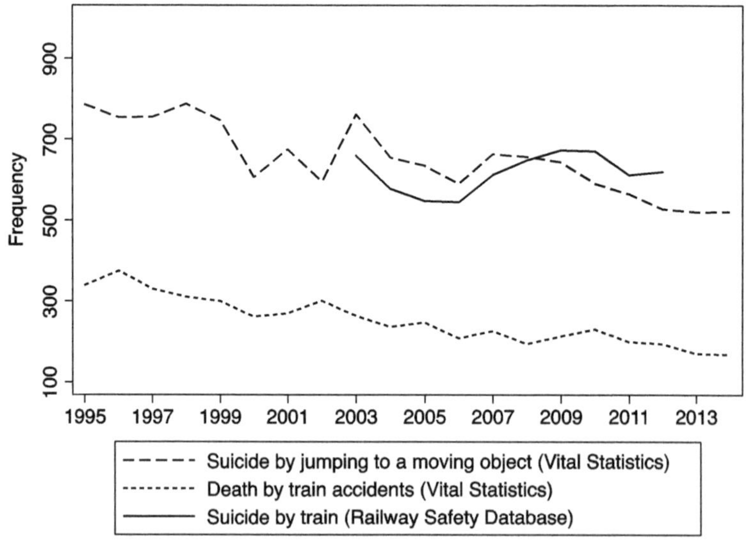

Fig. 1 Frequencies of deaths related to railways *Source* Vital statistics and railway safety database

attempted suicide, not just completed suicide, whereas the Vital Statistics data only included cases of completed suicides. The details of railway accidents included the time and place of occurrence, cause of accident, the number of injuries and deaths from the accident, and the length of delays. Using the search engine of the database, we chose accidents that involve “suicide” as a cause of accidents and counted the frequency per year between 2003 and 2012. The frequency did not include accidents that could not be officially accounted as a railway suicide due of a lack of information at the time of the accident. Thus, the frequency reported below might be an underestimate of the actual number of railway accidents.

The solid line in Fig. 1 shows the temporal shift in the frequency of railway accidents as a result of attempted and completed suicide. The frequency declined from 660 to 546 between 2003 and 2007, but jumped to 613 in 2007 and remained at around 650 since then. Importantly, the frequency varies greatly across regions. Figure 2 shows the same information separately by the Tokyo metropolitan area (accounting for 33% of the total population as of 2014) and the other areas. Half of the accidents took place in the Tokyo metropolitan area and the frequency has been increasing since 2003. In contrast, the number of accidents by railway suicides in the other regions such as the Osaka and Nagoya metropolitan area has been decreasing.

When comparing the frequency of deaths by X81 in the Vital Statistics and the frequency of railway accidents by suicide in the Railway Safety Database, their numbers and temporal patterns closely resemble each other. This indicates that the information in Fig. 1 is likely to accurately represent the actual frequency of railway suicides. In the last 10 to 15 years, the number of railway suicides per year in

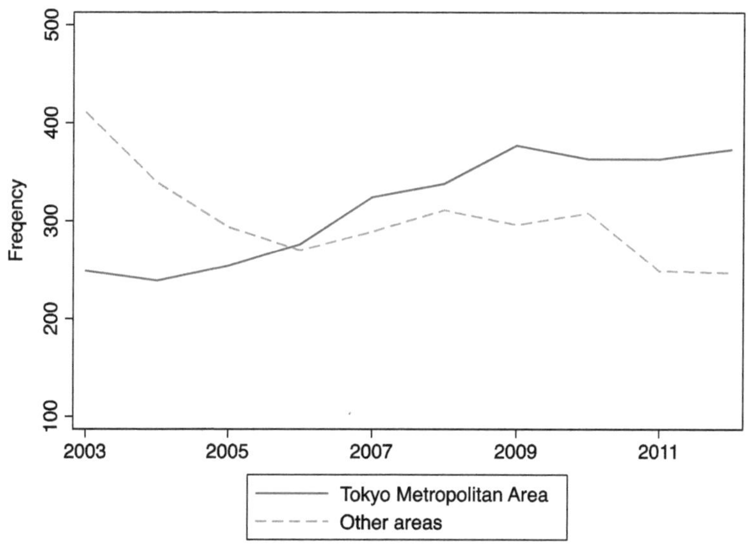

Fig. 2 Frequencies of suicides in Tokyo metropolitan area and other areas *Source* Railway safety database

Japan has been approximately 600 to 700, which means that 1 or 2 suicides occur at a station or crossing every day.

For the purpose of comparison, Fig. 1 includes a dotted line that represents the frequency of deaths by "pedestrian injured in collision with railway train or railway vehicle" that corresponds to V5 in ICD-10. This captures the number of unintentional deaths at stations and crossings, such as unintentional falling from the platform and contact with a running train. It is evident from Fig. 1 that the frequency of unintentional deaths at stations and crossings also declined during our study period, suggesting that intentional and unintentional deaths by trains have become less frequent in the last 20 years in Japan.

Next, we used the Vital Statistics data to examine demographic characteristics of those who died by X81, hereafter railway suicide, given that most deaths categorized in X81 were likely to be caused by railway suicide. We focus on railway suicides that occurred between 1995 and 2014 and grouped them into combinations of sex and eight age categories: 19 and below, 20–29, 30–39, 40–49, 50–59, 60–69, 70–79, and 80 years and above. We omitted those whose age was unknown from our analysis. Table 1 shows the percent of those who chose railway suicides as a method of suicide among all suicide victims in each age-group by sex. Table 1 reveals several interesting patterns. First, women were more likely to choose railway suicide as a method than men across all age categories. Second, when comparing across age-groups of railway suicide victims, the youngest cohort (below 19 years of age) was most likely to choose to die by railway suicide. Third, the percent of railway suicides decreases as victims become older. The older cohorts occupied only a small portion of the total number of railway suicides.

Finally, we used the Railway Safety Database to examine when railway suicides take place. When counting the frequency of railway suicides between 2003 and 2012 by day of the week, we found no distinctive pattern, as shown in Fig. 3. However, when counting the frequency by time of the day, Fig. 4 shows that the number of railway suicides increases as the day progresses. The number of trains operating is largest in the morning and evening, but the number of railway suicides is smaller between 6:00 and 8:00 a.m. The largest frequency is observed around 8:00 p.m., when many commuters return home. This might indicate that those who are exhausted are more vulnerable to the risk of suicide. Further, passengers returning home are likely affected by railway suicides.

Table 1 Percent of deaths by X81 by age groups and gender

	Total	–19	20–29	30–39	40–49	50–59	60–69	70–79	80–	Unknown
Male	1.81	8.50	2.71	1.97	1.27	1.15	1.58	1.83	0.61	15.96
Female	2.85	14.75	3.29	2.86	2.68	3.28	3.22	1.97	0.4	17.65

Source Vital Statistics (2012)
Note The data represent the number of deaths by X81 divided by the number of all suicide deaths (X60–X84) multiplied by 100. The last column includes the percent of deaths by those with unknown age

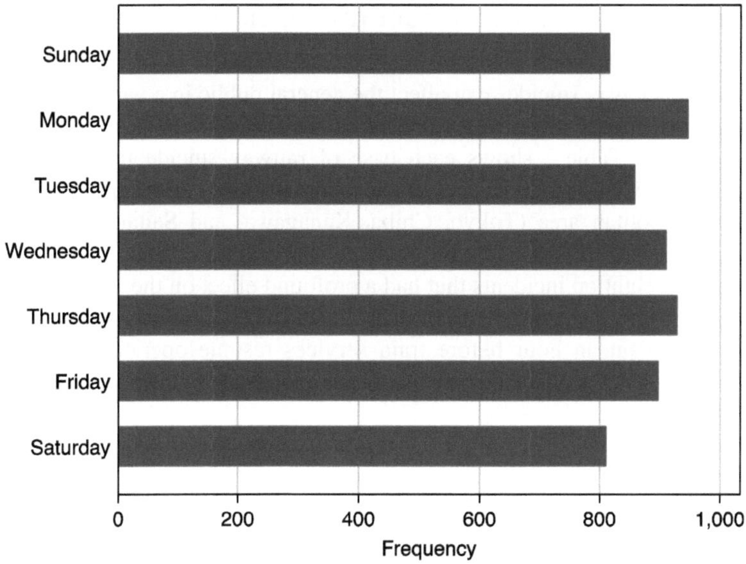

Fig. 3 Timing of railway suicides during a week: 2003–2012 *Source* Railway safety database

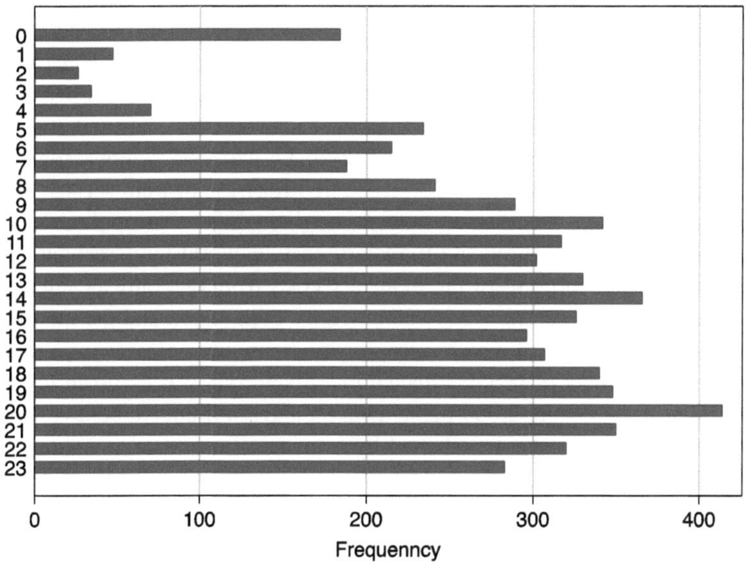

Fig. 4 Timing of railway suicides during a day: 2003–2012 *Source* Railway safety database. *Note* The y-axis is based on the 24 h clock

3 The Economic Costs of Railway Suicides

Railway and subway suicides can affect the general public in a variety of ways. We examined the impact of railway suicides by measuring delays and disruptions in train schedules. Table 2 shows each case of railway suicide posted in *Yomiuri Shimbun* articles, among all railway suicides that occurred in four prefectures in the Tokyo metropolitan area (Tokyo, Chiba, Kanagawa, and Saitama) in 2010. We must be aware that this list excludes incidents that had only minor effects and likely puts greater weight on incidents that had a profound effect on the transit system and passengers. Table 2 suggests that, in many cases, when a railway suicide occurred, it took more than an hour before train services resume operations and that the number of passengers affected by the suspension or delay of train services can reach 20,000 to 30,000.

Table 3 summarizes the number of train suspensions and delays and the length of delays in minutes, nationwide, between 2003 and 2012 when railway suicides occurred. The descriptive statistics in Table 3 were obtained from the Railway Safety Database and targets accidents that caused the suspension of train operations or delays longer than 30 min. Accordingly, the statistics did not reflect information on railway suicides that had not caused train suspensions or delays but may have had other repercussions. Table 3 shows that on average, when a railway suicide occurred, 18 train operations were suspended, while 28 trains were operated behind the schedule. Moreover, the average length of a delay was close to 70 min.

The report "Investigation on the effects caused by stroubles related to railway transportation", (Ministry of Land, Infrastructure, Transport, and Tourism 2009), published by the Investigation and Review Commission of the Railway Bureau, Ministry of Land, Infrastructure, Transport, and Tourism, analyzed the data on railway accidents and suicides in the Tokyo, Osaka, and Nagoya metropolitan areas. In the fiscal year 2007, suicide accounted for 61% of train service delays of more than 30 min and less than an hour in the three major metropolitan areas. The report estimated the total time and monetary costs incurred by passengers affected by railway suicides. In terms of the monetary costs from one railway suicide in the Tokyo metropolitan area, the mean value was 89 million yen and the median value was 77 million yen, both of which were very high amounts. However, in this rough estimation, the number of people affected in a given train was assumed to be 2,000 people. Even if there were 2,000 passengers on a given train, we believe that many more commuters could also be affected by a suspension or delay, as inferred from Table 3. In this estimation, the report focused only on the delays of more than 30 min and less than an hour. However, as delays of more than an hour could often occur in reality, we believe that the numbers presented here are moderately estimated figures. Moreover, because these numbers did not include the amount of various direct damages caused by railway suicides, we believe that they were the lowest possible estimated figures and that the actual social costs borne by train users were much higher.

Table 2 Detailed information on delays and disruptions in train schedules in 2010 in four prefectures (Tokyo, Chiba, Kanagawa, Saitama) in the Tokyo metropolitan area

Date of occurrence	Time	Location	Place	Number of trains canceled	Amount of time that train service was suspended (min)	Number of trains delayed	Amount of time service was delayed (min)	Affected population	Notes
Jan 6	PM 06:10	Tokyo	Between stations	63				180,000	
Jan 9	AM 10:37	Tokyo	Station	21				5,000	
Jan 13	PM 07:30	Tokyo	Station	36	120			39,000	
Jan 19	PM 02:40	Tokyo	Station		70			38,500	
Feb 11	PM10:20	Tokyo	Station		45			13,000	
Feb 24	PM 04:40	Tokyo	Station		59			35,000	
Mar 1	PM 08:45	Yokohama	Station		30				
Mar 2	PM 08:45	Saitama							
Mar 5	PM 06:15	Saitama	Station	12		17		29,000	
April 4	PM 09:35	Kanagawa	Station	4		11	65	4,400	
April 13	PM 03:15	Chiba	Station	10				11,000	
April 16	PM 08:30	Tokyo	Between stations		70			30,000	
April 24	*AM 07:00	Kanagawa	Between stations	10		16	55	2,2000	* Time when the body was discovered
May 2	AM 10:10	Kanagawa	Station	17			120	24,000	
May 10	PM 02:25	Kanagawa	Station	32				24,000	
May 30	PM 09:30	Kanagawa	Between station	16				7,000	

(continued)

Table 2 (continued)

Date of occurrence	Time	Location	Place	Number of trains canceled	Amount of time that train service was suspended (min)	Number of trains delayed	Amount of time service was delayed (min)	Affected population	Notes
May 30	AM07:45	Kanagawa	Between stations	23*				25,000*	* Two accidents on this day are combined to show these total figures
May 30	PM 03:00	Kanagawa	Station						
June 12	PM 05:05	Tokyo	Station					89,500	
June 21	AM 10:00	Saitama	Between stations	2		15	55	14,000	
July 12	AM 10:14	Kanagawa	Station	28				23,000	
July 26	PM 09:35	Kanagawa	Station	2		16	58	14,000	
Aug 2	AM 08:55	Tokyo			95			32,000	
Sep 2	PM 03:45	Saitama	Station	6		10	44	7,900	
Sep 20	PM 03:45	Kanagawa	Station	27				30,000	
Oct 1	AM 07:20	Tokyo	Between stations	62	70			85,000	
Oct 2	PM 11:20	Kanagawa	Between stations			14	30	5,000	
Oct 5	AM 08:50	Kanagawa	Station	10		12	60	13,000	
Oct 13	PM 04:40	Saitama	Station	6		16	60	10,500	
Oct 20	AM 11:45	Kanagawa	Station	8		14	60	15,000	
Oct/21	AM 06:35	Tokyo	Between stations		45			21,000	
Nov 1	AM 07:05	Kanagawa	Station	14		22	64	82,000	
Nov 19	AM 08:30	Tokyo	Station					63,000	
Nov 21	PM 05:00	Saitama	Station	2			50	21,000	

(continued)

Table 2 (continued)

Date of occurrence	Time	Location	Place	Number of trains canceled	Amount of time that train service was suspended (min)	Number of trains delayed	Amount of time service was delayed (min)	Affected population	Notes
Nov 24	PM 06:35	Kanagawa	Station	8		13	80	12,000	
Nov 25	AM 10:35	Kanagawa	Station	8		15	80	13,000	
Nov 25	AM 06:00	Kanagawa	Between stations	20		18	60	50,000	
Dec 14	AM 10:45	Saitama	Between stations			12	64	11,000	
Dec 18	AM 07:08	Saitama	Station	10		18	105	26,000	

Source Yomiuri Shimbun

Table 3 Descriptive statistics of the number of suspended and delayed trains and the length of delays in minutes between 2003 and 2012

	Mean	SD	Min	Max
N of suspended trains	18	26	0	266
N of delayed trains	28	40	0	921
Length of delays in minutes	69	43	0	1,416

Source Railway Safety Database

Railway suicides impose immense costs not only on train users but also on railway companies. Railway companies take different approaches as to whether they charge the families of suicide victims for train repair costs or for passengers' compensations, but when they do not charge the bereaved families, the railway companies must bear the full costs. Our interview with a railway company in the Tokyo metropolitan area in June 2012 suggests that when one jumps in front of a train, especially if the event occurs close to the last train of the day, there will be a delay in the allocation of trains, which must be finished before the first train begins operations the next day. As a consequence, station workers will be forced to work overtime and significant labor costs will be borne by the railway company.

In addition, railway suicides can have a profound psychological burden on railway company employees, including train operators. Previous studies have demonstrated that railway suicides impose a great psychological burden on the drivers who came across the suicides (Weiss and Farrell 2006; Farmer et al. 1992; Cothereau et al. 2004; Farmer et al. 1992; Kim et al. 2013; Limosin et al. 2006; Weiss and Farrel 2006). According to our interview with the railway company mentioned previously, a large number of passengers make complaints (sometimes unreasonable ones) to the station workers or the customer service center of the railway company when an accident involving a person occurs, which imposes a notable psychological burden on the employees who deal with such complaints.

4 Prevention Strategies and Their Effectiveness

To reduce disruptions to railway operations caused by suicides, railway operators in Japan started to adopt two major prevention strategies: the installation of platform screen doors (PSD) and blue light-emitting-diode (LED) lamps on platforms. We review our own research on the effectiveness of these two strategies.

4.1 Platform Screen Doors

Installing physical barriers on train platforms is considered to be one of the most effective measures to prevent railway suicide (Ladwig et al.2009; Law and Yip 2011; Mishara 2007). These doors open only when trains stop at stations, thereby limiting access to the platform by individuals who enter train tracks for the purpose of ending their lives. Because these doors can also prevent unintentional accidents, the installation of PSDs has become popular among railway operators in many places, including Copenhagen, Guangzhou, London, Taipei, Paris, Seoul, and Hong Kong. In Japan, the government has urged train operators to install PSDs as a safety measure, especially at stations that serve more than 100,000 passengers per day (235 stations as of 2013).

However, there is surprisingly little evidence on the effectiveness of such barriers for suicide prevention. To our knowledge, the only case that has been studied is the railway system in Hong Kong where one of the train operators (MTR Corporation) has started the installation of full-height (i.e. ceiling-to-floor) PSDs on three lines (TWL, KTL, and ISL) in 2002. According to two related studies, the number of suicides at stations with PSDs decreased after the installation of the doors, while the number of incidents remained unchanged at stations without PSDs (Law et al. 2009; Law and Yip 2011).

Ueda et al. 2015 sought to offer additional evidence for the effectiveness of PSDs in suicide prevention by using data from Japan. Japan presents a unique case because most of its train operators employ half-height, as opposed to full-height, PSDs whose effectiveness has yet to be studied. The half-height PSDs in Japan are chest-height, and in theory can be climbed over by an adult. In contrast, the full-height PSDs, such as the ones used in Hong Kong, extend from the ceiling to the floor of the platform. Thus, entry to train tracks is completely blocked. Given the prevalence of half-height PSDs in many parts of the world, evaluating their effectiveness constitutes an important research agenda.

We examined whether the installation of half-height PSDs has contributed to the reduction of the incidents of fatal and non-fatal railway suicide by using data from a railway company in the Tokyo metropolitan area.[1] This railway company maintains a database that records all incidents of accidents and suicides (both fatal and non-fatal) that occurred on its railway system. The information recorded in the database includes the date and time of incidents, station name/location, train number, a detailed description of incidents, the estimated number of passengers affected by the incident, and the number of trains that were delayed and cancelled as a result of the incident.[2] The data on suicides covered the period of April 2004 to March 2014, while the data on unintentional accidents covered the period of April 2005 to March 2014. The installation date of PSDs for each station was also made available by the train company.

Incidents of suicide were determined as such only when the motives for entering train tracks became evident based on the investigation by the police or by victims' own account. Both fatal and non-fatal incidents of suicide are included in our

[1]Following the request from the railway company, the name of the company will remain anonymous. In order to avoid the identification of the company, the number of lines in the company's train network will also remain undisclosed.

[2]The company removed information that can lead to the identification of victims from the data before releasing them to us.

analysis. As for accidents, included in the analysis are fall accidents that involved passengers falling onto the track area. The most common fall accidents were by drunken passengers who constituted 80% of all cases, followed by falls due to inattention (13%), sickness (6%), and collisions with other passengers (1%). Because the focus of this study is PSDs installed at stations, only incidents of suicides and accidents that occurred at stations are included in the analysis.

All stations of the network, except for the ones on the newest line that started operating in 2008 (8.7% of all stations), were included in the analysis. We excluded these new stations because their accident and suicide records were available only for a subset of years. Only one suicide occurred between 2008 and 2013 at these excluded stations. All of the stations on this line have half-height PSDs. After the exclusion of those stations, the number of stations included in the analysis was 168. We used monthly data for our analysis, and our unit of observation was the station-month. The total number of station-month observations totaled 20,160 (= 168 stations * 120 months).

The dependent variables were the number of suicides and accidents per station-month. The average number of suicides and accidents per station-month was 0.007 (s.d. = 0.084) and 0.079 (s.d. = 0.299), respectively. The minimum number was 0, while the maximum was 1 for suicide and 3 for accidents. The station with the largest number of suicides had a total of 7 suicides during the study period. The station with the largest number of accidents had a total of 74. The total number of suicides and accidents during our 10-year study period was 144 and 1,821, respectively.

The main independent variable was a dummy variable valued at 1 if the station had PSDs installed in a particular month. The railway company installed its first PSDs in 1991 when they opened a new line. Because the company could design these new stations with PSDs in mind, it installed full-height PSDs at these stations. The train operator has gradually retrofitted existing stations with half-height PSDs since then. At the beginning of our study period in April 2004, 19 of the 168 stations in our study had PSDs installed, and 52 stations were subsequently retrofitted with half-height PSDs at different timings. As of March 2014, 71 stations (42.76% of 168 stations) have PSDs. Among them, 73.24% had half-height PSDs and the rest had full-height PSDs.

The height of half-height PSDs is 1.3 m (51 in.; the doors are 1.2 m), which was not impossible for an adult to climb over. The half-height PSDs that the company installed did not have an alarm system that alerts train conductors or staff when somebody tried to climb over them when the train was not at the station.

We first report the average number of suicides and fall accidents per year by the availability of PSDs. Table 4 shows the total number of suicides and accidents in each year at stations with and without PSDs. It is evident that the number of suicides is much larger at stations without PSDs than those with PSDs. Yet, the installation of PSDs did not completely prevented suicide. In total, 7 suicides were observed at stations with PSDs. In contrast, no fall accidents occurred at stations with PSDs, while an average of 185 accidents per year occurred at stations without PSDs.

Table 4 Number of suicides and accidents by the presence of platform screen doors (PSDs)

	Stations without PSDs			Stations with PSDs		
Year	*N*	Suicide	Accident	*N*	Suicide	Accident
2004	1,758	19	–	258	0	–
2005	1,752	14	173	264	0	0
2006	1,675	13	190	341	0	0
2007	1,504	22	193	512	1	0
2008	1,441	14	213	575	2	0
2009	1,440	13	166	576	1	0
2010	1,411	14	199	605	1	0
2011	1,320	13	221	696	1	0
2012	1,241	6	213	775	0	0
2013	1,201	9	237	815	1	0

Note Table entries are the total number of suicides and unintentional fall accidents at 168 stations. Observations are station-month. The years refer to Japanese fiscal years (April–March). Data on accidents are not available for 2004

Next, we used a Poisson regression model based on a difference-in-differences (DID) approach. We regressed the number of suicides on an indicator variable, which equals 1 if the station had PSDs in a particular station-month observation. We did not estimate the effect of PSDs on the number of accidents because PSDs succeeded in the complete prevention of accidents.

In addition, in order to take into account the differences among stations (e.g., the number of passengers, the presence of express trains), we included station-specific dummy variables in the model. By including these dummies, we were able to separate the effect of PSDs on suicide from the effect of station-specific time-invariant unobserved factors. In addition, this method allowed us to estimate a temporal difference in the mean number of suicides before and after the installation of PSDs. Second, in order to take into account the effects of time-varying factors (e.g., macroeconomic conditions) that can also affect the frequency of railway suicide, the model included year-month-specific dummy variables (fixed effects). By including the year-month fixed effects, the effect of such time-varying common factors was taken into account, enabling us to isolate the effect of PSDs from those of other factors.

Table 5 reports estimation results by Poisson regression. The station and year-month fixed effects were included in the estimation but not reported in the table.[3] The regression coefficient associated with the PSD dummy variable was estimated to be negative, indicating that the number of suicides became lower after the installation of the PSDs compared to the period before the installation. To interpret the substantive effect of the PSDs, we computed the Incident Relative Ratio (IRR) at 0.240 with a 95% confidence interval 0.086–0.673. This suggests

[3]To address the potential heterogeneity and autocorrelation in the error terms within each station, standard errors were adjusted by using a heteroskedasticity-autocorrelation consistent estimator.

Table 5 Estimated effect of PSD on the number of suicides

	Coef	95% CI	P-value
Effect of PSD on suicides	−1.427	−2.458, −0.397	0.007
N	20,160		

Note Table entries are Poisson regression estimates. The dependent variables are the total number of suicides and accidents at each station per month. Data include 168 stations between April 2004 and March 2014. The 95% confidence intervals are based on robust standard errors. The station-specific and year-month-specific fixed effects are included in the estimate

that the introduction of PSDs resulted in a decrease in the number of suicides by 76% (CI: 33–93%).

In short, we found that PSDs were effective in reducing the number of railway suicides, but the half-height PSDs did not completely prevent people from entering tracks. During the study period, there were seven cases of suicide at stations with half-height PSDs. In five of these seven cases, passengers climbed over the PSDs. In one case, a passenger tried to enter the tracks through a staff-only door of the PSDs at the end of the platform. In the remaining case, it was not reported how the passenger entered the tracks. Among the five cases in which passengers climbed over the PSDs, two were female passengers. All the passengers were in their 20 and 30s. Thus, for individuals with physical strength and a strong intention to enter the track area, half-height PSDs could not serve as a complete barrier. In contrast, no suicides have been attempted at stations with full-height PSDs.

This suggests that the half-height PSDs are less effective than the full-height PSDs in preventing intentional entry to the train tracks. This is further supported by Chung et al. (2016) that assessed the effectiveness of installing half- and full-height platform screen doors by using 10-year monthly panel data between 2003 and 2012 from Seoul Metro, a major subway operator that functions throughout the Seoul metropolitan area in South Korea. Their analysis reported that the installation of full-height PSDs resulted in the elimination of subway suicides by completely blocking access to the track area, while half-height PSDs, which did not extend to the ceiling of the platform, were not as effective as full-height ones.

Note that the half-height PSDs have several features that make them attractive to train operators; they can be installed even when there is no structural support at the ceiling and can therefore easily be retrofitted to existing stations. In addition, they are lightweight and less costly than the full-height ones. For these reasons, 76.2% of stations with PSDs in Japan have half-height PSDs rather than full-height PSDs (as of March 2014). The findings from this study suggest that one way to increase the effectiveness of half-height PSDs in preventing suicide is to increase their height. The typical height of PSDs in Japan at 1.3 m is lower than that of half-height PSDs used in other places, such as Taiwan (1.5 m) or France (1.7 m).

4.2 Blue Lights

While PSDs have been shown to be highly effective for suicide prevention, their installation is often challenged by the high costs. The installation of these doors is generally very expensive and often requires the reinforcement of platforms due to their weight, imposing additional costs on railway companies.

More recently, as a less expensive alternative measure for suicide prevention, some major railway operators in Japan have started to install blue light-emitting-diode (LED) lamps on train platforms and at railway crossings in the expectation that they may have an effect of deterring suicides. For example, the West Japan Railway Company, one of the major railway companies in Japan, has begun installing blue lights at railway crossings in 2006 and the number of blue lamps reached 94 by the end of 2010. Similarly, the East Japan Railway Company, Japan's largest railway company, has put blue lamps at each end of the platforms at all 29 stations on the central train loop (the Yamanote line) in Tokyo as well as at other major train stations. Other railway operators followed suit hoping that this blue lighting will deter people from jumping into trains at stations and railway crossings.

The blue lamps were originally introduced in some towns and cities in Japan as street lights for the purpose of reducing crime rates. Although there has been no definitive scientific evidence, it is believed that the color of blue lights calms people down. Blue lights were introduced to platforms at train stations and railways crossings for a similar reason; they are expected to have a calming effect on people who are agitated.

In two studies (Matsubayashi et al. 2013, 2014), we studied the impact of blue lights on the number of suicides because finding a relatively easy and inexpensive method of preventing railway suicide benefits many cities and railway operators around the world that face problems of railway and metro suicides. As blue lights are easier and less expensive to install as compared to other measures, they can be a useful suicide prevention method if they are proven to be effective.

In addition to estimating the effectiveness of blue lights, we considered the substitution phenomenon, i.e., that an intervention for a particular place induces people at risk to look for a nearby place for suicide, resulting in no major reduction in the overall number of suicides after implementation. This possibility has been widely studied in the case of suicide by jumping from high sites (e.g., Law et al. 2014). After reviewing related studies, Pirkis et al. (2013) concluded that the physical barriers to prevent jumping from bridges or cliffs increased suicides at nearby sites by 44%, while the prevention effort generated an overall reduction in suicides by 28% at the study cites.

Importantly, less is known about the possibility of the substitution phenomenon in the case of railway and metro suicides. Despite increasing efforts to install physical barriers to prevent railway and metro suicides, only a single study has examined whether the installation of physical barriers generates the substitution phenomenon. Law et al. (2009) showed that the installation of platform screen doors prevented suicide with no substitution phenomenon in the subway system of

Hong Kong. Accordingly, it is crucial to examine the possibility that the installation of blue lights at a particular station shifted the incidents of suicide to its neighboring stations.

We obtained data on railway suicides and the installation of blue lights from a railway company in the Tokyo Metropolitan area.[4] The data included information on the location and timing of the installation of blue lamps as well as the number of suicides each year at 71 stations between 2000 and 2013. A year in this data set refers to the Japanese fiscal year, which runs from April to March. Thus, the data covered the period from April 2000 to March 2014. Hereafter, we mean the fiscal year when referring to a particular year. We used yearly data for our analysis, and our unit of observation was the station-year. The total number of station-year observations equaled 994 (= 71 stations * 14 years).

The dependent variable was the number of suicides per station-year. The average number of suicides per station-year was 0.16 (s.d. = 0.44). The maximum was 3, while the minimum was zero. For the study period, 853 observations were associated with no suicide. The station with the largest number of suicides had a total of 10 suicides during the study period.

The analysis included two sets of the independent variables. The first set of the independent variable represented whether or not a station had blue lights on the platform in a particular year. It was given the value of 1 when a station had blue lights on the platform in a particular year and 0 otherwise. The variable is coded 0 if a station had no blue light for the entire study period.

Because the unit of analysis was the station-year, the following adjustment of the data set was necessary when stations had cases of suicides in the same year that they installed blue lights. During the period of our study, we found six cases of suicides that happened at four stations where blue lamps were eventually installed in the subsequent month of the same year. Because these stations set up blue lights at the very end of the fiscal year, we recoded the year of the blue light installation as the following year. For example, in one case, a suicide happened in July 2009 and the blue light was installed in February 2010 at the station where the suicide happened. In this case, we recoded the year of blue light installation for this station as the 2010 fiscal year (April 2010–March 2011), not the 2009 fiscal year (April 2009–March 2010). This recoding ensures that the data set reflects the fact that the suicide happened before the blue light installation.

The number of stations where the blue lights were installed was 1 in 2008, 4 in 2009, 6 in 2010, 1 in 2011, 0 in 2012, and 2 in 2013. At all stations, blue lights were installed at the edges of the platforms. In addition, at some stations blue lights were also installed in the middle of the platform. The lights were on from sunset to sunrise, thus the effectiveness of blue lights should be limited to the hours after dusk. However, the following statistical analysis did not take into account whether

[4]Following the company's request, the name of the railway company remains anonymous in this study.

suicides occurred during the day or at night. This was because the data provided by the railway company did not contain information on the dates and times of suicides in most cases; only suicides that happened at stations with blue lights were recorded with the date and time of the incidents.

Using the variable on the installation of blue lights described above, we created a second set of independent variables that equal 1 if a station is located near a station with blue lights and 0 otherwise. For example, if there are three neighboring stations, A, B, and C, and station B had blue lights installed in 2009, this variable was assigned the value of 1 for A and C in 2009 and in the subsequent years. If the substitution phenomenon existed and people at risk looked for a nearby place for suicide, we should be able to see an increase in the number of suicides at stations A and C after blue lamps were installed at station B. Because the stations of the railway company in our study were located close to each other (it typically takes a few minutes to move to the next station), we considered the possibility that people at risk might go up to five stations away from the station with blue lamps on the same railway line. Thus, ultimately, we created five indicator variables in total that denoted whether a station was located within one to five stations away from the station with blue lamps in either direction.

We first report the average number of suicides per year before and after the installation of blue lamps. The averages were calculated for six groups of stations. The first group contains stations that had blue lights installed during the study period. The second group contains stations that were located next to the station with blue lights installed. The third to sixth groups contain stations that were located two to five stations away from the station with blue lights. The last group contains stations that had no station with blue lights within five neighboring stations in each direction of the same line. If the installation of the blue lamps generated the substitution phenomenon, there should be a decrease in the average number of suicides at the stations where the lamps were installed, while there should be an increase in the average number of suicides at nearby stations.

Table 6 presents the average number of suicides per year for each group of stations before and after the installation of blue lights. The number of station-years

Table 6 Average number of suicides before and after the installation of blue lights

	(1)	(2)	(3)	(4)	(5)	(6)	(7)
	Station with blue lights installed	One station away	Two stations away	Three stations away	Four stations away	Five stations away	Six and more stations away
Before	0.435 (115)	0.269 (182)	0.234 (201)	0.275 (189)	0.245 (200)	0.259 (220)	0.090 (546)
After	0.189 (53)	0.274 (84)	0.269 (93)	0.275 (91)	0.266 (94)	0.245 (102)	

Note Table entries are the average number of suicides per year before and after the installation of blue lights with the number of station-years in parentheses. Data represent the number of suicides at 71 stations between 2000 and 2013. The total number of observations is 994

is shown in parentheses. The shaded column refers to the group of stations that installed blue lights between 2008 and 2013. At these stations, the average number of suicides per year decreased from 0.435 to 0.189. The number in the post-installation period corresponds to 10 cases of suicides, among which nine incidents happened during the day when the blue lights were not on. The remaining single case occurred in the evening at a station with blue lights, but a person jumped from about 50 m from the edge of the platform and the station had blue lights at the end of the platform (0 to 15 m from the edge) and in the middle of the platform (80 m from the edge). Thus, it is unlikely that the person was under the blue lamps. This means that effectively only one case of suicide happened at these stations when blue lights were on, and even this single case happened at a location on the platform where the lights were not lit. In contrast, the remaining columns show no major increase or decrease in the average number of suicides before and after the installation of blue lights at nearby stations. It is worth emphasizing that the average number of suicides prior to blue light installation was higher in column (1) than in columns (2)–(6), while the opposite is true after the installation.

Next, to obtain a precise estimate on the substitution effect, we used a Poisson regression model based on a difference-in-differences (DID) approach. We regressed the number of suicides per year at each station on the indicator variable, which equals 1 if the station had blue lights as well as on the five indicator variables, which equal 1 if the station was located one to five stations away from a station with blue lights.

In addition, our regression model included two types of dummy variables. First, in order to take into account the differences among stations (e.g., the number of passengers, the population size of cities, and the types of platforms), we included station-specific dummy variables. By including these dummies, we could separate the effect of blue lights on suicide from that of these station-specific time-invariant unobserved factors. This method of estimation allowed us to estimate a temporal difference in the mean number of suicides before and after the installation of blue lights at the nearby stations. The regression coefficient obtained in this model ultimately reflects a difference in the change in the average number of suicides between two groups with and without the nearby stations where blue lights were installed. Second, because factors that vary over time (e.g., macroeconomic conditions) can also affect the total number of suicides, the model included dummy variables for each year. By including the year-specific dummies, the effect of such time-varying common factors was taken into account, enabling us to isolate the effect of blue lights from those of other factors.

Table 7 reports estimation results by Poisson regression. Note that the qualitative results reported below hold even when a linear model and spatial regression model were used instead (results not shown). The station- and year-specific dummy variables were included in the estimation, but they are not reported in the table. To address the potential heterogeneity and autocorrelation in the error terms within each station, standard errors were adjusted by using a heteroskedasticity-autocorrelation consistent estimator. We ran five regression models by adding each of the indicator variables on

Table 7 Estimated effect of blue lights on the number of suicides

	(1)	(2)	(3)	(4)	(5)	(6)
Blue lights	-0.983^{**} (0.320)	-1.256^{**} (0.348)	-1.278^{**} (0.384)	-1.318^{**} (0.334)	-1.321^{**} (0.334)	-1.356^{**} (0.361)
One station away		0.718 (0.347)	0.459 (0.430)	0.483 (0.418)	0.486 (0.444)	0.526 (0.434)
Two stations away			0.510 (0.455)	0.387 (0.475)	0.391 (0.465)	0.379 (0.471)
Three stations away				0.385 (0.315)	0.389 (0.346)	0.438 (0.350)
Four stations away					−0.018 (0.339)	0.040 (0.367)
Five stations away						−0.201 (0.313)
Constant	-17.871^{**} (1.050)	-18.114^{**} (1.053)	-18.223^{**} (1.062)	-18.320^{**} (1.064)	-18.329^{**} (1.062)	-18.301^{**} (1.063)
AIC	856.805	846.854	851.106	833.981	829.979	843.720

Note Table entries are Poisson regression estimates. The dependent variable is the total number of suicides per station-year

Data represent the number of suicides at 71 stations between 2000 and 2013. The total number of observations is 994. The station- and year-specific fixed effects are included in all estimations. Robust standard errors clustered by each station are shown in parentheses

*p-values < 0.05; **p-values < 0.01 (two-tailed tests)

nearby stations sequentially. If the substitution phenomenon occurred, the coefficients on the variables of nearby stations should be estimated to be positive.

Regardless of the specifications, the regression coefficients associated with the blue lamp dummy variable are consistently negative, indicating that the average number of suicides became lower after the installation of the blue lamps compared to the period before the installation. To interpret the substantive effect of the blue lights in model (6) with the full specification, we computed the Incidence Rate Ratio (IRR) to equal 0.258 with a 95% confidence interval 0.127–0.523. This suggests that the introduction of blue lights resulted in a decrease in the number of suicides by 74% (CI: 48–87%).

Column (2) of Table 7 shows that the coefficient associated with the indicator variable of one station away from the station with blue lights is positive (=0.718) with a 95% confidence interval 0.380–1.398. Yet, the size of the coefficients on the same variable become smaller in the remaining columns and the confidence intervals overlap zero. In columns (3)–(6), the estimated coefficients on the nearby stations are small and their confidence intervals overlap zero. In short, we found no systematic evidence for the substitution phenomenon that the installation of blue lights increased suicides at nearby stations.

The above analysis contained several limitations. First, we did not consider the possibility that people might choose to jump in front of a running train at a railway crossing, not from a station platform, or the possibility that people might go to a station of a different railway company. Considering these possibilities was not possible owing to the lack of data. Thus, we cannot conclude that the installation of blue lights resulted in an overall reduction in the number of suicides in the region.

Second, our findings do not imply that the blue lights are always effective for preventing railway suicide. They are expected to stop people at train platforms from jumping in front of trains at night, not during the daytime. In fact, as suggested by Ichikawa et al. (2014), suicide attempts at station platforms during the nighttime account for only 14% of all railway suicide attempts. Thus, the installation of blue lights may contribute to suicide reduction, but it is not necessarily the ultimate solution to the problem. There is a need to develop additional strategies to prevent suicide during the daytime and unintentional accidents.

Third, the generalizability of our findings remains limited. Our analysis relied on the data for a limited period of time from a single railroad company. Additionally, the findings did not reveal the underlying mechanism of why the installation of blue lights resulted in the smaller number of suicides at stations with the lights, while generating no substitution phenomenon at the nearby stations. Our findings are suggestive, but future research needs to examine the same hypothesis as ours with data from other railway companies that installed blue lights and explore the underlying mechanism from a psychological perspective. These future studies will help establish the external validity of our findings.

References

Chung, Y. W., Kang, S. J., Matsubayashi, T., Sawada, Y., & Ueda, M. (2016). The effectiveness of platform screen doors for the prevention of subway suicides in South Korea. *Journal of Affective Disorders, 194,* 80–83.

CIA Fact Book. 2016.

Cothereau, C., de Beaurepaire, C., Payan, C., et al. (2004). Professional and medical outcomes for French train drivers after "person under train" accidents: three year follow up study. *Occupational and Environmental Medicine, 61,* 488–494.

Farmer, R., Tranah, T., Odonnell, I., et al. (1992). Railway suicide—The psychological effects on drivers. *Psychological Medicine, 22*(2), 407–414.

Ichikawa, M., Inada, H., & Kumeji, M. (2014). Reconsidering the effects of blue-light installation for prevention of railway suicides. *Journal of Affective Disorders, 152–154,* 183–185.

Kim, H.-R., Yim, H. W., Jo, S.-J., et al. (2013). Major depressive disorder, panic disorder, and post-traumatic stress disorder in Korean subway drivers. *International Archives of Occupational and Environmental Health, 86,* 471–477.

Ladwig, K. H., Ruf, E., Baumert, J., et al. (2009). Prevention of metropolitan and railway suicide. In D. Wasserman & C. Wasserman (Eds.), *Oxford textbook of suicidology and suicide prevention* (pp. 589–594). Oxford: Oxford University Press.

Law, C. K., Yip, P. S., Chan, W. S., et al. (2009). Evaluating the effectiveness of barrier installation for preventing railway suicides in Hong Kong. *Journal of Affective Disorders, 114,* 254–262.

Law, C. K., & Yip, P. S. F. (2011). An economic evaluation of setting up physical barriers in railway stations for preventing railway injury: evidence from Hong Kong. *Journal of Epidemiology and Community Health, 65,* 915–920.

Law, C. K., Sveticic, J., & De Leo, D. (2014). Restricting access to a suicide hotspot does not shift the problem to another location. An experiment of two river bridges in Brisbane, Australia. Aust. N. Z. *Journal of Public Health, 38*(2), 134–138.

Limosin, F., Loze, J.-Y., Cothereau, C., et al. (2006). Aprospectivestudyofthepsychological effectsof "person undertrain" incidents ondrivers. *Journal of Psychiatric Research, 40*(8), 755–761.

Matsubayashi, T., Sawada, Y., & Ueda, M. (2014). Does the installation of blue Lights on train platforms shift suicide to another station?: Evidence from Japan. *Journal of Affective Disorders, 169,* 57–60.

Matsubayashi, T., Sawada, Y., & Ueda, M. (2013). Does the installation of blue lights on train platforms prevent suicide? A before-and-after observational study from Japan. *Journal of Affective Disorders, 147,* 385–388.

Mishara, B. L. (2007). Railway and metro suicides: understanding the problem and prevention potential. *Crisis, 28,* 36–43.

Pirkis, J., Spittal, M. J., Cox, G., Robinson, J., Cheung, Y. T. D., & Studdert, D. (2013). The effectiveness of structural interventions at suicide hotspots: a meta-analysis. *International Journal of Epidemiology, 42*(2), 541–548.

The Ministry of Land, Infrastructure, Transportation, and Tourism, the Government of Japan (2016). Annual Report on Rail Transportation Statistics.

Ueda, M. Sawada, Y., & Matsubayashi, T. (2015). The Effectiveness of Installing Physical Barriers for Preventing Railway Suicides and Accidents: Evidence from Japan. *Journal of Affective Disorders,178*, 1–4.

World Development Indicators. 2016.

Weiss, K. J., & Farrell, M. J. (2006). PTSD in railroad drivers under the federal employers' liability act. *Journal of the American Academy of Psychiatry and the Law, 34*(2), 191–199.

Chapter 7
Government Partisanship and Suicide

1 Introduction

Since the rise of the welfare state, the government has expanded its influence to many facets of our life. The functions of the government range from the provision of public goods to the redistribution of income, all of which can influence the quality of life. The extent to which government actions affect the life of citizens, however, depends on the ideology of government. Some parties believe in small government and try to minimize the influence of their actions on citizens' lives. At the opposite side of the ideological spectrum lie parties that support a large government role and active intervention into the lives of its citizens. Thus, for better or worse, government ideology should affect the lives of citizens.

Previous research shows that government partisanship greatly affects economic aspects of citizens' lives (Alesina et al. 1997; Bradley et al. 2003), yet little is known about the impact of government partisanship on the overall quality of their lives. This chapter shows that the parties serving in the government affects the well-being of citizens, which was measured by the reported level of happiness and suicide rates.

There are three primary ways that government partisanship can affect people's well-being. First, government partisanship affects the generosity of welfare provisions and the nature of redistributive policies. Left-wing parties tend to implement policies that alleviate economic difficulties of citizens, while right-wing parties tend to regard economic hardship as an individual matter and thus leave the solution to the market. Such ideological differences are reflected in actual policies. For example, Allan and Scruggs (2004) demonstrate that the generosity of welfare programs, such as unemployment and sickness replacement benefits, is higher under left-wing governments. Huber and Stephens (2001) show that the size of social expenditures is also larger under a left-wing government. In contrast, a right-wing government has the opposite

---

The content of this chapter was based on the published article: "Government Partisanship and Human Well-being" *Social Indicators Research* 107(1): 127–48, 2012.

Y. Sawada et al., *Economic Analysis of Suicide Prevention*, Creating a Society for All, DOI 10.1007/978-981-10-1500-7_7

effect on the generosity of welfare and social programs (Di Tella and MacCulloch 2002).

The expansion of social and welfare programs or an increase in welfare and social security spending can directly enhance the quality of life of those in need. Pacek and Radcliff (2008) show that welfare generosity is positively associated with the reported level of life satisfaction in Europe. In addition, an increase in spending on certain items, such as health care, can enhance the *physical*, not just economic, well-being of citizens. For example, infant mortality rates decrease when the amount of social security transfer and the spending on health increases, both of which are more likely to happen under left-wing governments (Chung and Muntaner 2006; Conley and Springer 2001).

Second, government partisanship can affect the well-being of citizens through macroeconomic policies. Alesina et al. (1997) argue that different political parties favor different macroeconomic policies because they represent different constituents. They show that left-party governments whose support tends to come from the lower class are likely to expand the economy, producing higher GDP growth rates and lower unemployment rates, but also higher inflation rates. In contrast, right-party governments that tend to rely on support from higher-class constituents are more likely to focus on fighting inflation, causing a recession and slowing down economic growth. Higher growth rates and lower unemployment rates alleviate economic difficulties of people in need. In fact, they are shown to improve the level of reported happiness (Di Tella et al. 2003).

Finally, the presence of a left-wing party in government can lead people to believe that the government produces policies in favor of people in economic need. This belief can increase the level of political efficacy that their voices are represented by the government and thus improve overall happiness especially among people in need and with left-wing ideology.

Building on these arguments, this chapter empirically tested whether government partisanship matters for the well-being of citizens. The previous discussions suggest that the presence of left-leaning parties in the government increases the satisfaction level of the economically disadvantaged through their social and macroeconomic policies that benefit the poor. Thus, we would expect that more left-leaning governments are associated with the increased level of well-being for those who are economically struggling. At the same time, we would expect that the well-being of citizens who are against redistributive programs, or those who do not benefit from these policies, stays constant or decreases when a left-wing government is in power.

We measured the well-being of citizens with two indicators of the quality of human life: subjective happiness level and suicide rates. Our first measure of a person's well-being used a reported level of life satisfaction in a large survey of people in European countries over the period of 1980–2002. The survey asked respondents how satisfied they are with their lives, and other studies have used the same survey question to answer related research questions (e.g., Alesina et al. 2004; Di Tella and MacCulloch 2005; Di Tella et al. 2003; Pacek and Radcliff 2008; Radcliff 2001). Using responses to the life satisfaction question, we tested whether the subjective happiness level was related to government partisanship. The advantage of using this survey was that it allowed us to directly examine the relationship between government partisanship and the happiness level of individuals, while controlling for the effects of other individual characteristics (e.g., their partisanship) as well as country-level characteristics such as government policies (e.g., the amount of social spending) and macroeconomic variables.

The second measure used to gauge the level of people's well-being was the suicide rate in 21 OECD countries from 1980 to 2004. Suicide is a deliberate act to express ultimate dissatisfaction with one's life. If we postulate that one engages in an act of suicide when his or her life satisfaction level becomes lower than a certain threshold, then the incidents of suicide can be regarded as cases where the level of personal well-being reaches the bottom end. Thus the overall suicide rate in a country reflects the health of its society as well as its underlying well-being. While both the reported happiness level and suicide rates are measures of human well-being, suicide rates may serve as a more objective, if extreme, indicator of society's well-being. In this part of the empirical analysis, we used country-level panel data of 21 OECD countries to estimate the relationship between government ideology and suicide rates. As in the individual-level analysis presented in the first part of the chapter, we also controlled for the effects of government actions and macroeconomic conditions on suicide rates. Given the importance of socio-demographic variables as determinants of the suicide rate, we also included various measures of society's underlying conditions in the estimation.

In both sets of analysis, we found statistically significant evidence suggesting that government partisanship greatly matters for the level of human well-being. Our empirical results indicate that as the share of left-wing or Christian Democratic parties in the government increased, people became happier and less suicidal. The results held after controlling for the effects of government policies, macroeconomic indicators, and other time-variant and invariant factors that can affect our dependent variables. The macroeconomic variables, such as GDP per capita and inflation rates, had a statistically significant impact on the level of subjective happiness and suicide rates, while the actual government policies, as measured by the size of social spending, had almost no effect on the dependent variables. The substantive impact of government partisanship was similar to that of the macroeconomic variables. These results suggest that the influence of government partisanship goes far beyond what it manifests itself in government policies (both macroeconomic and social).

Our study in this chapter contributes to the recent "happiness" literature in economics and political science. While Di Tella and MacCulloch (2005) present a brief test of how government partisanship affects the reported level of life satisfaction, our analysis is different from their work in that we relied on a more intuitive theoretical perspective, used a different and more appropriate definition of government partisanship, and controlled for the effects of government policies. In addition, we estimated the impact of government partisanship on both the subjective and objective measures of human well-being, not just the reported level of happiness. Another related paper, Radcliff (2001), also examines the impact of government partisanship on the reported level of life satisfaction. However, its empirical analysis was purely cross-national, which makes it difficult to control the impacts of cultural differences across nations.

The chapter is organized as follows. The second section reports the results of our individual-level analysis that uses the reported level of subjective happiness as a measure of well-being. The third section presents the country-level analysis in which suicide rates are used as an alternative measure of society's well-being. The final section includes discussion and concluding remarks.

2 Individual-Level Analysis

We first examined the impact of government partisanship on the well-being of citizens using individual-level survey data. We employed data from the Mannheim Eurobarometer trend file, 1970–2002.[1] The Eurobarometer is a series of surveys designed to assess citizens' view and knowledge on European unification, yet it also contains a question on life satisfaction of respondents. The study also contains other useful information about respondents, such as their political beliefs, social behavior, and demographic backgrounds. The Eurobarometer target individuals in member states of the European Union (initially the European Community) and those in Norway in some of the survey years. Each survey consists of approximately 1,000 face-to-face interviews in each country.

The Eurobarometer was a desirable data source for our empirical analysis for two reasons. First, it was one of the few longitudinal and cross-national survey projects that consistently included the same question on one's subjective well-being. This allowed us to make a within-country comparison. Second, the Eurobarometer has been used by the "happiness" literature (Alesina et al. 2004; Di Tella and MacCulloch 2005; Di Tella et al. 2003). Thus, we could compare and cross-check our findings with those in other studies.

Our analysis included survey respondents from 14 OECD countries that belonged to the European Union: Austria, Belgium, Denmark, Finland, France, Germany, Greece, Ireland, Italy, Netherlands, Portugal, Spain, Sweden, and the United Kingdom.[2] These countries were also included in our country-level analysis reported in the subsequent section. We focused on the years 1980 to 2002 because of the availability of country-level control variables needed for the analysis. In total, our analysis was based on 227 country-years.

The model for the individual-level analysis was given by:

$$\mathrm{s_{ijt}} = \beta_1 [Left]_{\mathrm{jt}} + \beta_2 [CD]_{\mathrm{jt}} + \lambda \mathrm{w_{jt}} + \gamma \mathrm{x_{ijt}} + \eta_{\mathrm{j}} \mathrm{T} + \phi_{\mathrm{t}} + \rho_{\mathrm{j}} + \varepsilon_{\mathrm{ijt}} \tag{1}$$

where s_{ijt} denotes a (latent) scale of subjective well-being of individual i in country j in year t; ρ_j is a country-fixed effect; φ is a year-fixed effect; and ε_{ijt} is an individual-specific error term. All time-invariant characteristics of country j are

[1]The data file is available at the ICPSR data archive (study no. 4357).

[2]In total, the Eurobarometer trend file includes 15 nations. Norway was excluded because its weight variable is not available.

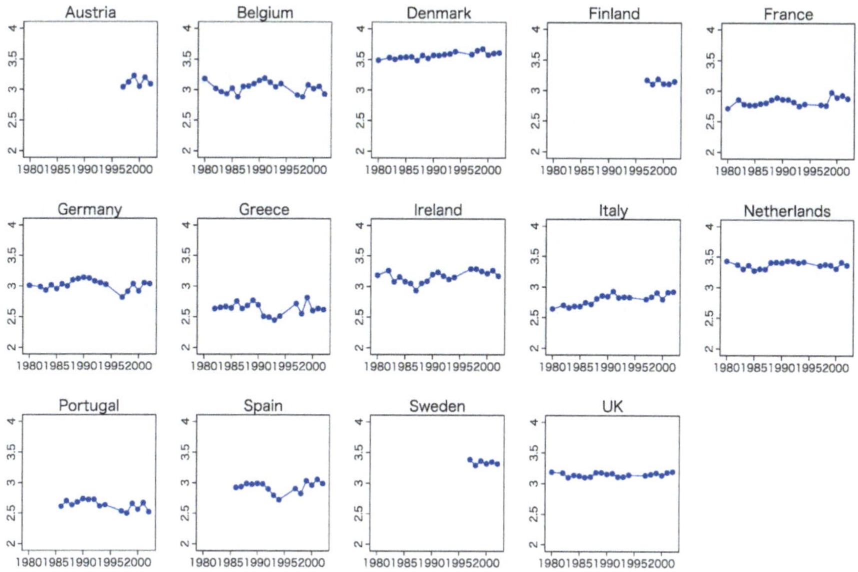

Fig. 1 Mean level of life satisfaction, 1980–2002

captured by ρ_j. In other words, the model accounted for the effects of all time-invariant cultural and social differences across countries. The model also controlled the effects of unobserved country-specific but time-varying characteristics by allowing a country-specific coefficient, η_j, for a linear time trend, T.[3]

Subjective well-being was measured by a survey question on life satisfaction. The question asked, "On the whole, are you very satisfied, fairly satisfied, not very satisfied, or not at all satisfied with the life you lead? Would you say you are…?" We coded 1 as "not at all satisfied"; 2 as "not very satisfied"; 3 as "fairly satisfied"; and 4 as "very satisfied.[4] Figure 1 displays temporal changes in the mean level of life satisfaction in 14 nations between 1980 and 2002.[5]

The same or similar "happiness" question has been extensively used for the purpose of measuring the level of well-being by scholars in economics, political science, psychology, and sociology over the last 10 years. The accuracy of the measure has been discussed at a great length in various studies (e.g., Frey and

[3]Substantive results do not change even if the country-specific time trend is removed from the model. Note that our model is equivalent to a random-intercept multilevel model. The presence of a group-level random component is taken into account by clustering standard errors by country-year.

[4]Our analysis excludes respondents who answered "don't know" and other respondents who did not provide any answer to this question. These respondents constitute less than 1% of the sample.

[5]Our analysis excludes surveys in 1996 and 1997 because the question on life satisfaction was not included in these 2 years.

Stutzer 2002; Kahneman and Krueger 2006).[6] Although some scholars express concerns about the use of survey responses as a measure of subjective well-being (Bertrand and Mullainathan 2001; Loewenstein and Ubel 2008), others offer evidence that suggests the validity and reliability of such measures.[7] For example, the reported level of happiness and life satisfaction is strongly correlated with other objective physical and psychological measures of well-being, as reviewed by Kahneman and Krueger (2006, 7–9). Krueger and Schkade (2008) show that the correlation between self-reported life satisfaction levels that are measured two weeks apart is sufficiently high. In the subsequent section, we used a more objective measure of human well-being in order to corroborate our findings in this section.

$[Left]_{jt}$ in Eq. (1) was our key explanatory variable. We measured government partisanship using the share of cabinet seats of leftist parties in country j in year t. This is the most conventional measure of left-party strength in government in political science and sociology (e.g., Allan and Scruggs 2004; Hicks and Swank 1992; Huber and Stephens 2001; Huber et al. 1993; Swank 2002). The cabinet share of leftist parties is a stronger predictor of welfare provision than the share of votes in elections and parliamentary seats (Huber et al. 1993). A similar measure of government partisanship is also used by past research in economics Di Tella and MacCulloch (2002, 2005). The $[Left]_{jt}$ variable ranged from 0 to 1, where larger values denoted a greater cabinet share of left-wing parties. The data of cabinet seats came from the Comparative Parties Data Set developed by Duane Swank.[8] Swank classified parties in 21 OECD nations into left, right, Christian Democratic, and center parties using expert judgment developed by Castles and Mair (1984).

In addition to $[Left]_{jt}$, Eq. (1) also included $[CD]_{jt}$ that measured the share of cabinet seats of Christian Democratic parties. Huber et al. (1993) and Huber and Stephens (2001) argue that Christian Democratic parties also play an important role in the formation of welfare policies that benefit lower- and middle-class individuals. Left-wing parties tend to promote a wide range of social service programs and labor participation of working-age population, while Christian Democratic parties tend to focus on social insurance and generous transfers. Huber and Stephens (2001, 39) note that both types of parties "are effective in keeping people out of poverty and are highly redistributive." Thus both left-wing and Christian Democratic parties were expected to increase the level of life satisfaction of those who were economically disadvantaged when they were in power. The cabinet share of Christian Democratic parties was also available from Swank's Comparative Parties Data Set.

The vector $\mathbf{w}_{jt}$ includes variables that capture time-varying characteristics of country j that were likely to be correlated with the partisan composition of

[6]See also the special issue on the "happiness" research in the *Journal of Public Economics*, vol. 92, 2008.

[7]Some of the objections to the use of survey questions include their variability (e.g., responses may be susceptible to changes in mood) and comparability (the reported well-being may not be comparable across people because people can adjust their responses based on their own implicit standards. See, for example, Loewenstein and Ubel (2008).

[8]The data are available on his web site. We accessed the web site on April 7, 2010.

government and the level of life satisfaction. Specifically, w_{jt} includes three sets of variables. The first set of variables represents the level and generosity of welfare programs. Prior research finds that leftist and Christian Democratic parties enhance the level of welfare provision and generosity (Allan and Scruggs 2004; Di Tella and MacCulloch 2002; Huber and Stephens 2001), and also that the level and generosity of welfare provisions increase the well-being of citizens (Di Tella et al. 2003; Minoiu and Andres 2008). The level of welfare provision was measured by total government social expenditures as a percentage of the Gross Domestic Product (GDP).[9] Following Di Tella et al. (2003), the level of welfare generosity was measured by unemployment benefit replacement rates that are equal to unemployment benefit entitlement divided by the corresponding wage. Higher values denoted higher replacement rates. Data on the replacement rates were available only for odd-numbered years; thus we used a linear interpolation for even-numbered years. The data on government expenditure and unemployment benefit replacement rates were obtained from the OECD Stat Extracts.

The second set of country-level variables captures economic characteristics of country *j* in year *t* such as the growth rate of real GDP per capita in constant dollars, the unemployment rate, and the inflation rate. These macroeconomic variables are likely to be correlated with both government partisanship (Alesina et al. 1997) and life satisfaction (Di Tella et al. 2003). The growth rate of real GDP per capita was obtained from the Penn World Table 6.3. The inflation rate was measured by an annual change in the consumer price index. The unemployment rate was measured by the percentage of the unemployed in the total labor force. The data for the inflation rate and the unemployment rate came from the OECD Stat Extracts.

The vector w_{jt} also includes socio-demographic variables such as the level of economic development, economic inequality, union density, female labor participation, the percent of dependent population, and the size of the total population. The level of economic development was measured by real GDP per capita in constant dollars. The data came from the Penn World Table 6.3. Economic inequality is measured by the Gini coefficient. It ranges from 0 to 1, where the larger values denoted a higher level of economic inequality. The data for the Gini coefficient came from the Standardized World Income Inequality Database (Solt 2009). Union density was measured by the percentage of union members among wage and salary earners. Female labor participation was measured using the percentage of the female civilian working population divided by the total size of the female labor force. Data for these two variables came from the OECD Stat Extracts. The percent of dependent population is equal to the sum of percentages of population under 15 years and over 65 years of age. The population data came from the World Health Organization (WHO) Mortality Database. We took a natural log of the real GDP per capita and total population size for our regression analysis.

[9]These social expenditures are spent on benefits with a social purpose, such as family assistance, support for children, cash benefits for low-income households, employment training, support for the elderly, and disability benefits.

Further, the vector x_{ijt} includes individual-level control variables. Building on the previous model of life satisfaction (Di Tella et al. 2003), we controlled the effects of individual characteristics, such as education and income levels, age, gender, marital status, and employment status. Education level was measured by four indicator variables that equals 1 if a respondent finished full-time education before turning age 14 years, between ages 15–18 years old, between ages 19–22 years, or if one is still studying, respectively. The base category is those who finished education before reaching age14 years. The level of income was measured by income quartiles that were defined for each country in each survey year. The base category is the first quartile. Age was measured in years. Gender was an indicator variable that equaled 1 if a respondent was female. Marital status was measured by five indicator variables that denoted whether a respondent was never married, married, divorced, separated, or widowed. The base category is the category "never married." Finally, the employment status was measured by three indicator variables that equal 1 if a respondent was self-employed, unemployed, or retired, respectively.[10] All summary statistics are presented in Table 1.

We employed an ordered logit regression model to estimate Eq. (1) because we did not directly observe a latent continuous scale of life satisfaction. Because our dependent variable is four discrete and ordered responses to the survey question regarding life satisfaction, we considered the probability that individual i chose one of the response categories as

$$\begin{aligned} P\left(s_{ijt}{}^{*} = 1\right) &= P(-\infty < s_{ijt} \leq \tau_1) \\ P\left(s_{ijt}{}^{*} = 2\right) &= P(\tau_1 < s_{ijt} \leq \tau_1) \\ P\left(s_{ijt}{}^{*} = 3\right) &= P(\tau_2 < s_{ijt} \leq \tau_2) \\ P\left(s_{ijt}{}^{*} = 4\right) &= P(\tau_3 < s_{ijt} \leq \infty \end{aligned}$$

where s_i^* denotes one of the observed response categories; s_i denoted a latent scale of life satisfaction in Eq. (1); andτ_1, τ_2, andτ_3 denoted the thresholds. We assumed that ε_{ijt} in Eq. (1) has a cumulative standard logistic distribution with mean 0 and variance $\pi^2/3$ and developed the joint likelihood function of all probabilities. In order to account for potential correlations among errors within a country in the same year, we clustered all standard errors by country-year.

Table 2 reports the estimated effects of government partisanship on the level of individual life satisfaction in Europe. All respondents were included in the analysis. We controlled for the effects of individual-level demographic attributes on happiness level in all models. The level of social spending and macroeconomic and socio-demographic variables were included in some of the specifications. All models also included country- and year-fixed effects. The estimated results in columns (1) and (2) suggest that as the government leaned to the left, citizens were generally more satisfied with their lives. The same positive effect can be found with

[10]Di Tella et al. (2003) also included the number of children, but we omit this variable due to a large number of missing cases in many survey years.

Table 1 Summary statistics for the individual-level analysis

	Mean	SD	Min	Max
Country-level variables				
Leftist party	0.378	0.392	0.000	1.000
Christian Democratic party	0.190	0.270	0.000	0.840
Social expenditure	0.220	0.044	0.110	0.305
Benefit replacement rate	0.321	0.151	0.003	0.625
GDP growth rate	0.023	0.023	–0.036	0.112
Unemployment rate	0.090	0.036	0.021	0.242
Inflation rate	0.027	0.014	–0.005	0.070
Log GDP per capita	9.986	0.216	9.347	10.444
Economic inequality	0.286	0.037	0.222	0.364
Female labor participation	0.561	0.116	0.345	0.786
Union density	0.396	0.203	0.082	0.822
Dependent population	0.334	0.019	0.299	0.412
Log population size	16.742	1.022	15.040	18.228
Individual-level variables				
Life satisfaction	3.044	0.761	1.000	4.000
Education to age: ≤ 14 years	0.283	0.450	0.000	1.000
Education to age: 15–18 years	0.377	0.485	0.000	1.000
Education to age: ≥ 19 years	0.259	0.438	0.000	1.000
Still studying	0.078	0.268	0.000	1.000
Income quartile 1	0.301	0.459	0.000	1.000
Income quartile 2	0.259	0.438	0.000	1.000
Income quartile 3	0.249	0.432	0.000	1.000
Income quartile 4	0.192	0.394	0.000	1.000
Age	43.962	17.717	15.000	99.000
Female	0.511	0.500	0.000	1.000
Married	0.638	0.481	0.000	1.000
Divorced	0.039	0.194	0.000	1.000
Separated	0.012	0.109	0.000	1.000
Widowed	0.083	0.277	0.000	1.000
Self-employed	0.069	0.253	0.000	1.000
Unemployed	0.055	0.228	0.000	1.000
Retired	0.190	0.393	0.000	1.000
N of observations	335653			

an increase in the share of Christian Democrats in the government; their presence in the government was associated with an increase in people's happiness level, even more so than the presence of leftist parties. Comparing columns (1) and (2), we could see that the estimated effects remain similar even if we included the government policy and macroeconomic conditions in the estimation.

Some of the country-level control variables have signs that one would expect. The level of female labor participation and the GDP growth rate had positive effects

Table 2 Effect of government partisanship on life satisfaction

	(1)	(2)	(3)
Country-level			
Leftist party	0.128* (0.061)	0.142* (0.055)	
Christian Democratic party	0.286* (0.138)	0.223* (0.126)	
Rightist party			−0.089* (0.046)
Social expenditure		−0.395 (1.313)	−0.184 (1.320)
Benefit replacement rate		−0.087 (0.423)	0.043 (0.384)
GDP growth rate		3.476* (0.860)	3.643* (0.866)
Unemployment rate		−4.505* (1.245)	−4.861* (1.241)
Inflation rate		0.493 (2.111)	0.295 (2.231)
Log GDP per capita	1.809* (0.535)	−0.107 (0.574)	0.006 (0.615)
Economic inequality	−2.269* (1.083)	−0.698 (0.990)	−0.717 (1.025)
Female labor participation	0.559 (0.834)	1.580* (0.922)	1.971* (0.994)
Union density	0.374 (0.952)	−0.705 (0.759)	0.052 (0.667)
Dependent population	2.231 (2.801)	−3.198 (3.221)	−5.471* (3.055)
Log population size	−0.576 (0.424)	−0.044 (0.352)	−0.152 (0.387)
Individual-level			
Education to age: 15–18 years	0.051* (0.017)	0.051* (0.017)	0.050* (0.017)
Education to age: ≧19 years	0.209* (0.020)	0.208* (0.020)	0.208* (0.020)
Still studying	0.573* (0.034)	0.573* (0.034)	0.573* (0.034)
Income quartile 2	0.326* (0.017)	0.326* (0.017)	0.326* (0.017)
Income quartile 3	0.551* (0.018)	0.552* (0.018)	0.552* (0.018)
Income quartile 4	0.813* (0.023)	0.815* (0.023)	0.814* (0.023)
Age	0.002* (0.001)	0.002* (0.001)	0.002* (0.001)

(continued)

Table 2 (continued)

	(1)	(2)	(3)
Female	0.083* (0.013)	0.084* (0.013)	0.084* (0.013)
Married	0.135* (0.019)	0.135* (0.018)	0.135* (0.018)
Divorced	−0.561* (0.033)	−0.562* (0.033)	−0.561* (0.033)
Separated	−0.601* (0.049)	−0.603* (0.048)	−0.603* (0.048)
Widowed	−0.218* (0.028)	−0.218* (0.028)	−0.218* (0.028)
Self-employed	0.045* (0.023)	0.044* (0.023)	0.044* (0.023)
Unemployed	−0.889* (0.039)	−0.890* (0.039)	−0.890* (0.039)
Retired	0.268* (0.026)	0.269* (0.026)	0.269* (0.026)
N of observations	335653		

Note Table entities are ordered logit regression estimates with standard errors in parentheses. Standard errors are clustered by country-year. The number of clusters is 227. The dependent variable is life satisfaction. Country- and year- fixed effects, and country-specific time trends are included in the models. The estimates for the cut points are not reported in the table. * $p < 0.05$ (one-tailed tests)

on the reported level of life satisfaction. Living in a country with a higher unemployment rate depressed one's happiness level, but the inflation rate and the level of economic inequality did not have any significant effect. Somewhat surprisingly, the size of social expenditures and the benefit replacement rate did not affect the happiness level of citizens. Consistent with Di Tella et al (2003), all individual-level control variables were estimated to have expected effects on the level of subjective well-being. Educated, affluent, older, female, married, self-employed, employed, and retired respondents were more satisfied with their lives.

Using the estimates in column (2), we computed the change in the probability of answering "very satisfied" when the key explanatory variables changed from one standard deviation below the mean to one standard deviation above the mean. The sizes of standard deviation are reported in Table 1. The probability of being "very satisfied" increases by 2% points when the cabinet share of leftist parties increased from one standard deviation below the mean to one standard deviation above the mean.[11] The probability of answering "very satisfied" also increased by 2% points

[11]In ordered logistic regression, the marginal effects are not constant across different values of the explanatory variables. They depend on both the values of all explanatory variables and the sizes of estimates associated with the explanatory variables. We compute these predicted probabilities by using the estimates in column (2) and setting country-level variables and age at their mean and setting the indicator variables at 0.

with the same magnitude of increase in the cabinet share of Christian Democratic parties.

For comparison, we also computed the change in the probability of being "very satisfied" when two macroeconomic variables, namely the GDP growth rate and unemployment rate, increased from one standard deviation below the mean to one standard deviation above the mean. An increase in the GDP growth rate was associated with a 2.6% point increase in the probability of being "very satisfied". The probability decreased by 6% points with a similar two standard deviation increase in the unemployment rate. This suggests that, compared to the effects of macroeconomic variables, government partisanship had a comparable effect on the level of human well-being, although the magnitude of partisan effects was somewhat smaller than that of the unemployment rate.

The results so far suggest that having a government with more cabinet seats occupied by left-wing parties and Christian Democratic parties was associated with happier citizens. But how about the effect of having a right-wing government? In column (3), we examined what happens to the happiness level of citizens when the seat share of right-wing parties increased in the government. The coefficient on the share of right-wing parties is negative, which suggests when that the government leaned toward the right, it decreased the overall life satisfaction in a nation.

Our analysis so far assumed that effects of government partisanship on subjective well-being were constant across the entire population. However, it is unlikely that all citizens reacted to government partisanship in the same way, because respondents with different ideological positions might react to government partisanship differently. Thus even if the *overall* effect of having a right-wing government on happiness level was negative in columns (3), it should have a different effect on the supporters of right-wing parties. In columns (1)–(3) in Table 3, we allowed the effect of government partisanship to differ by citizens' ideology. We expected that people with left-leaning ideology were more likely to report that their satisfaction level was high when leftist or Christian Democrats were in power compared to people with right-wing ideology. We determined the partisanship of respondents by referring to a question on their ideological positions in the Eurobarometer survey. Respondents located their ideological positions on a 10-point scale ranging from 1 to 10, where larger values denoted more conservative and right-wing positions. If their ideological score was between 1–3 on the left–right scale, we classified them as 'left' and those with an ideological score between 8–10 are called "right", and the rest of the respondents were categorized as "moderate" citizens.

According to Table 3, the effect of having a left-leaning party is positive for both "left" and "moderate" citizens. As one would expect, the effect of a left-leaning government is larger for "left" supporters, but it also had a statistically significant positive impact on the life satisfaction level of "moderate" citizens. The effect of having Christian Democrats in the government was also estimated to be positive for these two groups of citizens. As for the happiness level of conservative ("right") citizens, their happiness level did not seem to be affected by the presence of leftist parties or Christian Democrats in the government. The coefficient associated with

Table 3 Effect of government partisanship on life satisfaction by respondents' ideology and income level

	(1) Left	(2) Moderate	(3) Right	(4) Low	(5) High
Country-level					
Leftist party	0.350* (0.075)	0.151* (0.063)	−0.150 (0.093)	0.194* (0.056)	0.062 (0.065)
Christian Democratic party	0.345* (0.141)	0.260* (0.137)	0.055 (0.164)	0.178 (0.132)	0.267* (0.137)
Social expenditure	−0.651 (1.632)	−0.818 (1.563)	−1.371 (2.348)	−0.193 (1.357)	−0.691 (1.922)
Benefit replacement rate	−0.106 (0.569)	−0.035 (0.487)	0.604 (0.627)	−0.175 (0.479)	−0.039 (0.502)
GDP growth rate	2.880* (1.249)	3.270* (1.004)	3.835* (1.288)	3.397* (0.911)	3.545* (1.073)
Unemployment rate	−3.660* (1.516)	−3.700* (1.261)	−4.477* (1.915)	−4.655* (1.270)	−4.428* (1.549)
Inflation rate	1.993 (2.534)	−1.405 (2.589)	2.640 (2.429)	−0.839 (2.191)	2.060 (2.512)
Log GDP per capita	0.799 (0.790)	0.243 (0.687)	−2.117* (0.868)	−0.375 (0.612)	0.239 (0.701)
Economic inequality	−0.887 (1.366)	−1.054 (1.168)	0.563 (1.682)	−1.751* (1.054)	0.680 (1.492)
Female labor participation	1.017 (1.308)	1.910* (1.096)	0.427 (1.272)	0.778 (0.975)	2.747* (1.222)
Union density	0.584 (0.929)	−1.156 (0.886)	−1.355 (1.167)	−0.464 (0.776)	−1.119 (1.041)
Dependent population	2.401 (4.371)	−1.753 (3.718)	−21.419* (5.103)	−3.408 (3.384)	−3.083 (4.251)
Log population size	−0.042 (0.565)	−0.019 (0.411)	0.377 (0.561)	0.171 (0.419)	−0.375 (0.461)
Individual-level					
Education to age: 15–18 years	−0.005 (0.037)	0.034 (0.022)	0.083* (0.040)	0.026 (0.020)	0.080* (0.030)
Education to age: ≧19 years	0.173* (0.041)	0.216* (0.026)	0.218* (0.046)	0.227* (0.026)	0.200* (0.029)
Still studying	0.462* (0.059)	0.577* (0.043)	0.638* (0.076)	0.643* (0.044)	0.504* (0.045)
Income quartile 2	0.302* (0.033)	0.301* (0.017)	0.364* (0.043)	0.313* (0.016)	
Income quartile 3	0.551* (0.035)	0.527* (0.022)	0.522* (0.042)		
Income quartile 4	0.767* (0.042)	0.819* (0.024)	0.822* (0.048)		0.300* (0.017)
Age	0.000 (0.001)	0.002* (0.001)	0.004* (0.001)	0.004* (0.001)	−0.001 (0.001)

(continued)

Table 3 (continued)

	(1) Left	(2) Moderate	(3) Right	(4) Low	(5) High
Female	0.043 (0.027)	0.088* (0.017)	0.126* (0.031)	0.068* (0.014)	0.094* (0.020)
Married	0.218* (0.029)	0.125* (0.024)	0.113* (0.046)	0.095* (0.023)	0.226* (0.027)
Divorced	−0.321* (0.063)	−0.587* (0.042)	−0.710* (0.094)	−0.602* (0.039)	−0.377* (0.059)
Separated	−0.430* (0.100)	−0.630* (0.068)	−0.575* (0.180)	−0.570* (0.060)	−0.670* (0.109)
Widowed	−0.010 (0.062)	−0.227* (0.042)	−0.317* (0.064)	−0.245* (0.034)	−0.128* (0.062)
Self-employed	−0.043 (0.046)	0.077* (0.029)	−0.063 (0.056)	0.007 (0.032)	0.065* (0.030)
Unemployed	−0.918* (0.053)	−0.888* (0.043)	−0.863* (0.086)	−0.909* (0.042)	−0.771* (0.053)
Retired	0.272* (0.052)	0.299* (0.034)	0.270* (0.043)	0.194* (0.027)	0.435* (0.043)
N of observations	56779	183474	46879	187771	147882

Note Table entities are ordered logit regression estimates with standard errors in parentheses. Standard errors are clustered by country-year. The number of clusters is 227. The dependent variable is life satisfaction. Country- and year- fixed effects, and country-specific time trends are included in the models. The estimates for the cut points are not reported in the table. * $p < 0.05$ (one-tailed tests)

the *leftist party* is negative, but it is indistinguishable from zero. These results suggest that the positive coefficients in Table 2 were mainly driven by "left" and "moderate" citizens.

Next, because the likelihood of support for government actions by left-wing or Christian Democratic parties was likely to be correlated with people's income level, we tested whether the effect of government partisanship varied by respondents' income level. Columns (4)–(5) report estimation results when respondents with "low" and "high" levels of income were analyzed separately. We called respondents "high income" when their income quartile was 3 or 4 (defined for each country in each year). The estimation result suggests that having a left-wing party increased the life satisfaction level among people with low income level, but the presence of Christian Democrats in the government did not affect their happiness level. In contrast, respondents with relatively high income became more satisfied when Christian Democrats were in the government instead of left-wing parties [column (5)).

In Table 4, we estimated the effect of government partisanship on the level of life satisfaction by age groups. Government actions do not affect all citizens equally. For example, teenagers and those in their early 20 s receive little direct policy benefits, and thus we would expect that they do not care too much about government policies and ideology. In contrast, working-age citizens and seniors are more likely to rely on social securities than young citizens, and thus government ideology may matter more for these age groups. In column (1) of Table 4, respondents under age 24 were analyzed. Columns (2) and (3) contain results when those between 25 and 64 years of age and those 65 years of age and above were analyzed, respectively. These results suggest that government partisanship did not affect the life satisfaction level of young citizens, as expected. The positive effects of government ideology on happiness level were highest among working-age citizens [column (2)). Column (3) reports life satisfaction among seniors was influenced more by Christian Democratic parties than by leftist parties.

Table 4 Effect of government partisanship on life satisfaction by age groups

	(1)	(2)	(3)
	<24	25–64	≥65
Country-level			
Leftist party	0.109 (0.074)	0.165* (0.061)	0.102 (0.069)
Christian Democratic party	0.017 (0.129)	0.258* (0.133)	0.339* (0.171)
Social expenditure	0.388 (1.909)	−0.461 (1.396)	−0.873 (1.963)
Benefit replacement rate	−0.507 (0.580)	0.456 (0.458)	−1.827* (0.640)
GDP growth rate	3.436* (1.151)	3.767* (0.964)	2.637* (1.147)
Unemployment rate	−7.724* (1.565)	−3.321* (1.295)	−6.459* (2.005)
Inflation rate	−0.530 (2.418)	1.880 (2.367)	−4.668* (2.582)
Log GDP per capita	−0.779 (0.767)	0.554 (0.602)	−1.974* (0.836)
Economic inequality	−2.428 (1.762)	−0.384 (1.070)	−0.310 (1.526)
Female labor participation	0.748 (1.247)	1.923* (1.027)	1.419 (1.300)
Union density	−0.563 (1.103)	−0.758 (0.824)	−0.417 (1.206)
Dependent population	−9.761* (4.525)	−1.655 (3.371)	−0.001 (4.554)
Log population size	1.321* (0.587)	−0.536 (0.410)	0.272 (0.608)
Individual-level			
Education to age: 15–18	−0.054 (0.059)	0.041* (0.020)	0.100* (0.032)
Education to age: ≧19	0.106 (0.065)	0.210* (0.023)	0.235* (0.047)

(continued)

Table 4 (continued)

	(1)	(2)	(3)
	<24	25–64	≥ 65
Still studying	0.250* (0.061)	0.258* (0.055)	0.501* (0.215)
Income quartile 2	0.222* (0.042)	0.371* (0.020)	0.342* (0.031)
Income quartile 3	0.395* (0.037)	0.623* (0.025)	0.563* (0.036)
Income quartile 4	0.625* (0.039)	0.917* (0.031)	0.778* (0.059)
Age	−0.045* (0.006)	−0.000 (0.001)	0.014* (0.003)
Female	0.068* (0.029)	0.097* (0.014)	−0.070* (0.028)
Married	0.259* (0.036)	0.242* (0.023)	0.093* (0.052)
Divorced	−0.670* (0.183)	−0.431* (0.037)	−0.471* (0.078)
Separated	−0.649* (0.231)	−0.462* (0.050)	−0.639* (0.162)
Widowed	0.381 (0.417)	−0.203* (0.035)	−0.271* (0.052)
Self-employed	0.155* (0.083)	0.047* (0.023)	0.086 (0.107)
Unemployed	−0.967* (0.053)	−0.937* (0.041)	−0.291 (0.258)
Retired	−0.336* (0.196)	0.226* (0.034)	0.031 (0.029)
N of observations	52531	228190	55112

Note Table entities are ordered logit regression estimates with standard errors in parentheses. Standard errors are clustered by country-year. The number of clusters is 227. The dependent variable is life satisfaction. Country- and year- fixed effects, and country-specific time trends are included in the models. The estimates for the cut points are not reported in the table. * $p < 0.05$ (one-tailed tests)

3 Country-Level Analysis

The previous section showed that the presence of left-wing parties and Christian Democratic parties in government was strongly related to the reported level of citizen happiness. In this section, we employed another measure of human well-being in order to assess the effect of government partisanship on the life of citizens. Specifically, we examined the impact of leftist-party and Christian Democratic party government on suicide rates using country-level panel data.

The panel data came from 21 OECD nations between 1980 and 2004. Our analysis included Austria, Australia, Belgium, Canada, Denmark, Finland, France, Germany, Greece, Ireland, Italy, Japan, Netherlands, New Zealand, Norway, Portugal, Spain, Sweden, Switzerland, the United Kingdom, and the United States. These countries were chosen on the basis of availability of data.[12] Of the 21 nations, 14 were included in the individual-level analysis in the previous section. The total number of cases was 525. The model for the country-level analysis was given by:

$$\mathrm{s_{jt}} = \beta_1[\mathit{Left}]_{\mathrm{jt}} + \beta_2[\mathit{CD}]_{\mathrm{jt}} + \lambda \mathrm{w_{jt}} + \eta_{\mathrm{j}}\mathrm{T} + \phi_{\mathrm{t}} + \rho_j + \varepsilon_{jt} \tag{2}$$

where s_{jt} denotes the suicide rate in country j in year t. ρ_j is country fixed effects, while $\psi_\mathrm{t}$is year fixed effects. ε_jt is a country-year specific error term. All time-invariant characteristics of country j are captured by the country fixed effect, ρ_j. Further, any time-specific shock is captured by the year-fixed effect, ψ_t. As in Eq. (1), we also included the country-specific time trend, η_j T, in the model.

The suicide rate, s_{jt}, is the number of suicides per 100,000 persons in country j in year t. We computed the suicide rate for (1) total population; (2) total male population; (3) total female population; (4) male population from 25 to 64 years of age; (5) female population from 25 to 64 years of age; (6) young population under age 25 years; and (7) senior population over age 65 years. In the following analysis, we used the total suicide rate as well as the age- and gender-specific rates because the impact of government partisanship might differ for different age and gender groups.[13] The data for suicide and population size were obtained from the World Health Organization (WHO) Mortality Database.[14]

Using a suicide mortality rate is another way of measuring the subjective well-being of citizens. Suppose that there is a similar latent scale of individual happiness, s_j, as in Eq. (1). We formulated the decision to die by suicide as

$$s_i^* = 1 \text{ if} s_i < \tau_\mathrm{i}, \text{ 0otherwise,}$$

where s_i^* denotes an observable indicator variable that equals one if individual i dies by suicide and zero otherwise; s_i denotes a latent variable of happiness; and τ_i denotes a threshold. We assumed that citizens decide to die by suicide if their level of life satisfaction is below a certain unobservable threshold, τ_i. Because neither of the individual-level data, s_i^* nor s_i, was available, we used the aggregated suicide rate, $s_{jt} = \Sigma s_i^*$, in country j as a measure of happiness.

The use of suicide rates as a measure of well-being and happiness is justified by prior research. Oswald (1997, 1823–24) notes, "Suicides represent choices in response to (un)happiness that are intrinsically more compelling than replies made

[12]The data of government partisanship are unavailable for other OECD countries and non-OECD countries.

[13]We use the crude suicide rates for our analysis. The results are almost identical when we take a natural log of the suicide rates.

[14]The data are available at http://www.who.int/whosis/mort/download/en/index.html.

to happiness survey questions." Several studies have used the suicide rates as a measure of well-being and happiness (Flavin and Radcliff 2009; Minoiu and Andres 2008). In addition, Di Tella et al. (2003) report that higher levels of national reported well-being are associated with lower national suicide rates.

Figure 2 shows a trend in the total suicide rates between 1980 and 2004 in the countries included in our analysis. We can see from Fig. 2 that there was considerable within-country variation in suicide rates over time. Some countries, such as Austria, Denmark, Finland, Germany, Sweden, and Switzerland, experienced a large reduction in the suicide rate over the period of this study. A stark contrast can be found in Ireland and Japan, where there existed an increasing trend in the suicide rates. We exploited such within-country variation in the suicide rates to evaluate the impact of government partisanship on the quality of life.

Equation (2) includes a similar set of variables to Eq. (1). The key explanatory variables are the cabinet share of left-wing and Christian Democratic parties, $[Left]_{jt}$ and $[CD]_{jt}$. $\mathbf{w_{jt}}$ is a vector of time-varying country characteristics such as welfare effort and generosity (i.e., the percentage of welfare spending in the total GDP and the unemployment benefit entitlement rate), macroeconomic variables (i.e., the GDP growth rate, the unemployment rate, and the inflation rate), and other base control variables (i.e., real GDP per capita, economic inequality, female labor participation, union density, the percentage of dependent population, and the total size of population). We also added the divorce rate to $\mathbf{w_{jt}}$ as a control variable because a higher divorce rate is associated with a higher suicide rate (Minoiu and Andres 2008). The divorce rate equals the number of divorces per 1,000 persons.

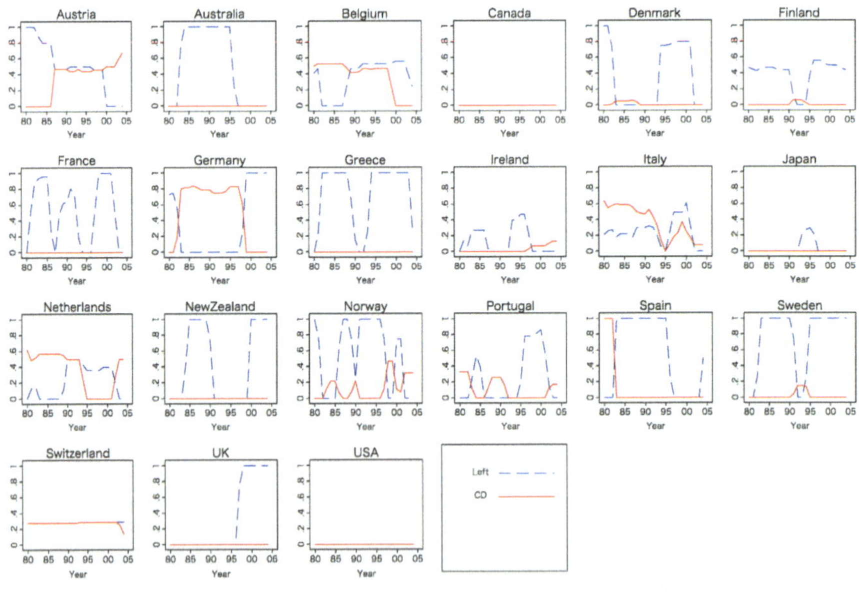

Government partisanship, 1980–2004

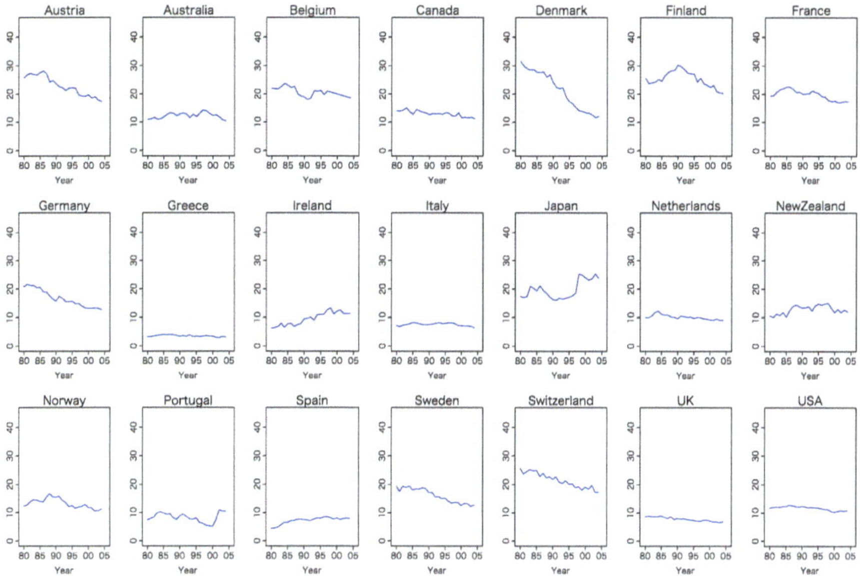

Fig. 2 Total suicide rates, 1980–2004

The divorce rate data were obtained from the OECD Stat Extracts. Summary statistics are presented in Table 5.

Table 6 reports the estimated results. In column (1), suicide rates of the entire population in each country were regressed on government partisanship as well as the policy-related variables, macro-economic variables, and socio-demographic characteristics of countries. The negative coefficient associated with the left-party government variable indicates that as the government became more left-wing, the overall suicide rates in the country tended to become low. The effect of Christian Democrats on the total suicide rates is indistinguishable from zero at the 0.05 level of significance. Welfare policies and macro-economic variables had no statistically significant impact on the suicide rates. We find that higher levels of economic inequality decreased suicide rates. Finally, higher divorce rates and female labor participation increased suicide rates.

The estimated coefficient associated with the presence of left-wing parties in the government suggests that the number of suicides per 100,000 decreased by 0.9 as the cabinet share of left-wing parties increased from 0 to 1. This is a large effect because the average total suicide rate per 100,000 persons was 20, as reported in Table 5. When leftist parties occupied all cabinet seats, countries with a population of 10 million people (e.g., Austria, Belgium, Portugal, and Sweden) had the suicide rate decreased by 90; countries with 50 million people (e.g., France, Italy, Spain, and UK) had the suicide rate decrease by 450; and countries with more than 100 million people (e.g., Germany and Japan) had the suicide rate decrease by more than 900.

Table 5 Summary statistics for the country-level analysis

	Mean	SD	Min	Max
Suicide rate: total	20.902	9.090	4.522	47.850
Suicide rate: male	21.352	9.389	4.602	49.308
Suicide rate: female	7.728	4.109	0.868	22.317
Suicide rate: male, 25–64 years old	26.617	12.206	5.041	66.261
Suicide rate: female, 25–64 years old	9.562	5.102	1.010	32.316
Suicide rate: youth, <25 years old	4.793	2.456	0.773	12.886
Suicide rate: senior, ≥65 years old	23.454	12.074	4.616	55.119
Leftist party	0.359	0.392	0.000	1.000
Christian Democratic party	0.127	0.224	0.000	1.000
Rightist party	0.390	0.406	0.000	1.000
Social expenditure	0.206	0.053	0.102	0.358
Benefit replacement rate	0.286	0.129	0.003	0.649
GDP growth rate	0.020	0.024	−0.089	0.112
Unemployment rate	0.076	0.040	0.002	0.242
Inflation rate	0.025	0.014	−0.009	0.085
Log GDP per capita	10.065	0.253	9.263	10.697
Economic inequality	0.286	0.043	0.003	0.392
Female labor participation	0.603	0.113	0.320	0.809
Union density	0.395	0.204	0.080	0.839
Divorce rate	2.038	0.995	0.000	5.300
Dependent population	0.335	0.018	0.299	0.412
Log population size	9.752	1.219	8.049	12.590
Number of Observations	525			

In columns (2)–(3), male and female suicide rates were analyzed separately. Suicide rates of both male and female groups decreased as the government ideology leaned toward the left. The noteworthy difference between the result in column (1) and the results here is that female suicide rates decreased when the share of Christian Democrats in the government went up. The male suicide rates also decreased with the increased presence of Christian Democrats in the government, but the coefficient is not statistically significant at the 0.05 level. Interestingly, female labor participation rate did not affect female suicide rates, but as more women entered the labor market, the male suicide rates went up.

In columns (4)–(7), we analyzed the relationship between government partisanship and suicide rates of various age and gender groups. Suicides rates among people aged between 25–64 exhibit a similar pattern to that of columns (2)–(3). The female suicide rates were negatively affected by the presence of left-wing and Christian Democratic parties, but an increase in Christian Democrats did not affect the male suicide rates.

Columns (6) and (7) report estimation results when suicide rates among young and old people were analyzed separately. The presence of Christian Democrats in the government was most negatively associated with the suicide rates of both

Table 6 Effect of government partisanship on suicide rates

	(1) Total	(2) Male	(3) Female	(4) Male 25–64	(5) Female 25–64	(6) Youth <25	(7) Senior ≥ 65
Leftist party	−0.865* (0.386)	−0.907* (0.399)	−0.520* (0.244)	−1.416* (0.557)	−0.714* (0.287)	−0.069 (0.237)	−0.392 (0.545)
Christian Democratic party	−1.165 (0.779)	−1.261 (0.809)	−1.210* (0.411)	−1.823 (1.137)	−1.526* (0.517)	−0.656* (0.345)	−1.839* (0.972)
Social expenditure	20.419 (14.612)	21.485 (14.891)	8.971* (4.724)	29.420 (24.130)	11.522 (8.563)	4.181 (5.283)	−0.850 (12.885)
Benefit replacement rate	4.102 (5.363)	4.159 (5.458)	−1.981 (2.568)	4.511 (8.015)	−1.416 (3.225)	1.873 (1.612)	−3.638 (3.721)
GDP growth rate	−9.090 (5.399)	−9.232 (5.557)	−0.193 (2.070)	−13.591 (7.979)	−1.058 (2.654)	−2.120 (1.925)	2.051 (4.393)
Unemployment rate	−9.133 (14.508)	−9.376 (14.871)	−4.653 (6.127)	−9.505 (20.671)	−2.288 (7.284)	−4.515 (4.016)	−4.465 (15.939)
Inflation rate	4.188 (11.401)	4.037 (11.628)	1.353 (5.491)	13.150 (17.799)	9.845 (6.914)	−4.670 (4.894)	4.284 (16.031)
Log GDP per capita	−14.560 (8.933)	−14.834 (9.096)	−3.982* (2.206)	−21.040* (11.695)	−5.106* (2.541)	−4.063* (2.311)	−9.896 (7.765)
Economic inequality	−8.266* (4.775)	−8.609* (4.881)	−0.496 (2.172)	−10.319 (6.818)	0.542 (3.120)	−0.294 (1.718)	−7.402 (5.784)
Female labor participation	−0.808 (7.619)	−0.534 (7.838)	0.428 (2.118)	1.955 (10.759)	−0.582 (3.798)	−4.586 (3.681)	4.254 (4.615)
Union density	17.870* (8.577)	18.259* (8.808)	0.320 (3.402)	15.727 (11.775)	−1.969 (3.389)	13.840* (5.360)	−8.122 (8.242)
Divorce rate	1.915* (1.031)	1.974* (1.056)	0.458 (0.292)	2.773* (1.232)	0.817* (0.464)	0.182 (0.409)	1.265 (0.963)
Dependent population	6.776 (40.462)	6.452 (41.488)	−20.251* (11.336)	19.379 (54.484)	−15.104 (14.548)	−13.801 (13.031)	−16.651 (45.735)
Log population size	1.249 (8.302)	0.550 (8.670)	3.297 (2.714)	4.507 (11.809)	4.615 (3.185)	−5.823* (2.949)	16.832* (8.978)
R^2	0.968	0.969	0.975	0.966	0.968	0.928	0.972

Note Table entities are fixed effects regression estimates and standard errors in parentheses. Standard errors are clustered by countries. Estimates are based on data from 21 OECD nations between 1980 and 2004. The dependent variables are the suicide rates. Country- and year-fixed effects and country-specific time trends are included in the models. The number of observations is 525. * $p < 0.05$ (one-tailed tests)

groups. The estimate indicates that the number of suicides per 100,000 decreased by 1.8 as the cabinet share of Christian Democratic parties increased from 0 to 1. However, left-wing parties do not seem to have had any effect on their suicide rates. It is interesting to note that an increase in the female labor participation was associated with more suicides among youth.

Table 7 reports the estimated results for the right-wing party government. We replaced the cabinet share of leftist and Christian Democratic parties with that of rightist parties and estimated the same model. Columns (1)–(5) show that the larger

Table 7 Effect of rightist-party government on suicide rates

	(1) Total	(2) Male	(3) Female	(4) Male 25–64	(5) Female 25–64	(6) Youth <25	(7) Senior ≥ 65
Rightist party	0.252 (0.359)	0.273 (0.366)	0.150 (0.213)	0.512 (0.506)	0.230 (0.285)	−0.058 (0.199)	−0.346 (0.421)
Social expenditure	19.613 (15.092)	20.606 (15.401)	8.044 (5.142)	28.163 (25.098)	10.364 (9.439)	3.636 (5.188)	−2.297 (11.692)
Benefit replacement rate	3.687 (5.769)	3.762 (5.885)	−1.922 (2.780)	3.941 (8.446)	−1.380 (3.539)	2.056 (1.734)	−3.777 (4.177)
GDP growth rate	−9.541* (5.397)	−9.708* (5.556)	−0.504 (2.111)	−14.313* (7.991)	−1.472 (2.726)	−2.208 (1.979)	1.695 (4.318)
Unemployment rate	−7.915 (14.344)	−7.990 (14.691)	−2.794 (6.529)	−7.432 (20.315)	0.028 (7.494)	−3.379 (4.171)	−2.251 (17.332)
Inflation rate	5.436 (11.120)	5.471 (11.324)	3.251 (5.369)	15.444 (17.523)	12.250 (7.108)	−3.644 (4.780)	5.758 (15.230)
Log GDP per capita	−14.865 (8.924)	−15.141 (9.085)	−4.073* (2.173)	−21.475* (11.630)	−5.236* (2.441)	−4.048* (2.309)	−10.170 (7.647)
Economic inequality	−9.195* (4.715)	−9.585* (4.831)	−1.226 (2.207)	−11.671 (6.909)	−0.382 (3.169)	−0.668 (1.684)	−8.922 (5.565)
Female labor participation	−4.029 (7.300)	−3.927 (7.496)	−1.980 (2.222)	−2.985 (9.970)	−3.704 (3.937)	−5.563 (4.077)	0.396 (4.045)
Union density	15.933* (9.070)	16.214* (9.322)	−1.065 (3.444)	12.642 (12.510)	−3.801 (3.633)	13.402* (5.169)	−9.804 (8.067)
Divorce rate	1.992* (1.024)	2.053* (1.049)	0.510* (0.290)	2.869* (1.222)	0.880* (0.467)	0.217 (0.417)	1.450 (0.961)
Dependent population	11.489 (38.456)	11.555 (39.431)	−15.179 (11.720)	26.596 (51.420)	−8.763 (15.848)	−10.851 (11.915)	−8.171 (43.446)
Log population size	1.256 (8.671)	0.514 (9.052)	2.882 (2.912)	4.464 (12.247)	4.126 (3.268)	−6.191* (3.030)	16.329 (9.811)
R^2	0.968	0.968	0.974	0.965	0.966	0.927	0.972

Note Table entities are fixed effects regression estimates with standard errors in parentheses. Standard errors are clustered by countries. Estimates are based on data from 21 OECD nations between 1980 and 2004. The dependent variables are the suicide rates. Country- and year-fixed effects, and country-specific time trends are included in the models. The number of observations is 525. * $p < 0.05$ (one-tailed tests)

the share of rightist parties in the cabinet was positively associated with the suicide rates, yet none of the coefficients were statistically significant at the 0.05 level. Columns (6) and (7) show that the presence of the right-wing party in the government was associated with a decrease in the suicide rates of the youth and seniors. However, again, the coefficients were not distinguishable from zero.

4 Conclusions

In contemporary democratic societies, the government intervenes in almost every aspect of human life. The government develops and implements policies that affect birth and death, marriage and divorce, education, economic activities, and even criminal activities. Prior research has investigated the effects of government partisanship on these consequences individually, but we have little evidence of how the government affects the overall quality of human life.

This chapter examined how government partisanship affects the quality of human life. We measured the quality of life using the reported level of life satisfaction and the suicide rates. We measured the nature of government actions using the partisan composition of the government. We argued that left-leaning governments representing lower-class constituents are more likely to develop policies that favor their constituents resulting in the expansion of welfare provisions, higher GDP growth rates, and lower unemployment rates. These economic consequences would improve the economic welfare of citizens and in turn increase their happiness, especially among lower-class individuals. In contrast, right-leaning governments representing higher-class constituents would be likely to generate policies that favor their constituents, resulting in smaller government spending and lower inflation rates. These economic consequences worsen the economic welfare of lower-class individuals, leading to a decrease in the level of happiness.

Our analysis, using data from OECD nations between 1980 and the early 2000s, showed that the presence of left-leaning parties in government is associated with an increase in the level of happiness. Our individual-level analysis using survey data showed that citizens were more likely to report they are satisfied with their lives when left-wing parties and Christian Democratic parties occupied a larger share of cabinet seats in the government of their country. The effects of government partisanship held even after we controlled for the impacts of welfare policies, macroeconomic conditions, other country- and individual-level characteristics, and country- and year-fixed effects. Government partisanship had a larger impact on citizens with a leftist ideology, in the lower class, and in older generations. Our country-level analysis using panel data of 21 nations confirmed the individual-level findings. The suicide rates tended to be lower when the cabinet share of left-wing and Christian Democratic parties increases.

Our study suggests that, in addition to macroeconomics (Di Tella and Oswald 2001; Di Tella et al. 2003), politics matters for the quality of life. Happiness depends not only on individual-level and macro-level economic success but also on government actions. Leftist and Christian Democratic parties develop public policies that alleviate the effect of economic success and failure on the happiness of individuals. These parties are more influential on the happiness of people who are supportive of policies pursued by those parties. In contrast, those parties have no impact on the happiness of people who are not in favor of policies pursued by left-wing and Christian Democratic parties. Importantly, we found the strong impact of left-wing and Christian Democratic parties after controlling for the impacts of welfare policies and macroeconomic variables. This means that these parties have other channels of policies that affect the quality of life.

References

Alesina, A., Roubini, N., & Cohen, G. D. (1997). *Political cycles and the macroeconomy*. Cambridge, MA: The MIT Press.

Alesina, A., Di Tella, R., & MacCulloch, R. (2004). Inequality and happiness: Are Europeans and Americans different? *Journal of Public Economics, 88*(9–10), 2009–2042.

Allan, J. P., & Scruggs, L. (2004). Political partisanship and welfare state reform in advanced industrial societies. *American Journal of Political Science, 48*(3), 496–512.

Bertrand, M., & Mullainathan, S. (2001). Do people mean what they say? implications for subjective survey data. *American Economic Review, 91*(2), 67–72.

Bradley, D., Huber, E., Moller, S., Nielsen, F., & Stephens, J. D. (2003). Distribution and redistribution in postindustrial democracies. *World Politics, 55*(1), 193–228.

Castles, F., & Mair, P. (1984). Left-right political scales: some 'expert' judgements. *European Journal of Political Research, 12,* 73–88.

Chung, H., & Muntaner, C. (2006). Political and welfare state determinants of infant and child health. Indicators: An analysis of wealthy countries. *Social Science & Medicine*, *63*(3), 829–842.

Conley, D., & Springer, K. W. (2001). Welfare state and infant mortality. *American Journal of Sociology, 107*(3), 768–807.

Di Tella, R., & MacCulloch, R. (2002). The determination of unemployment benefits. *Journal of Labor Economics, 20*(2), 404–434.

Di Tella, R., & MacCulloch, R. (2005). Partisan social happiness. *Review of Economic Studies, 72* (2), 367–393.

Di Tella, R., MacCulloch, R. J., & Oswald, A. J. (2003). The macroeconomics of happiness. *Review of Economics and Statistics, 85*(4), 809–827.

Flavin, P., & Radcliff, B. (2009). Public policies and suicide rates in the American States. *Social Indicators Research, 2*(1), 195–209.

Frey, B. S., & Stutzer, A. (2002). What can economists learn from happiness research? *Journal of Economic Literature, 40*(2), 402–435.

Hicks, A. M., & Swank, D. H. (1992). Politics, institutions, and welfare spending in industrialized democracies, 1960–1982." *American Political Science Review*, *86*(3), 658–674.

Huber, E., & Stephens, J. D. (2001). *Development and crisis of the welfare state: parties and policies in global markets*. Chicago: University of Chicago Press.

Huber, E., Ragin, C., & Stephens, J. D. (1993). Social democracy, Christian democracy, constitutional structure, and the welfare state. *American Journal of Sociology*, *99*(3), 711–749.

Kahneman, D., & Krueger, A. B. (2006). Developments in the measurement of subjective well-being. *Journal of Economic Perspectives*, *20*(1), 3–24.

Krueger, A. B., & Schkade, D. A. (2008). The reliability of subjective well-being measures. *Journal of Public Economics, 92*(8–9), 1833–1845.

Loewenstein, G., & Ubel, P. A. (2008). Hedonic adaptation and the role of decision and experience utility in public policy. *Journal of Public Economics, 92*(8–9), 1795–1810.

Minoiu, C., & Andres, A. R. (2008). The effect of public spending on suicide: evidence from US State data. *Journal of Socio-Economics, 37*(1), 237–261.

Oswald, A. J. (1997). Happiness and economic performance. *Economic Journal, 107*(445), 1815–1831.

Pacek, A., & Radcliff, B. (2008). Assessing the welfare state: The politics of happiness. *Perspectives on Politics, 6*(02), 267–277.

Radcliff, B. (2001). Politics, markets, and life satisfaction: The political economy of human happiness. *American Political Science Review, 95*(4), 939–952.

Solt, F. (2009). Standardizing the world income inequality database. *Social Science Quarterly, 90* (2)–242.

Swank, D. (2002). *Global capital, political institutions, and policy change in developed welfare states*. New York: Cambridge University Press.

Chapter 8
Economic and Welfare Policies and Suicide

1 Introduction

In the previous chapter, we focused on government partisanship as an overall indicator of what policies the government implements. Our analysis using cross-national data demonstrated that suicide rates tend to decrease when a leftist party or a Christian Democratic party is in power, as these parties expand welfare policies and promote macroeconomic policies for higher economic growth, both of which are influential on the quality of life of those in need. Our findings imply that government policies are strongly associated with the overall risks of suicide in society.

Yet, those findings do not reveal what specific types of government policies are important in lowering suicide rates. In other words, it remains unclear whether suicide rates indeed show a decline when the government enforces policies to improve the economic conditions of those who suffer from unemployment and poverty.

This chapter highlights the roles of economic and welfare policies adopted by local governments that are expected to understand people's economic needs within their jurisdiction in a more comprehensive and systematic way than the national government. Specifically, we developed the panel data of 47 prefectures in Japan between 1982 and 2006 to examine how the expansion and shrinkage of economic and welfare policies are associated with changes in suicide rates.

The content of this chapter was based on "Welfare and Economic Policies and Suicide Rates: Analysis of Prefecture-Level Data in Japan" *Nihon Keizai Kenkyu* (2013).

Y. Sawada et al., *Economic Analysis of Suicide Prevention*, Creating a Society for All, DOI 10.1007/978-981-10-1500-7_8

2 Relationship Between Economic and Welfare Policies and Suicide Rates

Government economic policies, when effective, promote economic growth and improve people's living conditions. For example, if the government attempts to rejuvenate the economic conditions of an area through public projects, this will create employment opportunities, which will lead to a decline in the number of jobless people; and ultimately the income level of the entire area is likely to go up. Furthermore, public projects may also stimulate business activities, which may improve the economic conditions of self-employed workers who own businesses. Because economic insecurity is one of the leading causes of suicide, as discussed in Chap. 2, effective economic policies by local governments are expected to reduce the risk of suicide by mitigating such economic insecurity especially among those who are struggling.

Moreover, government welfare policies, if expanded, will increase the number of people who can benefit from such safety nets and directly improve the quality of lives of people in poverty. For example, if financial assistance is offered to people who have lost their income and their home, it should contribute to mitigating their hardships in life at least for a certain period of time. Considering that the large number of people choose to die by suicide because of economic hardships and that suicide rates among the unemployed are extremely high (see Chap. 2), the expansion of welfare policies, including income assistance, is expected to have a substantial positive effect on reducing suicide rates. Welfare policies can also enrich community medical facilities and services and thus enhance the possibility that those with suicidal thoughts can receive a variety of medical assistance, which may lead to a decline in suicide rates.

In this chapter, we developed hypothesis that suicide rates tend to decrease as the local government invests more for economic and welfare policies. This hypothesis was tested against the data for 47 prefectures in Japan between 1982 and 2006. The number of observations was 1,175 (=47 prefectures ×25 years). As indicators of economic policies, we used the annual amount of public investments and the expenditure for unemployment relief in each prefecture. As indicators of welfare policies, we used the annual amount of expenditures for income assistance, child and senior welfare, and public health.

3 Data and Method

We used the following model:

$$[Suicide]_{it} = \beta[Policy]_{it} + \lambda \mathbf{w}_{it} + \gamma_i T + \varphi_t + \rho_i + \varepsilon_{it} \tag{1}$$

where the outcome variable $[Suicide]_{it}$ was the suicide rate per 100,000 population in year t in prefecture i. We transformed the suicide rate into a natural log. To take into consideration the possibility that the effects of government policies vary by age and gender, we used the suicide rates by six subpopulation groups such as (1) all aged under 64, (2) men aged under 64, (3) women aged under 64, (4) all aged 65 and over, (5) men aged 65 and over, and (6) women aged 65 and over. The shifts in suicide rates by age in 47 prefectures can be found in Fig. 1 in Chap. 4.

$[Policy]_{it}$ was the explanatory variable including economic policies and welfare policies adopted by each prefectural government. As indicators of economic policies, we used the expenditure for public investments and the expenditure for unemployment relief. Public investments refer to public projects implemented by the national and local governments to build community infrastructures and industrial infrastructures, as well as to conserve national land. Investments in community infrastructures include construction of local roads, establishment of water and sewage systems, public welfare projects, and establishment of educational facilities. Investments in industrial infrastructures include construction of national and prefectural roads, ports, and airports. Kondo (2008) notes that investments in community infrastructures rank the highest (approximately 40–50%) among the public investments in Japan from 1970 to 2003, followed by investments in industrial infrastructures (around 20%). Investments in agriculture, forestry, fishing, and national land conservation account for only around 10%. Here, we calculated the amount of public investments per person by dividing the total amount invested in each fiscal year in each prefecture by the population of that prefecture. To measure the total amount of expenditures related to unemployment relief, we used the total amount spent on unemployment relief in each prefecture and each municipality. We obtained the amount per person by dividing the total amount by the population. The per capita amount of public investments and unemployment relief were transformed into a natural log in our regression analysis.

As indicators of welfare policies, we used the expenditure for social welfare, the expenditure for welfare for senior welfare, the expenditure for child welfare, the expenditure for income assistance, and the expenditure for public health. The expenditure for social welfare includes expenses related to welfare services for the disabled and the operation and management of welfare facilities, whereas the expenditures for senior welfare includes expenses related to elderly care and facilities for the aged. The expenditure for child welfare includes the child allowance, expenses for child welfare facilities, and expenses related to support for single-parent households. The expenditure for public health refers to healthcare-related costs, such as expenditures for mental health and environmental health. We obtained the amount per person by combining the total amount spent by each prefecture and all municipalities within that prefecture, divided by the total population. We transformed this amount per person into a log.[1] Considering the natures of these expenditure categories, it would be reasonable to expect that the

[1]For all monetary variables, we adjusted prices for inflation by using the Consumer Price Index to take into consideration the effects of commodity prices. Further, we obtained the per capita amount of senior welfare by dividing the expenditure by the size of population aged 65 years and over and the per capita amount of child welfare by dividing the expenditure by the size of population aged 15 years and below.

expenditure for child welfare had an effect on the suicide rate among people aged 64 and under and the expenditure for senior welfare had an effect on the suicide rate among people aged 65 and over. On the other hand, other expenditure categories might affect all population groups irrespective of age and gender.

Figure 1 shows the temporal shifts in the amount of expenditures related to economic policies (dashed lines) and welfare policies (solid lines) by the prefectures. For economic policies, we used the total amount of expenditures per person for public investments and unemployment relief, whereas for welfare policies, we used the total amount of expenditures per person for social welfare, welfare for the aged, child welfare, livelihood assistance, and public health. The unit is 1,000 yen. Figure 1 suggests that the average amount of expenditures for these two types of policies varied significantly by prefecture and that the amount of expenditures in each prefecture also varied significantly depending on the period. The expenditures for economic policies increased in the mid to late 1990s and took a downward turn after that in all prefectures. On the other hand, the expenditures for welfare policies were increasing every year at a constant rate. Descriptive statistics related to the amounts of expenditures are compiled in Table 1.

As described in the previous section, suicide rates are hypothesized to decline as the expenditures for economic and welfare policies increase. For example, an increase in the amount spent on public investments will lead to an increase in the number of public projects in an area, which will eventually stimulate the area's business and economy. As a result, the local economy expands, and any decline observed in the unemployment rate of the area will probably lead to a decline in the suicide rate. An increase in the expenditure for income assistance is likely to contribute to lowering the number of suicides due to economic hardship.[2]

Expanding economic and welfare policies not only affect the economic conditions, but are expected to contribute to the improvement of an area's healthcare facilities and administrative services. Because many suicide victims suffer from mental illness, improved healthcare facilities and services will allow patients with

[2]The base amount of income assistance in each area is decided by the Minister of Health, Labour and Welfare; the municipalities are not allowed to set the amount on their own. However, because the base amount is sometimes revised by a municipality at different times, the expenditure per person for income assistance (obtained by dividing the total amount of expenditure for livelihood assistance by the total population of the prefecture) can change. At the same time, the decision as to whether income assistance for those who are in poverty and who have applied for such assistance should be provided is primarily left up to the municipalities or welfare offices. Therefore, it is possible that the expenditure per person for income assistance changes depending on the payment rate of income assistance. If the operating organization sets the payment rate higher, then the expenditure per person for income assistance should increase, whereas if the rate is set lower, then it should decrease. The effect of the payment rate itself is controlled for separately as the ratio of recipients of income assistance, as discussed later.

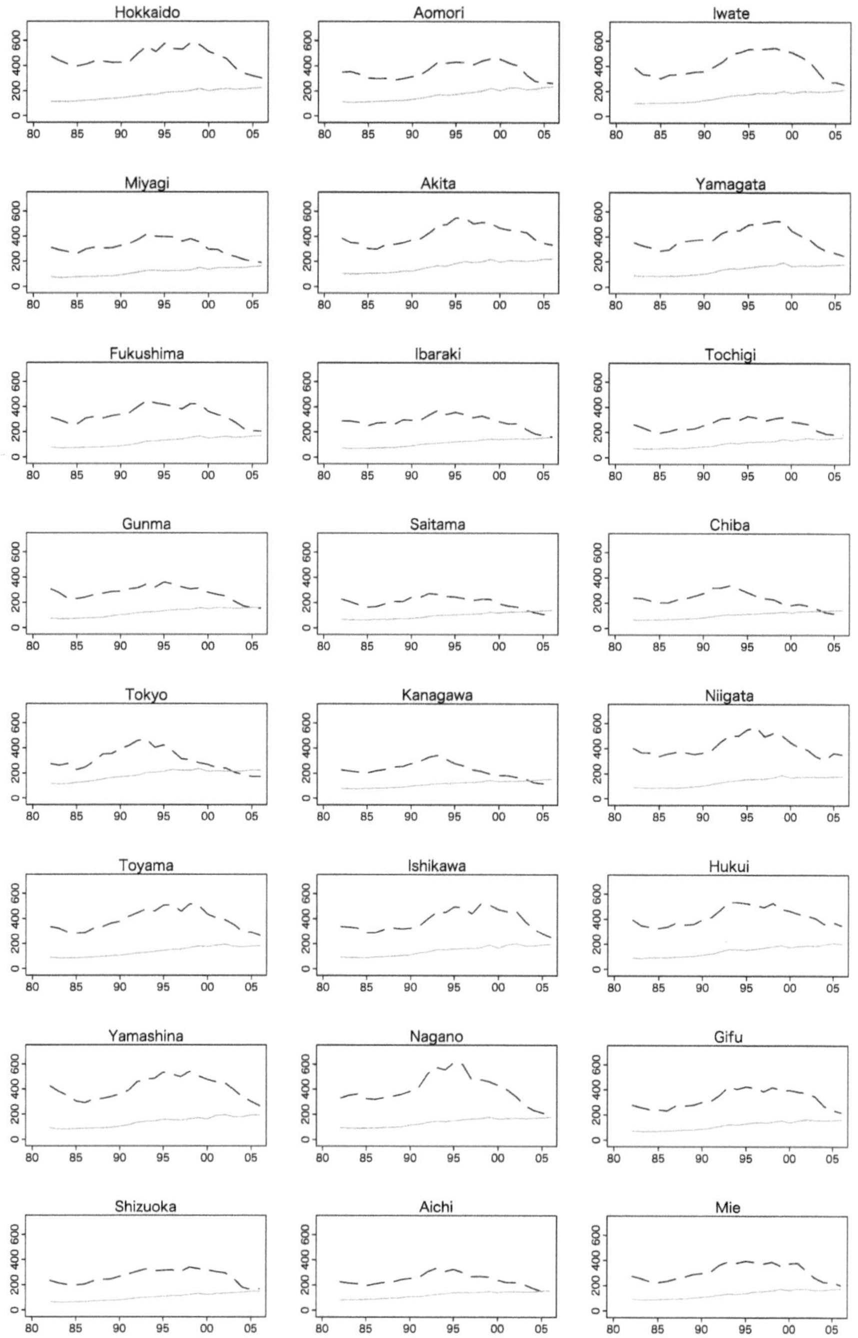

Fig. 1 Per capita expenditures for economic and welfare policies by prefecture

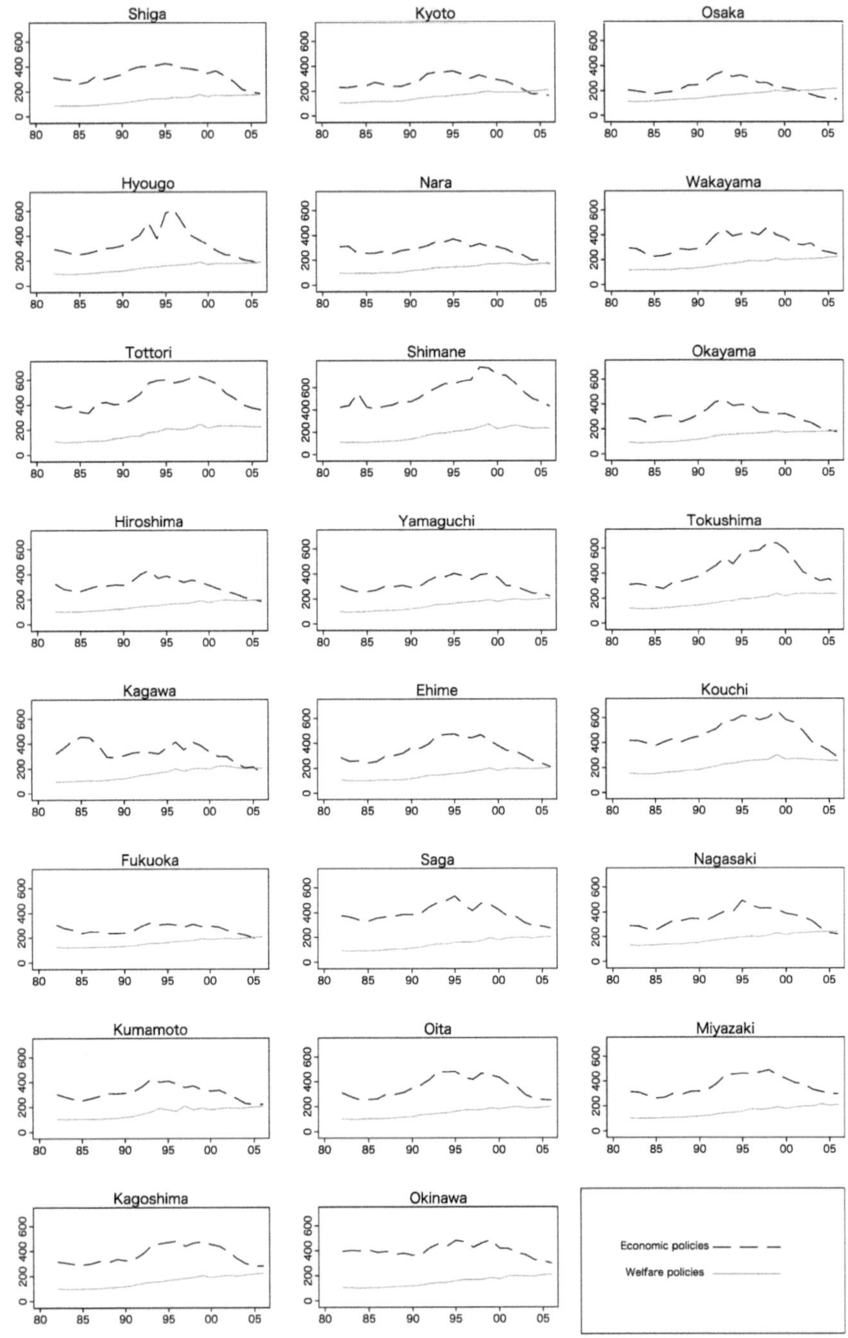

Fig. 1 (continued)

Table 1 Summary statistics

	Mean	SD	Min	Max
Suicide rates by all aged under 64, per 100,000	18.453	4.833	8.761	40.069
Suicide rates by men aged under 64 per 100,000	27.364	8.626	12.655	65.068
Suicide rates by went aged under 64 per 100,000	9.599	1.889	2.544	18.630
Suicide rates by all aged over 65 per 100,000	38.391	11.729	15.541	88.506
Suicide rates by men aged over 65 per 100,000	48.664	13.419	15.763	130.882
Suicide rates by women aged over 65 per 100,000	31.349	12.897	4.000	91.429
Per capita expenditure for public investment (log)	12.693	0.314	11.561	13.573
Per capita expenditure for unemployment relief (log)	2.062	7.088	-13.340	9.757
Per capita expenditure for social welfare (log)	10.040	0.442	8.894	10.984
Per capita expenditure for income assistance (log)	9.387	0.581	8.246	10.835
Per capita expenditure for child welfare (log)	11.992	0.481	10.867	13.079
Per capita expenditure for senior welfare (log)	12.004	0.280	11.246	12.894
Per capita expenditure for public health (log)	10.765	0.269	10.152	11.529
Per capita income (log)	14.767	0.172	14.297	15.380
Unemployment rate	0.040	0.015	0.014	0.123
Gini coefficient	0.222	0.016	0.183	0.302
Fiscal strength index	0.472	0.227	0.197	1.640
Rate of households receiving public assistance per 1,000	8.846	5.620	1.771	39.267
Rate of individuals receiving employment insurance benefits per 1,000	30.188	11.269	6.224	85.940
Divorce rate per 1,000	1.583	0.433	0.790	2.940
Rate of single-female-parent households per 1,000	14.083	3.532	8.918	30.959
Rate of elderly one-person households per 1,000	54.153	23.156	12.284	135.087
Population size (log)	14.492	0.723	13.311	16.354
Urbanization rate	0.490	0.185	0.234	0.994
Proportion population aged 15 and below	0.175	0.032	0.113	0.293
Proportion population aged 65 and over	0.160	0.045	0.066	0.275
N	1,175			

Note The statistics are based on the panel data of 47 prefectures between 1982 and 2006. We transformed the suicide rates into a natural log in our regression analysis

mental illness to receive more support, which may lower the risks of these patients.[3]

In Eq. (1), $\mathbf{w}_{it}$ refers to socioeconomic characteristics of each prefecture for each year, all of which are likely to affect both the suicide rate and the formation of government policies. We will not be able to determine whether the changes in the policies of our interest affected the suicide rate or if changes in socioeconomic characteristics affected the suicide rate unless we controlled for the effects of those

[3]According to the police data discussed earlier, of 15,802 suicide victims whose reasons and motive have been clarified in the year 2010, 7,020 people died by suicide due to depression and 2,637 people due to schizophrenia or other mental disorders.

characteristics. For example, suppose a prefecture where the unemployment rate went up. As a response to recession in this prefecture, the prefectural government was likely to increase public investments so as to improve the economic conditions and ultimately reduce the number of jobless people. If this is true, the amount of public investments will be larger in a year with a higher unemployment rate, while it will be smaller in a year with a lower unemployment rate. Furthermore, the unemployment rate is shown to have a direct positive relationship with the suicide rate, regardless of the amount of public investments by the government (see Chap. 2). Taken together, the suicide rate might decrease as a result increased public investments in a given year, while it might increase as a result of a higher unemployment rate that leads to a larger amount of public investments. This means that public investment's effect of lowering the suicide rate may be offset by the unemployment rate's effect of boosting the suicide rate. Thus, unless we took into consideration the effect of the unemployment rate in our analysis, we were not able to identify the exact relationship between public investments and the suicide rate. To address this problem, we controlled the effect of unemployment rates in our regression analysis. This approach is equivalent to examining the relationship between public investment and suicide rates in years with a low unemployment rate (such as under 2%) and in years with a high unemployment rate (2% or over) separately. In this approach, because the unemployment rate remains almost at a constant level within each analysis, we can control for the level of the unemployment rate and then reveal the relationship between public investments and the suicide rate more accurately. Note that the same problem can occur with other socioeconomic characteristics that can affect public policies and the suicide rate, aside from the unemployment rate.

The socioeconomic characteristics of prefectures in $\mathbf{w}_{it}$ includes income per capita, overall unemployment rate, Gini coefficient, financial strength index, rate of those receiving public assistance, rate of those receiving employment insurance benefits, divorce rate, rate of single-female-parent households, percent of elderly one-person households, population size, degree of urbanization, and percent of population aged under 15 and population aged 65 and over, for each prefecture and each year. Income per capita equals the amount of taxable income divided by taxable population. The unemployment rate was obtained by dividing the number of totally unemployed persons by the labor force population. The Gini coefficient measures income inequality within each prefecture and was calculated using the annual income average of decile groups of all households. A higher Gini coefficient indicates greater income inequality. The rate of those receiving public assistance equals the number of welfare recipients per 1,000 people. The rate of those receiving employment insurance equals the number of recipients of employment insurance benefits per 1,000 persons insured for employment insurance benefits. The divorce rate was obtained by calculating the number of divorces per 1,000 people. The rate of single-female-parent households and that of elderly one-person households were obtained by calculating the number of single-female-parent households and the number of one-person households aged 65 and over per 1,000 households, respectively. The degree of urbanization was obtained by dividing the population living in densely populated areas by the total population. We used natural logs of the total population and income per capita in our regression analysis.

Data for the Gini coefficient, the unemployment rate, the number of single-female-parent households, the number of elderly one-person households, and the population living in densely populated areas were surveyed only once every 5 years. Therefore, we obtained the values for the years with no surveys by linear interpolation.[4] Because the interpolated values may contain errors, we need to be careful when interpreting the estimated results.[5]

An increase in per-capita income is expected to lower the suicide rate, whereas the higher unemployment rate is expected to increase the suicide rate. The rate of recipients of income assistance is included to control for the effects of the area's economic conditions, but an increase or decrease in this ratio may be directly associated with the suicide rate. This is because if the rate of those receiving income assistance goes up, it means that many more people are trapped in poverty and would receive financial support. The financial strength index was used to measure the financial conditions of each prefecture. It can also serve as an indicator of how much the prefecture can afford to allocate to unemployment relief and welfare policies from its financial resources. Furthermore, an increase in the divorce rate, the rate of single-female-parent households, the rate of recipients of employment insurance benefits, and the rate of elderly one-person households may lead to an increase in the suicide rate. The rate of single-female-parent households was used as a control variable when analyzing the suicide rate among those younger than 65, and the ratio of elderly one-person households is used similarly when analyzing the suicide rate among those aged 65 and over. These data sets were all obtained from the "System of Social and Demographic Statistics of Japan, the basic data for prefectures (1975–2008)" provided by the Statistics Bureau, Ministry of Internal Affairs and Communications.[6] The descriptive statistics are compiled in Table 1.

---

[4]In terms of the annual income average of decile groups of all households, we used the quinquennial data from 1979 onward. We calculated the values for 2005 and 2006 based on the trends from 1999 and 2004. For other variables, we used the quinquennial data from 1980 onward. We used values calculated based on the trends from 2000 to 2005 as the data for 2006.

[5]We must be careful when interpreting the variable that may accompany sudden fluctuations in circumstance, such as household income and the number of single-female-parent households. To see what effects the interpolated data had on the estimated results, we first re-estimated the model after removing the interpolated variables from the model. Next, we re-estimated the model by removing the data for 2005 and 2006. Lastly, for the overall unemployment rate, we re-estimated the model by using the overall unemployment rates in 10 areas calculated by the Labor Force Survey and aggregating the other data by area (1983–2006). Because we were able to obtain results similar to those presented in Chap. 3 for all the additional analyses, we believe that the analysis results presented in this chapter are robust.

[6]The data were provided by the Statistical Information Institute for Consulting and Analysis as data for purchase. We referred to the National Economic Accounting published by the Cabinet Office for income of prefectural residents prior to 1996.

Lastly, φ_t in Eq. (1) represents the year effects, while ρ_i represents the prefecture-fixed effects unique to each prefecture. By including the year effects, we could control for the effects of annual socioeconomic fluctuations at the national level, such as the effects of macroeconomic policies and business cycle that might affect the entire country. By including the prefecture-fixed effects, we could control for the effects of time-invariant characteristics of prefectures, such as the effects of social norms related to suicide, and climate and geographic conditions.

The inclusion of the prefecture-fixed effects in Eq. (1) means that we exploited changes in the economic and welfare policies and the suicide rate within each prefecture. For example, in the case of Hokkaido presented in Fig. 1, the amount of expenditures for economic policies peaked in the latter half of the 1990s. If an increase in the amount of expenditures for economic policies tends to accompany a decline in the suicide rate, then the suicide rate in the latter half of the 1990s is expected to be lower than that in other periods, such as the 1980s or the 2000s. If such a tendency is observed not only in Hokkaido but in all 47 prefectures, the amount of expenditures and the suicide rate will be estimated to have a negative relationship in general. Therefore, the estimated coefficients reported in the next section were not obtained through direct comparison of different prefectures. We also added $\gamma_i T$ to the model to take into consideration the effects of linear trends unique to each prefecture.

4 Estimated Results

This section presents the estimated results on the effects of economic and welfare policies on the suicide rate of each population group. As discussed earlier, the effects of economic and welfare policies may vary by gender and age. Therefore, we estimated six separate regression models by using the suicide rates of six subpopulation groups.

Table 2 shows the estimated results for the suicide rates of men and women aged 64 and under, while Table 3 shows the results for the suicide rates among men and women aged 65 and over. The prefecture-fixed effects, the year-fixed effects, and the prefecture-specific time trends are not shown in the tables but were included in all the models. Standard errors were clustered at the prefecture. The number of observations is 1,175. We used the panel unit root test developed by Levin et al. (2002) and confirmed that all the dependent variables were stationary.

Table 2 Economic and welfare policies and suicide rates by population under 64

	(1) Total	(2) Male	(3) Female
Per capita expenditure for public investment (log)	−0.117** (0.045)	−0.124** (0.050)	−0.119 (0.085)
Per capita expenditure for unemployment relief (log)	−0.001* (0.001)	−0.002** (0.001)	0.000 (0.001)
Per capita expenditure for social welfare (log)	0.002 (0.054)	0.036 (0.063)	−0.089 (0.086)
Per capita expenditure for income assistance (log)	0.065 (0.085)	0.049 (0.096)	0.083 (0.114)
Per capita expenditure for child welfare (log)	0.097 (0.104)	0.123 (0.135)	0.042 (0.158)
Per capita expenditure for public health (log)	−0.005 (0.039)	−0.031 (0.048)	0.073 (0.081)
Per capita income (log)	−0.146 (0.157)	−0.185 (0.192)	−0.016 (0.172)
Unemployment rate	6.534** (1.673)	8.680** (1.940)	−1.357 (3.405)
Gini coefficient	−0.361 (0.678)	−0.652 (0.759)	0.598 (1.249)
Fiscal strength index	0.037 (0.070)	−0.002 (0.084)	0.091 (0.109)
Rate of households receiving public assistance per 1,000	−0.009** (0.003)	−0.011** (0.004)	−0.000 (0.006)
Rate of individuals receiving employment insurance benefits per 1,000	0.002 (0.001)	0.001 (0.001)	0.002 (0.002)
Divorce rate per 1,000	0.152** (0.063)	0.127 (0.080)	0.216** (0.093)
Rate of single-female-parent households per 1,000	0.021 (0.013)	0.022 (0.016)	0.027 (0.020)
Population size (log)	0.272 (0.428)	0.251 (0.554)	−0.181 (1.006)
Urbanization rate	−1.219 (0.913)	−1.899* (1.007)	0.278 (1.272)
Proportion population aged 15 and below	−0.419 (1.311)	−0.093 (1.279)	−0.148 (2.823)
Proportion population aged 65 and over	1.392 (1.832)	−0.277 (2.286)	4.655 (2.972)
R^2	0.909	0.916	0.517
N	1,175		

Note Table entries are linear regression estimates with standard errors in parentheses. The standard errors are clustered by prefecture. The outcome variables are the suicide rates per 100,000 in a natural log. All models include the prefecture- and year-fixed effects and the prefecture-specific linear time trends

$^{*}p < 0.10$, $^{**}p < 0.05$, $^{***}p < 0.01$ (two-tailed tests)

Table 3 Economic and welfare policies and suicide rates by population over 65

	(1) Total	(2) Male	(3) Female
Per capita expenditure for public investment (log)	−0.061 (0.065)	−0.019 (0.094)	−0.087 (0.083)
Per capita expenditure for unemployment relief (log)	0.002 (0.001)	0.002 (0.002)	0.002 (0.002)
Per capita expenditure for social welfare (log)	0.112 (0.093)	0.209* (0.106)	0.006 (0.126)
Per capita expenditure for income assistance (log)	−0.245* (0.134)	−0.217 (0.171)	−0.259 (0.160)
Per capita expenditure for senior welfare (log)	−0.060 (0.102)	−0.066 (0.110)	−0.093 (0.137)
Per capita expenditure for public health (log)	−0.026 (0.078)	0.010 (0.094)	−0.069 (0.106)
Per capita income (log)	−0.174 (0.198)	−0.046 (0.216)	−0.317 (0.331)
Unemployment rate	−0.334 (2.645)	1.861 (3.322)	−2.906 (4.285)
Gini coefficient	−0.102 (1.245)	−0.891 (1.486)	0.726 (1.488)
Fiscal strength index	0.046 (0.160)	0.009 (0.181)	0.124 (0.217)
Rate of households receiving public assistance per 1,000	0.007 (0.006)	−0.001 (0.008)	0.014 (0.009)
Rate of individuals receiving employment insurance benefits per 1,000	−0.001 (0.002)	0.001 (0.002)	−0.004 (0.003)
Divorce rate per 1,000	0.054 (0.091)	0.115 (0.108)	−0.017 (0.096)
Rate of elderly one-person households per 1,000	−0.004 (0.009)	0.002 (0.013)	−0.014 (0.009)
Population size (log)	−1.122 (0.953)	−1.366 (0.970)	−0.832 (1.404)
Urbanization rate	0.734 (1.406)	2.116 (1.938)	−1.688 (1.870)
Proportion population aged under 15 and below	2.139 (2.317)	3.098 (3.110)	0.907 (2.571)
Proportion population aged 65 and over	−4.071 (3.865)	−5.213 (5.685)	−2.371 (3.211)
R^2	0.822	0.633	0.828
N	1,175		

Note Table entries are linear regression estimates with standard errors in parentheses. The standard errors are clustered by prefecture. The outcome variables are the suicide rates per 100,000 in a natural log. All models include the prefecture- and year-fixed effects and the prefecture-specific linear time trends

$^{*}p < 0.10$, $^{**}p < 0.05$, $^{***}p < 0.01$ (two-tailed tests)

Table 2 suggests that there is a negative relationship between the amount of public investments and the suicide rate.[7] The coefficients associated with this variable were estimated to be negative in all three columns, both with the suicide rates by the total population and with the gender subgroups. Yet the estimated coefficients are statistically significant at the 0.05 level only in the models with the suicide rate among the total population and men. The effect size of public investments appears to be nontrivial. According to the result in the column (1) of Table 2, for example, if the amount of public investments increased by 10%, the suicide rate among men and women combined per 100,000 people was estimated to go down by about 1.1%. Public investments are likely to affect the suicide rate by lowering the unemployment rate and increasing the income level in the prefecture. The effects of these two variables have been controlled for in our regression analysis and therefore an increase in the amount of public investments might have an impact on the suicide rates through additional mechanisms other than the improvement in these economic variables.

As similar to the effect of public investments, the relationship between the expenditure for unemployment relief and the suicide rate among the population aged under 64 is also negative, though it is statistically significant only at the 0.10 level. Our additional analysis using the gender-specific suicide rates in Columns (2) and (3) indicates that this effect was driven primarily by the lowered suicide rate among men. The coefficient of the expenditure for unemployment relief is significant at the 0.05 level in column (2), while it is no longer significant among women aged 64 and under in column (3). This is probably because those who benefit from unemployment relief in Japan are mostly men.

Interestingly, the amount of expenditures for welfare-related policies, such as the expenditure for income assistance, has no statistically significant relationship with the suicide rate among the population aged 64 and under. Yet, the higher ratio of recipients of income assistance is linked with a decline in the male suicide rate. Because the economic conditions, such as the income level and unemployment rate within the prefecture, were controlled for in the model, if more people in need of income assistance begin to receive such assistance, then the suicide rate is expected to show a decline. Taken together, the estimation results in Table 2 indicate that expanding economic policies brought about a significant influence on suicide prevention for men younger than 64, but reinforcing welfare policies also might play an important role.

---

[7]Because the amount of public investments is not an exogenous variable, it is difficult to discuss the causal relationship in the estimation using the fixed effect model. We also performed an additional analysis using the GMM estimator to estimate the dynamic panel models by Arellano and Bond (1991), but we obtained results similar to those presented in Tables 2 and 3. Upon doing so, we inserted the suicide rate and the amount of public investments from a quarter before as well as all the variables included in the estimated equation (except for the amount of public investments) into the right side of the equation and used the data from two quarters before as manipulated variables. In this estimation, we only used the data from 1984 to 2006, because there are some missing values in the suicide rates of the year 1981 in some prefectures. The estimation was made using the xtabond2 of Stata through the one-step method.

When focusing on the control variables, we find several interesting patterns. First, the higher unemployment rate (especially among men) accompanied an increase in the suicide rate, which matches findings from previous studies. Second, the income inequality within the prefecture, as measured by the Gini coefficient, had no direct relationship with the suicide rate. Third, the higher divorce rate accompanied an increase in the suicide rate among women. Fourth, the degree of urbanization related to the male suicide rate; if a prefecture was more urbanized, the suicide rate tended to go down. Because the prefecture-level fixed-effect was included in the presented model, these results were not obtained through comparison between a more-urbanized prefecture and a less-urbanized prefecture.

Table 3 examines the influence of these variables on the suicide rates by those aged 65 and over. The amount of public investments, which had a negative relationship with the suicide rate among the population aged under 64, had no significant relationship with the suicide rate among the population aged 65 and over. This is probably because those aged 65 and over did not directly benefit from public investments, such as expansion of employment opportunities. Because many in this generation are likely to be non-workers, the expenditure for unemployment relief was also unrelated to the suicide rate among the elderly.

Turning to the welfare-related variables, we find a negative relationship between the per-capita amount of income assistance and the suicide rate among the total population aged 65 and over (significant at the 0.10 level). This result contrasts with the result obtained from the analysis of the data of the population aged under 64. We also find that the greater expenditure for social welfare accompanied an increase in the suicide rate among men aged 65 and over. However, this should be interpreted as that the expenditure for social welfare will increase when the suicide rate is high, rather than increasing the expenditure for social welfare itself will boost the suicide rate.

5 Summary

In this chapter, we used the data on economic and welfare policies adopted by local governments to examine how they affect the suicide rate. Our analysis using the prefecture-level data from 1982 to 2006 suggests that economic and welfare policies had an important relationship with the suicide rates of the regions. The amount of public investments and unemployment relief had a negative relationship with suicide rates; this relationship was especially evident in the case of men aged under 64. The results also indicated the possibility that the expansion of welfare policies, such as income assistance, would lower the suicide rate among the population aged 65 and over. The suicide rate among the population aged under 64 had a strong association with economic policies, whereas welfare policies might be more effective than economic policies in lowering the suicide rate among the population aged 65 and over. In other words, our findings indicate that reinforcement of income assistance is more important for the population aged 65 and over, which means that different suicide prevention strategies must be taken according to the age composition of the population of each prefecture.

Overall, our analysis indicates that economic and welfare policies are likely to play an important role as suicide prevention measures. Yet it may not be realistic to simply reinforce economic and welfare policies to reduce the suicide rate. However, the results of the analysis presented in this chapter show that implementation of policies that would mitigate economic insecurity, whatever the form that may take, could be one of the prescriptions for lowering the suicide rate.

References

Arellano, M., & Bond, S. (1991). Some tests ofspecification for panel data: monte carlo evidence and an application to employment equations. *Review of Economic Studies, 58*, 277–297.

Kondo H. (2008). Syakaishihonseibi ni okeruseijikeizaigakuteki sokumen. *Financial Revue 2008*, 68-92.

Levin A., Chien-Fu L., & Chia-Shang J. C.(2002). Unit Root Tests in Panel Data: Asymptotic and Finite-Sample Properties. *Journal of Econometrics, 108*, 1–24.

The Statistics Bureau, Ministry of Internal Affairs and Communications, the Government of Japan. (Various years). System of Social and Demographic Statistics of Japan, the basic data for prefectures (1975 to 2008).

Chapter 9
The Effect of Government Suicide Prevention Programs

1 Introduction

Suicide poses a serious challenge on all modern societies and governments are expected to play a major role in its prevention. The previous two chapters showed that policy choices of the government have a crucial influence on the risk of suicide among the population. Yet our measures of policy choices, such as government partisanship in Chap. 7 and economic and welfare policies in Chap. 8, are not a direct and immediate suicide prevention effort. They were hypothesized to affect the lives of vulnerable population in society and thus their suicidal risks.

This chapter highlights the importance of government suicide prevention efforts that directly affect the risks of suicide among vulnerable population. First, we evaluated the effectiveness of comprehensive suicide prevention programs developed by the national government in 21 Organization for Economic Co-operation and Development (OECD) nations by using panel data between 1980 and 2004. Second, we examined the effectiveness of suicide prevention programs by subnational governments by using panel data of 47 prefectures between 2000 and 2013 in Japan. Third, we examined the effectiveness of public awareness campaigns by using panel data between 2010 and 2012 from Nagoya City in Japan. Overall, our analysis demonstrates that the government's effort helps to reduce suicide rates.

The content of this chapter was based on the published articles: "The Effect of Government Suicide Prevention Programs on Suicide Rates." *Social Science & Medicine* 73: 1395–1400, 2011; "The Effect of Public Awareness Campaigns on Suicides: Evidence from Nagoya, Japan." *Journal of Affective Disorders* 152–154: 526–529, 2014.

Y. Sawada et al., *Economic Analysis of Suicide Prevention*, Creating a Society for All, DOI 10.1007/978-981-10-1500-7_9

2 The Effect of National Suicide Prevention Programs on Suicide Rates in 21 OECD Nations

A number of countries have developed comprehensive suicide prevention programs as a collective political effort. According to the WHO European monitoring surveys on national suicide prevention programs, 17 of 37 member states that responded to the surveys have launched national suicide prevention initiatives as of 2004 (World Health Organization Regional Office for Europe, Copenhagen 2002). Among those 17 nations, Finland was the first country to launch a nationwide suicide prevention program in 1992 (De Leo and Evans 2003). Comprehensive national programs for suicide prevention are also seen outside of Europe. Australia and New Zealand established national programs to prevent suicide among young people in the 1990 s (De Leo and Evans 2003; Taylor et al. 1997). In Asia, Japan and South Korea enacted legislation in the 2000s that sets up a comprehensive suicide prevention program to tackle the growing problem of suicide, according to the Japanese Cabinet Office and the Korean Ministry of Health and Welfare.

Despite the prevalence of nationwide suicide prevention programs around the world, no prior research has offered a systematic test of their effectiveness using cross-national data. Do nationwide programs for suicide prevention reduce the suicide rate? To answer this question, we evaluated whether government intervention through a comprehensive suicide prevention program had a notable impact on the total suicide rate as well as the age- and gender-specific suicide rates in subsequent years, using panel data from 21 developed nations between 1980 and 2004.

Table 1 National suicide prevention programs as of 2004

Nations with a national suicide prevention program
Australia (1995, expanded in 1999)
Denmark (1998)
Finland (1992)
France (1998)
Germany (2003)
Ireland (2001, expanded in 2005)
New Zealand (1998, expanded in 2004)
Norway (1994)
Sweden (1995)
United Kingdom (2002)
United States (2001)
Nations without a national suicide prevention program
Austria
Belgium
Canada
Greece, Italy
Japan (initiated in 2006)
Netherlands
Portugal, Spain
Switzerland

Table 1 lists the countries included in our analysis by the presence of a nationwide suicide prevention program as of 2004. If countries "have countrywide integrated activities carried out by government bodies," we coded countries as having a national program for suicide prevention using an elite survey conducted by the World Health Organization Regional Office for Europe Copenhagen (2002, 8). As reported in Table 1, 11 nations had nationwide programs for suicide prevention as of 2004. Austria developed a national plan for suicide prevention in 2000, but it has not been approved and implemented by the national government. Belgium has an official document on suicide prevention but conducts a comprehensive program only in the Flemish region (World Health Organization Regional Office for Europe, Copenhagen, 2002). Ireland initiated a prevention program when the government developed the "Health Strategy" in 2001, which it subsequently expanded into a comprehensive program in 2005. The Netherlands developed a national policy on suicide prevention in 1989 (Taylor et al. 1997), but the expert survey by the WHO Regional Office for Europe (2002) suggests that the government had implemented no action at the national level as of 2002. In this chapter, we followed the definition of the expert survey by WHO. Both Australia and New Zealand initiated prevention programs for youth and expanded them for the entire population later. Both Finland and Norway completed their national programs in 1998, but we assume that they have a spill-over effect on suicide rates after 1998 because the infrastructure for suicide prevention remains. Thus, we treated Finland and Norway as having suicide prevention programs after 1992 and 1994, respectively.

These national suicide prevention strategies shared common themes. They included "public education, responsible media reporting, school-based programs, detection and treatment of depression and other mental disorders, attention to those abusing alcohol and drugs, attention to individuals experiencing somatic illness, enhanced access to mental health services, improvement in assessment of attempted suicide, postvention, crisis intervention, work and unemployment policy, training of health professionals, and reduced access to lethal means" (Anderson and Jenkins 2005, 249).

At the same time, specific components and the focus of the nationwide suicide prevention programs could differ across countries. Taylor et al. (1997) summarized the differences in the components of the national programs across five countries with respect to the degree of community involvement, the targeted demographic groups, the agencies that were involved, and the themes of intervention. While we anticipated that the differences in the national programs played an important role because some prevention methods are more useful than others (Mann et al. 2005), this part of the analysis did not explore these differences. Instead, our focus lied on testing whether the initiation of any comprehensive program by the government caused any change in the rate of death by suicide.

2.1 Data and Method

Our analysis used panel data from 21 OECD countries between 1980 and 2004. Our dataset included Australia, Austria, Belgium, Canada, Denmark, Finland, France,

Germany, Greece, Ireland, Italy, Japan, Netherlands, New Zealand, Norway, Portugal, Spain, Sweden, Switzerland, the United Kingdom, and the United States. These countries and years were chosen on the basis of the availability of data. Data on national suicide prevention programs and other control variables for our regression analysis were not available for other OECD countries (i.e., Chile, Czech Republic, Estonia, Hungary, Iceland, Israel, South Korea, Luxembourg, Mexico, Poland, Slovak Republic, Slovenia, and Turkey) and non-OECD countries. The data on suicide rates were unavailable for some nations after 2004. The total number of observations included in our analysis was 525, representing the data of 21 countries over a period of 25 years.

We estimated a statistical model by assuming that suicide rates in each country were determined as a linear function of the presence of national suicide prevention programs and other time-specific factors such as macroeconomic and political conditions and socio-demographic characteristics in each nation. Then, the model to be estimated is written as:

$$s_{jt} = \beta[Prevention]_{jt} + \lambda w_{jt} + \eta_j T + \phi_t + \rho_j + \varepsilon_{jt} \quad (1)$$

where S_{jt} denotes the suicide rate in country j in year t. $[Prevention]_{jt}$ is an indicator variable that equals 1 after country j has a national suicide prevention program in place in year t, and 0 otherwise. The variable equals 0 if a country initiated no nationwide suicide prevention program between 1980 and 2004. If national programs for suicide prevention had an anticipated effect of reducing suicide rates, β associated with $[Prevention]_{jt}$ in Eq. (1) should be negative. The vector w_{jt} in (1) includes all control variables that capture time-varying characteristics of country j in year t that can affect suicide rates. Such variables include the macroeconomic conditions (e.g., unemployment rate), government partisanship, welfare policies, and socio-demographic characteristics of a county. They are explained in more detail below. ρ_j is the country-fixed effect, while ϕ_t is the year-fixed effect. ε_{jt} is a country-year-specific error term. We also include the country-specific time trend $\eta_j T$ in the model. All time-invariant characteristics of country j are captured by the country-fixed effect, ρ_j.

Time-invariant characteristics include stable and potentially unobservable cultural norms and beliefs that could be related to suicide rates and suicide prevention strategies. Since we included the fixed effect for each country in Eq. (1), our estimation exploited variations within each country. In other words, we tested whether there was a statistically meaningful difference in the suicide rates before and after the implementation of suicide-prevention programs. Those countries without a nationwide prevention program were included as a control group. Thus, the comparison was not made across countries but, rather, within each country.

Any time-specific shock was captured by the year-fixed effect, ϕ_t. Year-fixed effects could capture the effects of the global availability of antipsychotic drugs and antidepressants, global economic depression, and any other major events that occurred in a particular year that might be associated with the implementation of national suicide prevention strategies and suicide rates. The omission of the year-fixed effect would cause a bias in the coefficient of primary interest.

The suicide rate, S_{jt} equals the number of suicides per 100,000 persons in country j in year t. We compute the suicide rate for the (1) total population; (2) total male population; (3) total female population; (4) male population under 24 years old; (5) male population from ages 25 to 64 years; (6) male population ages 65 years and over; (7) female population under age 24 years; (8) female population from ages 25 to 64 years; and (9) female population over ages 65 years and over. In the following analysis, we used the total suicide rate as well as the age- and gender-specific rates. The impact of national suicide prevention programs might differ across different age and gender groups because demographic groups with higher suicide rates such as men and the elderly were more likely to be affected by the implementation of comprehensive national programs (De Leo 2002) and also because some national programs specifically targeted high-risk groups (e.g., young men). The data for suicide and population size were obtained from the WHO Mortality Database as of July 2010. Data on the number of suicides were unavailable for some years in a few countries. We linearly interpolated values for those years. Levin, Lin, and Chu's unit root test with a trend variable for panel data (Levin et al. 2002) indicates that most of our dependent variables were stationary.

In Eq. (1), $[Prevention]_{\mathrm{jt}}$ is our key explanatory variable. The coefficient associated with this variable measures whether there was a statistically meaningful difference in the suicide rates before and after the implementation of national suicide-prevention programs. This variable takes a value of 1 when a country j has a suicide prevention program in year t. To code this variable, we identified the beginning year of the program by consulting several sources such as De Leo and Evans (2003), Taylor et al. (1997), and the World Health Organization Regional Office for Europe, Copenhagen (2002). When no relevant information was found in these documents, we consulted official documents published by the national governments. It is challenging to identify the exact year of the initial implementation of some national programs. In this chapter, we defined a national program as having begun when the respective government first published an official document or enacted a law that set up a nationwide strategy for suicide prevention. In the subsequent section, we conducted a robustness check to assess whether our coding of the prevention programs derived the estimated results reported.

As control variables, the vector w_{jt} in (1) includes variables that capture the time-varying characteristics of country j that are likely to be correlated with the initiation of the national suicide prevention program and the suicide rates. Specifically, w_{jt} includes three sets of variables. The first set of variables represents the political features of country j in year t, such as government partisanship and welfare policies. We measured government partisanship using the share of cabinet seats of leftist parties and Christian Democratic parties. The cabinet shares of these parties have a strong impact on the formation of welfare policies (Allan and Scruggs 2004; Huber and Stephens 2001) and the level of human well-being (Radcliff 2001). The cabinet shares of leftist and Christian Democratic parties range from 0 to 1, where larger values denote greater cabinet shares. The data pertaining to cabinet seats came from the Comparative Parties Data Set developed by Duane Swank. Swank classified parties in 21 OECD nations into left-leaning, right-leaning, Christian Democratic, and center parties using expert judgment developed by Castles and Mair (1984).

In addition to government partisanship, we also took into account the level and generosity of welfare provisions. Prior research has found that the level and generosity of welfare provisions increase the well-being of citizens (Di Tella et al. 2003; Minoiu and Andres2008). The level of welfare provision was measured by total government social expenditures as a percentage of the gross domestic product (GDP). These social expenditures are spent on benefits with a social purpose, such as family assistance, support for children, cash benefits for low-income households, employment training, support for the elderly, and disability benefits. Following Di Tella and MacCulloch (2002), the level of welfare generosity was measured by unemployment benefit replacement rates that are equal to the unemployment benefit entitlement divided by the corresponding wage. Higher values denote higher replacement rates. Data on the replacement rates are available only for odd-numbered years; thus, we used a linear interpolation for even-numbered years. The data on government expenditures and unemployment benefit replacement rates were obtained from the OECD Stat Extracts (OECD 2010).

The second set of control variables captures the economic characteristics of country *j* in year *t* such as the growth rate of real GDP per capita in constant U.S. dollars, the unemployment rate, and the inflation rate. These macroeconomic variables are likely to be correlated with the well-being of citizens (Di Tella et al. 2003) and might affect the initiation of suicide prevention programs. The growth rate of real GDP per capita was obtained from the Penn World Table 6.3 (Heston, Summers, and Aten 2009). The inflation rate was measured by an annual change in the consumer price index. The unemployment rate was measured by the percentage of the unemployed in the total labor force. The data for the inflation rate and the unemployment rate came from the OECD Stat Extracts.

Other control variables include socio-demographic variables such as the level of economic development, economic inequality, union density, female labor participation, divorce rate, the percent of the dependent population, and the size of the total population. The level of economic development was measured by real GDP per capita in constant dollars. The data came from the Penn World Table 6.3. The level of economic inequality was measured by the Gini coefficient. It ranges from 0 to 1, where the larger values denote a higher level of economic inequality. The data for the Gini coefficient came from the Standardized World Income Inequality Database (Solt 2009). The union density was measured by the percentage of union members among wage and salary earners. The female labor participation was measured by the size of the female civilian working population divided by the total size of the female labor force. The divorce rate is the number of divorces per 100,000 persons. Data for the last three variables come from the OECD Stat Extracts. The percent of dependent population is equal to the sum of percentages of the populations under age 15 years and age 65 years and over. The population data come from the WHO Mortality Database. We took a natural log of the real GDP per capita and the total population size for our regression analysis. All summary statistics are presented in Table 2.

Table 2 Summary statistics

	Mean	SD	Min	Max
Suicide rate: total	14.397	6.439	2.940	31.583
Suicide rate: male	21.352	9.390	4.602	49.308
Suicide rate: female	7.728	4.109	0.868	22.317
Suicide rate: male, age under 24 years	7.462	4.027	1.241	20.985
Suicide rate: male, age 25–64 years	26.616	12.207	5.041	66.261
Suicide rate: male, age over 65 years	38.933	19.314	8.388	93.660
Suicide rate: female, age under 24 years	2.000	1.033	0.138	6.137
Suicide rate: female, age 25–64 years	9.562	5.103	1.010	32.316
Suicide rate: female, age over 65 years	13.127	8.992	1.231	44.147
Left party	0.359	0.392	0.000	1.000
Christian Democratic party	0.127	0.224	0.000	1.000
Social expenditure	0.206	0.053	0.102	0.358
Benefit replacement rate	0.286	0.129	0.003	0.649
GDP growth rate	0.020	0.024	-0.089	0.112
Unemployment rate	0.076	0.040	0.002	0.242
Inflation rate	0.025	0.014	-0.009	0.085
Log GDP per capita	10.065	0.253	9.263	10.697
Economic inequality	0.286	0.043	0.003	0.392
Female labor participation	0.603	0.113	0.320	0.809
Union density	0.395	0.204	0.080	0.839
Divorce rate	2.038	0.995	0.000	5.300
Dependent population	0.335	0.018	0.299	0.412
Log population size	9.752	1.219	8.049	12.590
Number of Observations	525			

All variables except for the following are measured in proportion from 0 to 1: Suicide rates equal the number of death by suicide per 100,000 persons

Log GDP per capita equals the log of GDP per capita in constant U.S. dollars. Economic inequality equals the Gini coefficient

Log population size equals the log of the total population

Divorce rate equals the number of divorces per 100,000 person

2.2 Results

Table 3 reports the results of the estimation. To address the potential heterogeneity and autocorrelation within each nation and contemporaneous correlation across nations, standard errors are estimated by using Driscoll and Kraay's (1998) covariance matrix estimator. In column (1), the suicide rates of the entire population in each country were regressed on the indicator variable of national suicide prevention programs as well as on political variables, macroeconomic variables, and the socio-demographic characteristics of countries. The negative coefficient associated with national suicide prevention programs indicates that, after the

Table 3 Effect of national suicide prevention programs on suicide rates

	(1)	(2)	(3)	(4)	(5)	(6)	(7)	(8)	(9)
	Total	Male	Female	Male, under 24	Male, 25-64	Male, over 65	Female, under 24	Female, 25-64	Female, over 65
National suicide prevention program	−0.886* (0.386)	−1.427* (0.513)	−0.374 (0.215)	−1.330* (0.500)	−0.999 (0.603)	−3.457* (1.030)	−0.276* (0.088)	0.026 (0.323)	−1.709* (0.608)
Left party	−0.663* (0.276)	−0.849* (0.293)	−0.504* (0.144)	−0.047 (0.238)	−1.376* (0.370)	−0.027 (0.573)	−0.029 (0.126)	−0.715* (0.179)	−0.519 (0.297)
Christian Democratic party	−1.191* (0.482)	−1.224* (0.457)	−1.200* (0.245)	−0.973* (0.379)	−1.797* (0.712)	−0.097 (1.017)	−0.293* (0.119)	−1.526* (0.384)	−2.261* (0.574)
Social expenditure	15.217 (9.666)	22.029* (7.483)	9.113* (2.615)	6.872 (4.743)	29.800* (10.675)	−12.168 (10.623)	2.209 (3.008)	11.512* (3.995)	9.353* (4.232)
Benefit replacement rate	0.924 (3.589)	3.966 (2.263)	−2.032 (0.981)	4.351* (1.620)	4.375 (3.196)	−1.079 (5.789)	−0.927 (0.772)	−1.413 (1.274)	−5.932* (2.565)
GDP growth rate	−4.655 (3.211)	−9.265 (4.462)	−0.202 (1.811)	−3.422 (2.830)	−13.615 (7.109)	−3.475 (7.040)	−0.768 (1.602)	−1.058 (2.625)	5.564 (3.303)
Unemployment rate	−4.688 (8.998)	−5.756 (9.758)	−3.705 (4.759)	−0.935 (4.899)	−6.971 (14.201)	1.656 (11.312)	−4.009 (2.784)	−2.353 (7.241)	−2.802 (6.184)
Inflation rate	5.134 (8.174)	7.914 (7.592)	2.368 (2.301)	−3.627 (6.452)	15.863 (12.402)	23.244 (17.655)	−1.278 (2.306)	9.775* (4.006)	−0.034 (6.394)
Economic inequality	−4.891 (3.285)	−9.347* (3.129)	−0.689 (1.149)	−2.728 (1.341)	−10.835* (4.532)	−14.673* (4.748)	1.361* (0.631)	0.555 (1.058)	-5.913 (3.363)
Log GDP per capita	-8.729 (5.117)	−13.866* (3.340)	−3.728* (1.325)	−5.641* (2.165)	−20.362* (4.475)	−10.872 (5.545)	−1.311 (0.784)	−5.123* (1.627)	−6.137 (3.826)
Union density	0.692 (4.491)	0.827 (5.901)	0.784 (1.874)	−5.438 (5.775)	2.908 (7.322)	9.289 (10.867)	−2.107 (1.582)	−0.606 (3.002)	7.879* (3.288)
Female labor participation	7.634 (5.140)	15.867* (3.378)	−0.307 (2.009)	22.383* (4.651)	14.053* (3.904)	−18.960 (10.153)	2.374 (1.547)	−1.926 (3.547)	−8.482 (4.744)

(continued)

Table 3 (continued)

	(1)	(2)	(3)	(4)	(5)	(6)	(7)	(8)	(9)
	Total	Male	Female	Male, under 24	Male, 25-64	Male, over 65	Female, under 24	Female, 25-64	Female, over 65
Divorce rate	1.289 (0.626)	2.128* (0.669)	0.498 (0.261)	0.440 (0.366)	2.881* (0.778)	3.298* (1.420)	0.089 (0.136)	0.814 (0.414)	0.402 (0.416)
Dependent population	−9.644 (23.658)	2.324 (17.595)	-21.332* (7.197)	−25.691* (8.414)	16.490 (26.080)	−0.028 (39.560)	−6.904* (2.984)	−15.029 (10.128)	−48.641* (19.794)
Log population size	2.443 (4.559)	0.990 (5.014)	3.413 (2.408)	−9.676* (3.240)	4.814 (5.981)	28.609* (9.192)	−1.306 (1.013)	4.607 (2.589)	12.366* (5.835)
Adjusted R^2	0.975	0.974	0.979	0.927	0.971	0.967	0.811	0.972	0.963

Table entities are fixed effects regression estimates and standard errors in parentheses
Standard errors are estimated by Driscoll and Kraay's (1998) covariance matrix estimator
Estimates are based on data from 21 OECD nations between 1980 and 2004
The dependent variables are the suicide rates
Country and year-fixed effects and country-specific time trends are included in the models
The number of observations is 525
*$p < 0.05$ (two-tailed tests)

government initiated a national program for suicide prevention, the overall suicide rates in the country decreased. The coefficient is statistically significant at the 0.05 level. The other control variables have no statistically significant impact on the suicide rates when the total suicide rates are analyzed.

The estimated coefficient associated with national suicide prevention programs in column (1) suggests that the number of suicides per 100,000 decreased by 0.886 after national programs for suicide prevention were initiated. This is a large effect because the average total suicide rate per 100,000 persons is 21, as reported in Table 2. This suggests that, since the nationwide programs for suicide prevention were initiated, countries with a population of 10 million people (e.g., Sweden) have seen the number of deaths by suicide decrease by 89 per year on average. In countries with 50 million people (e.g., the UK), the number of deaths by suicide decreased by 445; and in countries with more than 100 million people (e.g., Germany), an estimated 890 suicides were prevented because of the comprehensive national suicide prevention programs.

In columns (2)–(3), male and female suicide rates were analyzed separately. The suicide rates of males were estimated to have decreased after the government initiated a national suicide prevention program. In contrast, the national suicide prevention program had no statistically significant impact on the overall female suicide rates at the 0.05 level.

In columns (4)–(9), we analyzed the effect of the suicide prevention programs on the suicide rates of various age and gender groups. The most notable effect can be found among the elderly [columns (6) and (9)); column (6) indicates that suicide prevention programs were most effective in preventing suicides among the elderly male population. The number of suicides per 100,000 seniors decreased by about 3.5 after national programs for suicide prevention were initiated. Although the magnitude is slightly lower, the programs also have had a statistically significant impact on the suicide rate of senior women (column (9)). According to columns (4) and (7), the suicide prevention programs also had a negative impact on the suicide rates among populations younger than age 25 years. Interestingly, even among youth, the suicide rates of the male population were more responsive to the prevention programs than those of the female population, but their effectiveness was estimated to be statistically significant for both male and female young populations. By contrast, the suicide rates of working-age groups, regardless of gender, do not seem to have responded to the introduction of national prevention programs. According to columns (5) and (8), the estimated coefficients on the prevention program are indistinguishable from zero for both the male and female working-age groups.

2.3 *Discussion*

Our analysis evaluated how government-led comprehensive suicide prevention programs affected suicide rates in 21 OECD nations between 1980 and 2004. Our panel data analysis shows that the suicide rates became lower after the government initiated a nationwide suicide prevention program. The impact of the nationwide programs was particularly strong on the suicide rates of the youth and elderly. Notably, the suicide rates are not very high among the youth, yet the prevention programs in some countries such as Australia and New Zealand were indeed working. However, these strategies seem to have a limited effect on the suicide rates of working-age populations, and our analysis also suggests that suicide prevention strategies should target working-age populations more effectively. Although one may not be able to make a causal argument based on this analysis, the findings strongly suggest that a negative relationship existed between suicide rates and the introduction of suicide prevention programs.

One of the notable findings of this study was that the presence of national suicide prevention programs had a larger effect on the suicide rates of men than on those of women. We find two potential reasons as to why the effectiveness is asymmetrical across gender groups. First, some of the suicide prevention strategies included a goal to reduce access to firearms and/or to improve firearm education (e.g., in the United States and Sweden), and firearm suicide is much more common among men than among women (Ajdacic-Gross et al. 2008). Thus, male suicide rates were more likely to be affected by the effort to restrict access to firearms. Limiting access to firearms has been shown to reduce firearm suicides (e.g., Chapman et al. 2006; Baker and McPhedran 2006). Second, some of the national programs specifically targeted male subpopulations (e.g., in the United Kingdom and Ireland), such as young men, and these targeted efforts might have had intended consequences. However, these observations are somewhat speculative, and we need to wait for more refined analysis in the future to fully understand why the programs are most effective in reducing male suicide rates.

We conducted a few robustness checks of our analysis. First, we re-estimated the model by dropping one of the countries sequentially. This works as a check to see whether the coding of the prevention program for any particular country is driving the results reported in Table 3. The results were almost identical to those in Table 3. Second, because there are often various ways to define the implementation years of national programs, we used alternative definitions of the "year of implementation" and conducted the same analysis. For example, we coded Australia as having begun a national program in 1995 in the main analysis, but we used 1999 as the initial year in this robustness check because this was when the target population was expanded to include the entire population. The analysis using these alternative definitions yielded substantively similar results. Finally, we took a 1-year lag of the prevention program and re-estimated the model with the lagged indicator variable because the prevention program might not have had an immediate impact on the suicide rates in the first year. The results using the lag were similar to those shown in Table 3. These results are available upon request.

We also examined the presence of nonlinear trends by including quadratic and cubic terms of the country-specific time trend. According to the Akaike Information Criterion (AIC), the inclusion of those terms improves our model specification, but the new results do not differ from the original ones. Because our goal does not lie in approximating the trend of suicide rates in each nation, we decided not to include the quadratic or cubic terms of the trends in the baseline model.

Our analysis has a couple of limitations. First, the study did not investigate how particular components of prevention programs affected suicide rates. Ideally, we should track all specifics of national suicide prevention policies and examine their impacts on suicide rates. However, it is extremely challenging to collect data on specific aspects of prevention programs for all nations. Due to this limitation, we decided to assess whether the presence of national suicide prevention programs reduced suicide rates, which has not been systematically tested in the past. More refined analysis is an agenda for future studies.

The second limitation of our study is potential simultaneity. One may argue that the national prevention strategies were implemented in response to the suicide rates in preceding years. This potential simultaneity can pose a challenge to our estimation, especially when suicide prevention programs are likely to be implemented when suicide rates are already declining. This is because it can be difficult to distinguish the effect of national programs from that of the decreasing trend. In this chapter, we addressed the issue of potential simultaneity by including the country-specific linear time trends. While these time trends and the inclusion of other covariates took care of some simultaneous relationships between the national programs and suicide rates, our statistical analysis might not allow us to completely untangle this simultaneous relationship. Thus, the findings should be interpreted carefully.

3 Effect of Government Suicide Prevention Program on Suicide Rates in Japan

Our empirical analysis in the previous section did not define Japan as a country with a comprehensive suicide prevention program because our study period ranged from 1980 to 2004. The Japanese government enacted the Basic Law on Suicide Countermeasures in 2006 and started engaging proactively in suicide prevention as a part of national policy. Following the Basic Law, the national government published the General Principles of Suicide Prevention Policy in 2008 and revised it twice in subsequent years. The General Principles outline prevention programs that the government should pursue and encourage subnational governments to expand their efforts and implement their own programs.

While the Japanese government launched the suicide prevention program, the country experienced a decline in the number of suicides. As discussed in Chap. 1, the annual number of suicides increased sharply by more than 8,000 to exceed 30,000 in 1998 and continued to stay at this level for about 10 years. The number started declining in 2010 and decreased to 24,417 in 2016, according to Vital Statistics. At a glance, the government's active engagement in suicide prevention since 2008 was followed by the sharp decline in suicides. Thus, drawing on our

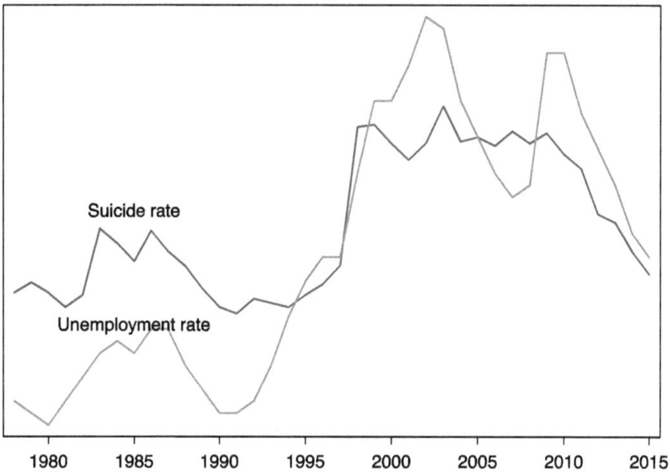

Fig. 1 Unemployment and suicide rates in Japan, 1978–2015

findings in the previous section of this chapter, one might be tempted to conclude that the government-led suicide prevention program was effective.

This conclusion might be invalid because the economic situation turned upward around 2012 and thus might also contribute to the decline in the number of suicides, given the strong linkage between economic situations and suicides as shown in Chap. 2. Figure 1 shows the temporal shift in the unemployment rate and the suicide rate between 1978 and 2015. It is evident that they moved together, suggesting that the decline in suicides could be explained, at least partly, by the improved economy in Japan.

This section examines the effectiveness of the government-led programs for suicide prevention in Japan by using data at the sub-national level between 2000 and 2013. The data came from 47 prefectures that received financial assistance from the national government to initiate or expand their own prevention programs. We tested whether the larger amount of spending for suicide prevention was associated with a decline in suicide in the prefectures while taking into account the influences of economic conditions.

3.1 Data and Method

Before the establishment of the Basic Law on Suicide Countermeasures and the General Principles of Suicide Prevention Policy, local governments in Japan played only a minor role in suicide prevention. According to a 2002 survey of all prefectures and major cities, only eight jurisdictions (13.6% of the total) reported that they engaged in suicide prevention at that time (Japan Support Center for Suicide Countermeasures 2008). As a response to the establishment of the Basic Law in

Table 4 Per capita expenditures for suicide prevention programs by 47 Japanese prefectures between 2009–2013

	Mean	SD	Min	Max
Total expenditure	33.903	21.587	0.282	165.188
Log expenditure for face-to-face consultations	1.262	0.766	0.000	3.618
Log expenditure for telephone consultations	1.143	0.680	0.000	2.928
Log expenditure for training of gatekeepers	1.433	0.696	0.000	3.780
Log expenditure for public awareness campaigns	2.540	0.712	0.000	4.268
Log expenditure for local needs	1.810	0.895	0.000	4.218

Expenditures are measured in Japanese Yen.

2006 that states local governments "have the duty to formulate and implement policy measures which are adapted to the conditions of the applicable region," many local governments only started to develop a suicide prevention program, yet their engagement was not sufficient. In addition, the number of suicides stayed around the same level between 2006 and 2009 as before even after the government launched the suicide prevention program.

As a result of this situation, the national government created the "Emergency Reinforcement Fund for Suicide Prevention in Local Areas" (henceforth, the Fund) in 2009 that was valued at ¥10 billion. The Fund aimed to support local governments for 3 years to implement their own suicide prevention measures that were designed for local demands. The Fund was allocated to all 47 prefectures on the basis of population size and suicide counts. The prefectures spent the Fund to design their own prevention measures or distribute a part of it to municipalities and nongovernmental organizations (NGOs) in their jurisdictions. The Fund was later extended with the supplement of an extra ¥1.75 billion in 2010, ¥3.7 billion in 2011, and ¥3.0 billion in 2012.

The prefectural governments were expected to spend the Fund to implement one or more of the following five types of projects: (1) support for face-to-face consultations; (2) support for telephone consultations; (3) training of gatekeepers; (4) public awareness campaigns, and (5) projects for local needs. The last type includes projects that improve suicide prevention measures in a particular region, such as patrolling a hot spot, providing an emergency shelter, and managing a community group for families of suicide victims. Table 4 summarizes the annual amount of the Fund per capita spent for each type of projects between 2009 and 2013. The data were obtained from the Ministry of Health, Labour, and Welfare.[1]

We examined whether the Fund allocated to 47 prefectures decreased the suicide rates in their jurisdictions. We developed a panel dataset of 47 prefectures that included information about the Fund, economic and welfare policies, and economic conditions between 2000 and 2013. Using this dataset, we estimated the following simple regression model:

[1]The data are available at http://www.mhlw.go.jp/stf/seisakunitsuite/bunya/0000134741.html.

$$[Suicide]_{jt} = \alpha[Prevention]_{jt} + \beta[Economy]_{jt} + \gamma_j T + \varphi_j + \rho_j + \varepsilon_{jt}, \quad (2)$$

where the outcome variable $[Suicide]_{jt}$ is the suicide rate per 100,000 population in year t in prefecture j. We transformed the suicide rate into a natural log. To take into consideration the possibility that the effects of the prevention efforts varied by age and gender, we used the suicide rates by six subpopulation groups such as (1) all aged under 59, (2) men aged under 59, (3) women aged under 60, (4) all aged 60 and over, (5) men aged 60 and over, and (6) women aged 60 and over. The data were obtained from death records in the Vital Statistics of Japan compiled by the Ministry of Health, Labour, and Welfare.

$[Prevention]_{jt}$ includes the amount of the Fund allocated to each prefecture in year t. Our first analysis used the total amount of the allocation, while the second analysis used the amount for the five types of projects separately. We obtained the amount per person to take into consideration the differences in population sizes among the prefectures and then transformed it into the natural log. Because the Fund was initiated in 2009, we assigned the value of one to the years between 2000 and 2008.[2]

$[Economy]_{jt}$ represents two types of variables that have a direct or indirect relationship with the economic conditions of prefecture j. The first type of variables measures government policies that were likely to influence the economy of prefecture j. Specifically, it includes the total expenditures by the prefectural government and the expenditure for public investments. These variables are important because economic and welfare policies have some influences on the suicide rates as shown in Chap. 8 and they are likely to affect economic conditions. Our analysis in this chapter used the total expenditure by the prefectural government rather than the expenditure for subcategories such as unemployment relief and income assistance because we sought to capture the overall effects of government economic and welfare policies. The expenditure for public investments was defined in the same manner as in Chap. 8. (Please see pages 167-168.) We calculated the expenditures per capita and then transformed them into the natural log. The correlation coefficient between the total expenditures and the expenditures for public investments was -0.4.[3] These data sets were obtained from Shakai Jinko Toukei Taikei (the System of Social and Demographic Statistics of Japan, the basic data for prefectures), Todofuken Kessan Jokyo Shirabe (Report on Accounting Information of Prefectures), and Gyosei Toushi Jisseki (Results of Public Investments).

The second type of variables in $[Economy]_{jt}$ measures the economic conditions of prefecture j in year t. It includes income per capita, overall unemployment rate, and total population size. Income per capita equals the amount of taxable income divided by taxable population. The unemployment rate was obtained by dividing the number of totally unemployed persons by the labor force population. We used natural logs of income per capita and population size in our regression analysis. The

[2]The value of 1, not 0, was assigned for the purpose of log transformation.

[3]We used the per capita amount in log.

data on income came from Kenmin Keizai Keisan (Prefecture Accounts Statistics), while the data on the unemployment rate came from Rodoryoku Chousa (Labor Force Survey). The population size came from Jyumin Kihon Daicho Jiko Ido Houkoku (Report on Migration from Basic Resident Register).

Equation (1) includes φ_t which represents the year-fixed effects, unique to each year, while ρ_j represents the prefecture-fixed effects unique to each prefecture. By including the year effects, we controlled for the effects of annual socioeconomic fluctuations at the national level, such as the effects of macroeconomic policies and business cycle that might affect the entire country. By including the prefecture-fixed effects, we controlled for the effects of time-invariant characteristics of prefectures, such as the effects of social norms related to suicide, and climate and geographic conditions. The inclusion of the prefecture-fixed effects means that we exploited changes in the variables within the prefectures. We also added $\gamma_j T$ to the model to take into consideration the effects of linear trends unique to each prefecture.

3.2 Results

Table 5 presents the estimation results that used the total expenditures for suicide prevention programs by the prefectural governments. The outcome variables are the log of the suicide rates by (1) men aged 59 years and under, (2) women ages 59 years and under, (3) men aged 60 years and above, and (4) women aged

Table 5 Effect of total expenditures for suicide prevention programs on suicide rates in 47 Japanese prefectures, 2000–2013

	Male ≤ 59	Female ≤ 59	Male ≥ 60	Female ≥ 60
Log total expenditure for suicide prevention	−0.005 (0.014)	−0.013 (0.031)	−0.000 (0.017)	−0.037 (0.033)
Log total government expenditure	-0.183^{**} (0.081)	-0.302^{*} (0.166)	−0.061 (0.088)	-0.319^{*} (0.173)
Log expenditure for public investment	0.008 (0.074)	0.230 (0.173)	0.042 (0.089)	0.143 (0.147)
Unemployment rate	0.028^{*} (0.017)	0.008 (0.032)	0.060^{***} (0.019)	−0.009 (0.029)
Log income per capita	-0.423^{**} (0.207)	−0.342 (0.380)	−0.052 (0.253)	0.191 (0.334)
Log population size	0.697 (1.938)	4.029 (3.280)	3.696^{*} (1.970)	0.947 (2.669)
Adj. R^2	0.818	0.323	0.753	0.563
N	611			

Table entries are linear regression estimates with standard errors in parentheses. The standard errors are clustered by prefecture. The outcome variables are the suicide rates per 100,000 in a natural log. All models include the prefecture- and year-fixed effects and the prefecture-specific linear time trends

$^{*}p < 0.10$, $^{**}p < 0.05$, $^{***}p < 0.01$ (two-tailed tests)

60 years and above. The prefecture-fixed effects, the year-fixed effects, and the prefecture-specific time trends are not shown in the tables but were included in all the models. Standard errors were clustered at the prefecture. The number of observations is 611.

Table 5 shows that the total expenditures for suicide prevention programs were estimated to have a negative coefficient, yet it is not statistically significant at the conventional levels. The suicide prevention programs initiated in 2009 seem to have had little influence on the suicide rates. In contrast, the economic variables appear to be significantly correlated with the suicide rates. More specifically, column (1) shows that the total expenditure by the prefectural governments is estimated to have a negative and statistically significant relationship with the suicide rates among males aged 59 years and under. The size of the coefficient suggests that the 1% increase in the total expenditure is associated with about a 0.18% decrease in the suicide rates. The total expenditures in columns (2) and (4) had a larger influence on women, but the coefficients are only marginally significant. In addition, column (3) reports that as the unemployment rate increased by 1%, the suicide rates among men aged 60 years and over decreased by 0.6%. Finally, per capita income is also negatively and significantly correlated with the suicide rates among males aged 59 years and under. A 1% increase in per capita income is associated with a 0.4% decrease in the suicide rate.

Next, we used the expenditures for the five types of suicide prevention measures and included them separately in a regression model. Table 6 reports the estimation results. We find that no suicide prevention program has a statistically significant relationship with the suicide rates. Similar to the results in Table 5, the economic variables were estimated to have a negative influence on suicide rates.

3.3 Discussion

We tested the hypothesis that the larger expenditures for suicide prevention programs by prefectural governments were associated with a reduction in suicide rates by using the data between 2000 and 2013. Our analysis shows little supportive evidence for this hypothesis, suggesting that the possibility that the significant reduction in the suicide rates in Japan since 2010 might not be explained by the suicide prevention efforts by prefectural governments.

Our analysis is limited in several ways. Most importantly, the study period of our analysis was short and covered only 5 years (i.e., 2009–2013) where the Fund for suicide prevention was distributed to 47 prefectures. This short period of time might not allow us to identify the effect of prevention efforts in the prefectures. In addition, arguably, the amount of expenditures for suicide prevention might not be an ideal measure to evaluate the effect of prevention efforts. It might be more useful to look at the number and context of actual prevention programs. Thus, we believe that it is too early to conclude that the economy, rather than the government's suicide prevention effort, accounts for the dramatic decline in suicide in the last several years in Japan.

Table 6 Effect of expenditures for five types of suicide prevention programs on suicide rates in 47 Japanese prefectures, 2000–2013

	Male ≤ 59	Female ≤ 59	Male ≥ 60	Female ≥ 60
Log expenditure for face-to-face consultations	0.002 (0.024)	0.029 (0.036)	−0.003 (0.024)	−0.002 (0.032)
Log expenditure for telephone consultations	0.021 (0.017)	−0.002 (0.036)	−0.005 (0.019)	0.031 (0.027)
Log expenditure for training of gatekeepers	−0.013 (0.017)	0.013 (0.042)	−0.006 (0.023)	−0.002 (0.040)
Log expenditure for public awareness campaigns	0.002 (0.016)	−0.037 (0.033)	0.007 (0.018)	−0.028 (0.039)
Log expenditure for local needs	−0.009 (0.013)	−0.011 (0.034)	0.001 (0.010)	−0.024 (0.018)
Log total government expenditure	−0.174** (0.079)	−0.344* (0.182)	−0.053 (0.090)	−0.317* (0.186)
Log expenditure for public investment	0.007 (0.075)	0.233 (0.177)	0.040 (0.088)	0.147 (0.148)
Unemployment rate	0.027 (0.017)	0.007 (0.033)	0.060*** (0.020)	−0.010 (0.029)
Log income per capita	−0.436** (0.202)	−0.340 (0.381)	−0.051 (0.251)	0.164 (0.354)
Log population size	0.851 (1.972)	2.945 (3.579)	3.913* (1.964)	0.515 (2.931)
Adj. R^2	0.817	0.322	0.751	0.561
N	611			

Table entries are linear regression estimates with standard errors in parentheses. The standard errors are clustered by prefecture. The outcome variables are the suicide rates per 100,000 in a natural log. All models include the prefecture- and year-fixed effects and the prefecture-specific linear time trends

*$p < 0.10$, **$p < 0.05$, ***$p < 0.01$ (two-tailed tests)

4 The Effect of Public Awareness Campaigns on Suicides in Nagoya City, Japan

In addition to the prevention efforts by the national and prefectural governments, many municipal governments in Japan started implementing their own prevention programs since the enactment of the Basic Law on Suicide Countermeasures. Their programs were built on the General Principles of Suicide Prevention Policy that was first documented in 2007 and revised in 2012, as discussed previously. One of the most popular programs designed by municipal governments has been a public awareness campaign that aims to "encourage every citizen to be aware of and monitor potential suicide victims, as suggested by the General Principles of Suicide Prevention Policy. More specifically, municipal governments seek to

> Develop public awareness programs through educational activities, advertising campaigns, etc., to promote public understanding about every citizen's role in suicide prevention measures by dispelling society's mistaken but common belief that suicide, multiple debts, depression and other suicide-related phenomena are shameful and dishonorable, a feeling which underlies a person's anxieties and prevents him/her from seeking help; by making people realize that the risk of being driven to suicide is something that can happen to anyone and that it is appropriate for someone in such circumstances to seek help; and by making them realize that there may be persons contemplating suicide among their own acquaintances and that they should speak to them, listen to them, refer them to a professional as necessary, monitor them and seek appropriate assistance in a crisis (the General Principles of Suicide Prevention Policy, p 13).

Public awareness campaigns about depression and suicide have been viewed as highly effective strategies in preventing suicide. The guidelines for suicide prevention set forth by the United Nations (1996) and World Health Organization (2011), for example, encourage conducting campaigns that aim to promote public awareness with regard to mental health and suicidal behavior.

Despite the popularity of public awareness campaigns as suicide prevention programs worldwide and in Japan, their effectiveness has not yet been established. A review article by Mann et al. (2005) reported that public education and awareness campaigns have little effect on suicidal acts, depression, and treatment-seeking behavior. Similarly, a more recent review by Dumesnil and Verger (2009, 1203) also concluded that, "no study has clearly demonstrated that such campaigns help to increase care seeking or to decrease suicidal behavior." The null finding on the effectiveness of such campaigns should be a serious concern for policymakers and practitioners worldwide who seek an effective suicide prevention program.

Using one of the public awareness campaigns by a municipal government in Japan, this subsection reports the results of our analysis that tested whether public awareness campaigns could actually reduce suicidal risks. We compared the number of suicides before and after a city-wide campaign in Nagoya, Japan, in which promotional materials were distributed to its residents. We examined whether more frequent distributions of promotional materials are associated with a reduction in the number of suicides in the months following such distributions.

4.1 Public Awareness Campaign in Nagoya

The city of Nagoya is located in Aichi Prefecture in the central part of Japan. Nagoya is the fourth largest city in Japan with a population of 2.3 million (as of February 2013). According to Vital Statistics compiled by the Ministry of Health, Labour, and Welfare, 448 people died by suicide in 2010, which corresponds to a suicide rate of 20.3.

The city government of Nagoya launched a public awareness campaign as part of its city-wide suicide prevention program in 2009. The campaign was designed to heighten the awareness of depression and promote care-seeking behavior among local residents. The city distributed promotional materials to commuters at major train stations and on the streets of the city in February, March, May, and June of 2010, 2011, and 2012. During these campaign months, the materials were handed out to commuters and pedestrians by paid staff members and volunteers every morning and evening of Monday to Friday. Only one location was targeted each morning or evening of the day. For example, the materials were handed out at station A in the morning of February 1st in 2010 and station B in the evening of the same day. The primary target of the campaign were middle-aged male residents of the city because 50% of total suicides were attributed to this population group. However, the material was distributed without discrimination and as a result, all those walking by had a chance to receive the pamphlet. During the period from April 2011 to March 2012, a total of 0.25 million materials were distributed at 41 different locations for 80 days.

The promotional material consisted of a hand-sized pamphlet that contained plastic bandages. It showed information regarding the symptoms of depression, its treatment options, and a message encouraging those with mental health issues to seek assistance. The back side of the pamphlet listed several telephone numbers for personal consultations, not solely about their mental health, but also about personal debt and other economic concerns. The material also encouraged them to visit a website launched by the city government for more detailed information about consultations and medical services. The pamphlet was called "Kokoro no Bansoukou," which generally translates to a first-aid or plastic bandage for mental health.

4.2 Data and Method

To test the effectiveness of the public awareness campaign described above, we created monthly panel data. We measured the frequency of the distribution of promotional materials per month in each of the 16 different wards (i.e., administrative jurisdictions in the city) by counting the total number of campaign sessions within the ward. We recoded the frequency as zero for the other months of the years because no activity occurred. This ward-specific, monthly data was then merged with the monthly data of suicides in each ward. The unit of observations is a ward-month. Our data covered January 2010 to December 2012 and the number of observations is thus 576 (16 wards $\times$36 months).

The frequency of campaign activities per month in 16 wards was measured in the following way. First, we counted the frequency of distributions at each location (e.g., station or street) per month, treating the morning and evening sessions separately. For example, if the materials were handed out at a particular station in both the morning and the evening of the same day, and no additional distribution was carried out at this station within the same month, the number of campaign activities at this station was coded as two. Second, we identified the physical address of the locations where the campaign activities were conducted and classified them into corresponding wards. Nagoya Station, the largest station in the city, for example, is located in Naka ward. For a few stations that were located at the border of two wards, we coded the number of activities as 0.5 per session for both wards. Third,

Table 7 Number of distributions in 16 wards of Nagoya, Japan

	2010				2011				2012			
Ward	Feb	March	May	June	Feb	March	May	June	Feb	March	May	June
Chikusa	11	0	8	0	6	2	3	4	3	3	3	4
Higashi	6	1	2	4	6	0	3	4	4	4	4	3
Kita	5	0	3	0	3	0	2	5	2	4	3	3
Nishi	1	0	1	0	1	0	0	2	1	1	1	1
Nakamura	2	9	0	10	1	9	5	6	8	5	7	5
Naka	9	29	11	23	14	18	18	9	12	11	17	8
Showa	2	0	1	1	1	1	2	1	2	1	0	3
Mizuho	0	0	2	0	2	0	0	1	1	1	1	2
Atsuta	1	5	0	8	0	8	3	3	2	4	5	3
Nakagawa	0	1	0	1	0	2	1	2	1	3	1	2
Minato	0	2	0	1	0	1	0	0	1	0	0	1
Minami	0	1	0	0	0	1	0	1	0	1	0	1
Moriyama	1	0	0	0	0	0	0	0	0	0	0	1
Midori	0	1	2	1	2	1	0	2	3	2	0	2
Meito	2	0	2	3	3	2	1	3	2	2	2	3
Tenpaku	2	0	2	1	1	4	1	5	2	1	0	4

The distributions of the promotional materials are counted as 1 if the distribution was carried out in the morning or evening in a ward. We aggregated the total number of distributions per ward per month. All other months are coded as 0

we aggregated the number of activities per month per ward. Table 7 reports the total count of campaign activities in each ward during the campaign months. The mean number of distributions was 2.77. All other months that are not displayed in the table are coded zero because no distribution was carried out. As is evident, there were substantial variations in distributions both across ward and time.

The monthly data on the number of suicides in each ward was taken from the suicide statistics compiled by the National Police Agency. In addition to the total number of suicides, we also obtained gender-specific suicide data because the campaign primarily targeted the male population. and thus the effect of the campaign may have varied across gender. The average number of suicides per ward-month during the period of our study is 2.56 for the total population (1.71 for the male population and 0.85 for the female population).

To examine the effect of the campaign, we estimated a Poisson regression model where the dependent variable, S_{iym}, is the number of suicides in ward i in month m of year y. We chose to use the suicide counts, rather than suicide rates, as our outcome variable because the population characteristics of the wards remained almost constant during our study period (36 months). The main independent variable, D_{iym}, equals the frequency of campaign activities in ward i in month m of year y. In order to capture a potential long-term effect of the campaign, we also included lagged values of D_{iym} in the estimation. We set the number of lags to be five based on the AIC. This means that we measured the impact of campaign activities on the number of suicides over the subsequent five months.

The Poisson model also included ward-specific, month-specific, and year-specific fixed effects in the model. The ward-specific fixed effects capture the effects of time-invariant observed and unobserved characteristics of wards that could be related to the suicide count. Thus, our estimation compared the number of suicides before and after the campaigns and the comparison was not made across wards. The month-specific effects capture the seasonal effect of suicides, while the year-specific effects capture the effects of economic depression and any other major events that happened in Nagoya in a particular year.

4.3 Results

Figure 2 reports adjusted Poisson regression IRRs with 95% confidence intervals. Standard errors were clustered by the wards. The top panel of reports the result for the total count of suicides as the outcome variable, while the middle and bottom panels report the results for the male and female populations, respectively.

The top panel shows that the total number of suicides decreased 2 months after the campaigns. The IRR for a ward that had a campaign activity 2 months earlier was estimated to be 0.971 (95% CI: [0.957, 0.985]), where the reference is the months with no campaign activity. Substantively, this estimated effect is equivalent to a reduction in the count of total suicides by 1 if the promotional materials were distributed on 15 weekdays per month. A similar result was observed 4 months after the distribution Fig. 2.

The effect of the campaign varied by gender. The middle panel of Fig. 2 shows that the distribution of promotional materials had an intended effect on the count of male suicides. The campaign did not have an immediate effect, but the IRRs are consistently below one once 2 months have passed since the distribution of promotional materials. The effect of the campaign lasts for 4 months, but not more than 5 months. The bottom panel shows that the campaign had a limited effect for the female population. The only statistically significant reduction in the number of suicides was observed in the second month during the post-distribution period.

4.4 Discussion

We examined whether a public awareness campaign can reduce the number of suicides using an original dataset from Nagoya, Japan. Our findings suggest that the public awareness campaign had an intended effect of reducing the suicide counts of the target group, namely the male residents of the city, from the second to fourth months after the program's implementation. Since half of the total suicides in the city were attributed to the middle-aged male residents of the city, we may safely conclude that the program has effectively achieved its outcomes.

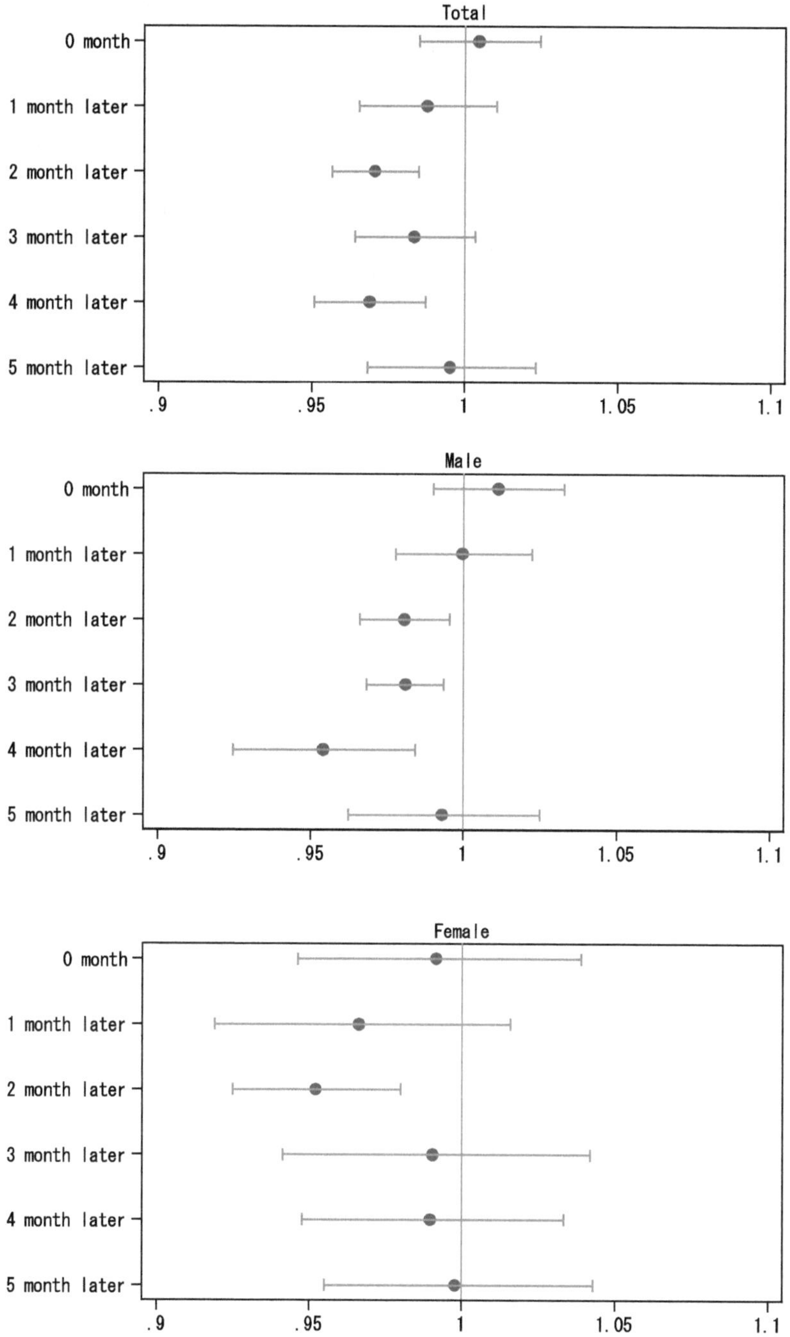

Fig. 2 Estimated effects of public awareness campaign on suicides. Note: Adjusted Poisson regression incidence rate ratios with 95% Confidence Intervals

The estimated effect of the public awareness campaign should be regarded as a lower-bound estimate because the recipients of the campaign materials may not reside in the ward where they were distributed and thus, its effect may not be confined to that specific ward.

It is worth emphasizing that the timing and frequency of distribution in each location was decided by the city government primarily for logistical reasons, and was thus exogenously given. In addition, it is unlikely that the findings of this paper are entirely explained by the effects of other types of campaigns that were conducted during the same period. This is due to the fact that the timing of the distribution is a crucial factor in our model, whereas other campaigns were conducted continuously without such specific timing.

We conducted several robustness checks on our findings. First, in order to exclude the possibility that an outlier observation was driving the results, we dropped each of the wards from the analysis and then estimated the same model with the remaining 15 wards. It did not change the substantive results. Second, we alternated the number of lags between 3 and 7, and confirmed that the results were not sensitive to the number of lags.

Admittedly, this study has several potential limitations. It did not answer why the campaign reduced suicide. It also remains unclear why the campaign seems to have had such a long delayed effect. Although more detailed data is necessary in order to fully answer these important questions, at least the number of phone calls to consultation services and access to the city's campaign website increased during the months of the campaign (data not shown). While this does not directly tell us whether the use of such services or websites prevents some potential suicides, it suggests that more people made use of the resources provided by the city after the awareness campaign.

The findings suggest that public awareness campaigns can reduce the risk of suicide. To understand why and when such campaigns are effective, further research is needed to investigate the underlying channels and mechanisms carefully, such as if such campaigns can also reduce the symptoms of depression or promote visitations to a doctor's office, thereby reducing the risk of suicide.

Acknowledgements We thank Finn Gjertsen for informing us of an error in our analysis in the analysis reported in the second section of this chapter.

References

Ajdacic-Gross, V., Weiss, M. G., Ring, M., Hepp, U., Bopp, M., Gutzwiller, F., et al. (2008). Methods of suicide: International suicide patters derived from the WHO mortality database. *Bulletin of the World Health Organization, 86*, 726–732.

Allan, J. P., & Scruggs, L. (2004). Political partisanship and welfare state reform in advanced industrial societies. *American Journal of Political Science, 48*, 496–512.

Anderson, M., & Jenkins, R. (2005). The challenge of suicide prevention: An overview of national strategies. *Disease Management and Health Outcomes, 13,* 245–253.

Baker, J., & McPhedran, S. (2006). Gun laws and sudden death: Did the Australian firearms legislation of 1996 make a difference? *British Journal of Criminology, 47,* 455–469.

Francis, Castles, & Mair, P. (1984). Left-right political scales: some 'expert' judgements. *European Journal of Political Research, 12,* 73–88.

Chapman, S., Alpers, P., Agho, K., & Jones, M. (2006). Australia's 1996 gun law reforms: Faster falls in firearm deaths, firearm suicides, and a decade without mass shootings. *Injury Prevention, 12,* 365–372.

De Leo, D. (2002). Struggling against suicide. *Crisis, 23,* 23–31.

De Leo, D., & Evans, R. (2003). International Suicide Rates: Recent trends and implications for Australia. Technical report, Australian Government Department of Health and Ageing, Canberra.

Di Tella, R., & MacCulloch, R. (2002). The determination of unemployment benefits. *Journal of Labor Economics, 20,* 404–434.

Di Tella, R., MacCulloch, R. J., & Oswald, A. J. (2003). The macroeconomics of happiness. *The Review of Economics and Statistics, 85,* 809–827.

Dumesnil, H., & Verger, P. (2009). Public awareness campaigns about depression and suicide: a review. *Psychiatric Services, 60,* 1203–1210.

Heston, A., Summers, R., & Aten, B. (2009). Penn World Table Version 6.3. http://pwt.econ.upenn.edu/phpsite/pwt63/pwt63form.php.

Huber, E., & Stephens, J. D. (2001). *Development and crisis of the welfare state: Parties and policies in global markets.* Chicago: University of Chicago Press.

Japan Support Center for Suicide Countermeasures. (2008). Report on Suicide Prevention Programs by Prefectures and Major Cities.

Levin, A., Lin, C.-F., & Chu, C.-S. J. (2002). Unit root tests in panel data: Asymptotic and finite-sample properties. *Journal of Econometrics, 108,* 1–24.

Mann, J. J., et al. (2005). Suicide prevention strategies: A systematic review. *Journal of American Medical Association, 294,* 2064–2074.

Minoiu, C., & Andres, A. R. (2008). The effect of public spending on suicide: Evidence from U.S. state data. *The Journal of Socio-Economics, 37,* 237–261.

Radcliff, B. (2001). Politics, markets, and life satisfaction: The political economy of human happiness. *American Political Science Review, 95,* 939–952.

Solt, F. (2009). Standardizing the world income inequality database. *Social Science Quarterly, 90,* 231–242.

Swank, D. H. (2010). *Comparative parties data set.* http://www.marquette.edu/polisci/documents/part19502006.xls.

Taylor, S. J., Kingdom, D., & Jenkins, R. (1997). How are nations trying to prevent suicide? An analysis of national suicide prevention strategies. *Acta Psychiatrica Scandinavica, 95,* 457–463.

The Organisation for Economic Co-operation and Development. (2010). *OECD Stat Extracts.* http://stats.oecd.org/Index.aspx.

United Nations. (1996). Prevention of Suicide: Guidelines for the Formulation and Implementation of National Strategies. New York: U.N. Department of Policy Coordination and Sustainable Development.

World Health Organization (2010). Suicide Prevention. http://www.who.int/mentalhealth/prevention/suicide/suicideprevent/en/.

World Health Organization (2011). Suicide prevention. http://www.who.int/mental_health/prevention/suicide/suicideprevent/en/.

World Health Organization Regional Office for Europe Copenhagen (2002). *Suicide Prevention in Europe: The WHO European monitoring survey on national suicide prevention programmes and strategies.*

Erratum to: Rationale Behind Suicide Prevention Policies

Erratum to:
Chapter 2 in: Y. Sawada et al., *Economic Analysis of Suicide Prevention*, Creating a Society for All,
https://doi.org/10.1007/978-981-10-1500-7_2

The original version of the book was inadvertently published prematurely before incorporating the final corrections in Chap. 2 due to an error in the production process. The version supplied here has been corrected and approved by the author.

The updated online version of this chapter can be found at
https://doi.org/10.1007/978-981-10-1500-7_2

Y. Sawada et al., *Economic Analysis of Suicide Prevention*,
Creating a Society for All, https://doi.org/10.1007/978-981-10-1500-7_10

FSC
www.fsc.org
MIX
Papier aus verantwortungsvollen Quellen
Paper from responsible sources
FSC® C105338

If you have any concerns about our products,
you can contact us on
ProductSafety@springernature.com

In case Publisher is established outside the EU,
the EU authorized representative is:
Springer Nature Customer Service Center GmbH
Europaplatz 3, 69115 Heidelberg, Germany

Printed by Libri Plureos GmbH
in Hamburg, Germany